INDIAN DEPREDATIONS
IN
UTAH

BY
PETER GOTTFREDSON

Indian Depredations in Utah
by Peter Gottfredson

First Published 1919
Published 2002 by Fenestra Books
Foreword Copyright © 2002 Phillip B. Gottfredson
All Rights Reserved.

International Standard Book Number:
1-58736-127-2
Library of Congress Control Number:
2002109647

Published by Fenestra Books™
610 East Delano Street, Suite 104
Tucson, Arizona 85705 U.S.A.
www.fenestrabooks.com

FOREWORD

I never met my great-grandfather Peter Gottfredson, and I only became acquainted with him through the family histories, which were kept and passed down. It is with pride that we, my brother David E. Gottfredson and I, honor Peter by re-publishing his book which we grew up with as children and on into adulthood. Our father, Merrill Edward Gottfredson, kept a copy of the book, and Merrill at times encouraged us to read it. Merrill knew Peter and spoke of him with great fondness and respect. Merrill felt it was important for us to remember what our forefathers had gone through, so that we could then have a better sense of who we are.

Indian Depredations in Utah explores the clash of two cultures, those of the Native Americans and the European settlers of the mid-1800s, in a most factual way. The book reveals in both cultures the extreme difficulty each had in understanding one another's ways. It also shows how the most bizarre of circumstances can bring out the best and the worst in humanity, regardless of culture or ethnic background. What seemed right to the one was seen as wrong by the other. Yet through the confusion, one can see the common virtues each held dear, regardless of their individual beliefs. These virtues were the stuff which formed close and lasting relationships between the two cultures, in spite of the egregious acts each committed against the other.

Needless to say, we cannot change what took place in the past, but we can learn from our mistakes and use our knowledge of the past to better our understanding of the present. Arguably, much in the way of progress has been accomplished between the Native Americans and the whites, and yet there remains much more to be done. During the opening ceremonies of the 2002 Winter Olympics, I watched with pure amazement as the Native Americans flawlessly performed their ceremonial blessings upon the athletes and upon the games, and I pondered the spectacle with tears of humility for the recognition they so greatly deserved but barely received. They, with the greatest of dignity and unwavering pride, stood before millions of spectators with an honor I believe most people could only begin to comprehend. As time passes and much recognition is lavished upon others, not a word of credit is given to Native Americans. As I said, there remains much to be done.

Indian Depredations in Utah is not about who was right and who was wrong. It simply is an account of what happened and why. At least this was the intention of Peter Gottfredson.

Early Recognition of The Book

On June 24,1970, Merrill Gottfredson, grandson of Peter Gottfredson, wrote an article honoring Peter. It was published in the *Provo Herald* newspaper. Merrill wrote:

I take pride in the fact that he was my grandfather, and why not? For I loved him very much. During World War I, he lived in our home and this happened to be at the same time he was finalizing this book. I see him now. His head held high in lofty thought, his steel gray eyes piercing his objectives. Determination loomed upon his brow as he set out on foot "just one more time" to harvest the last few kernels of information for his book.

Peter was a friend of the Indians in the early days and knew Chief Walker and Chief Blackhawk well. Peter got along with them well and learned their language and won their respect, and was the guest of Chief Blackhawk on several occasions. It is my guess that this was one of the deciding factors in wanting to write this history, for he liked them in spite of the fact that it later became his duty to fight wars against them. I know it saddened him to do so.

Peter worked for the railroad at the time of the driving of the "Golden Spike." He was awarded a badge of honor at the grand celebration and witnessed the driving of the Golden Spike at Promontory Point.

In Peter's later years, he served as a precinct judge; justice of the peace; and Sevier County Commissioner; and during his tenure of office, he promoted and helped build the new county courthouse. He cleared land and operated his farm, raised livestock, and served as a railroad stationmaster. He fashioned a newfangled surveying instrument and surveyed the eight-mile-long Venice canal. He served as a committeeman with those who named towns, places, and things throughout the valley, including Fishlake and Koosharem, Utah.

But then he set up a blacksmith shop intending to do some custom work, and this was his Waterloo!!! He met with an accident, which almost cost him limb and life, and put him permanently out of business occupationally. His doctor said, "Might as well bury him with his arm on as with it off." But the patient did not die. With three fingers stiff and clutched in the palm of his hand, and his index finger pointed forward towards his typewriter, he commenced and finished what was to him "the most important work of his life, *Indian Depredations in Utah.*"

On June 13, 1962, Kathryn D. Groesbeck wrote an article for the *Provo Herald* regarding Peter Gottfredson.

Back in 1919, Peter Gottfredson (1846-1934) had published his priceless collection of information about Utah-Indian warfare, his history of *Indian Depredations in Utah.* Long out-of-print, the book required twenty years in the making.

Most of those who responded to Mr. Gottfredson's request for aid in the collecting of the history he compiled where ones who had actually taken an active part when Indian troubles took place in Utah, about fifty years before the book was published. Mr. Gottfredson realized the great necessity of obtaining first-hand information while there were yet those living who could give it to him.

Mr. Gottfredson wrote that it was his wish that his little book of 352 pages would "fill an important place in the history of our fair state." Surely it has done so.

The Journey Begins in Denmark, 1857

Have you ever become so weary of your life that you wished you could just leave it all behind and take off on a journey into the unknown? Imagine yourself being just ten years of age and having parents that did just this very thing. You board a sailing ship and leave everything behind—friends, family, and life as you know it—to venture over 7000 miles into the vast unknown. While aboard a sailing ship on rough seas for a month, winter storms dictate that the ship has to return to shore and venture out again when weather permits. Then again the voyage continues with 500 other passengers crammed together in a tiny vessel. You witness the captain kill a shipmate with a hook on the end of a rope; you're so sickened that you go to the rail of the ship and vomit. The captain is overtaken and tied up as punishment for cruelty to passengers and crew.

Peter Gottfredson was just ten years of age when he, his brothers Hans (age 8) and Joseph (age 4), his sister Martha Christine (age 6), and his parents Jens and Karen, in pursuit of an adventure driven by their dreams and deep religious convictions, left their home in Denmark and traveled over land and sea to a desert place called Utah. Along the way, Peter's mother died, and his father remarried. A daughter was born. They named her Platine, after the Platt river. Platine's birth was premature, and she clung to life for three days. Peter buried his baby sister in the wilderness, along the banks of the Platt River.

In today's culture, this would send most folks back home asking God's forgiveness for being so damned foolish for putting their family in harm's way, but obviously this was not the case for Peter Gottfredson and his family. I guess it's safe to say that when you're thousands of miles from home and your only means of travel are by horseback and on foot, you instead ask God to give you the strength to forge on, for maybe there's something ahead that will, in some way, ease the searing pain of unintentional, uncalculated misfortune. And as Peter and his family continue on with the adventure, he struggled to reconcile this business of exploration and destiny with the loss of his family.

For Peter, this was only the beginning of a life of struggle and witnessing the darkest side of humanity. What lay ahead of Peter and his family would make the loss of his mother and sister appear as perhaps a blessing more than a tragedy. And in the end, Peter compiled and chronicled what he called *Indian Depredations in Utah*. For twenty years he did so because he felt deeply that future generations must not loose the truth in the matters of the Indian depredations in Utah. For he understood the fact that as stories are told and re-told, it is in the nature of mankind to embellish, distort and 'sweep under the carpet' the facts as they truly took place.

A Man of Ethics

Throughout the course of Peter's life, he was as common as any man of his time, working hard to support himself and his family. He visualized having a nice house and home. He lived by a simple code honor: an honest day's pay for an honest day's work. Peter achieved these things and was known to be an honorable man of his time. Curiously, Peter left little behind which could indicate that he had been emotionally crippled by all of the tragedy he had encountered; moreover, he left behind a legacy of incredible courage, strength, and character. His character was forged from the flames of conflict. As Peter witnessed the clash of cultures between the white settlers and the Native Americans, as one side strove to conquer the other through bloodshed and violence, Peter quite often found himself in the awkward position of being somewhere in the middle, and a friend to both.

Hearing about Peter from my father as I grew up gave me a strong sense of Peter as a person of great ethics and values. Peter would want his readers to learn one very important lesson he wrote about in a poem.

> If the years afore you have been lived a'right
> Your feet will be nimble; your eyes will be bright;
> You will truly be loved though your hair may be white,
> When you are eighty.
>
> But if it should be that you're faded and worn,
> By the battles you've fought and the burdens you've born,
> By a smile you will win, not by looking forlorn
> When you are eighty.

If you choose with care the seeds you sow,
You will reap with pleasure the crops you grow,
The things I tell you are things I know because I am eighty.

Bear in mind, as you journey into the western experience, that, as a pioneer, all you may have owned were the clothes on your back, a horse for travel, a gun for acquiring food and for protection, and perhaps a wagon and a couple of oxen to pull it. For food, there were no grocery stores; you ate what you killed with your gun. You made your own ammunition for your gun. If necessary, you ate your horse and oxen. You drank from the streams. When you found a place to call home, you bartered for more food such as cattle or sheep. To do this, you may have traded your wagon for a cow, traded the milk for some chickens, and traded the eggs for some flour, salt and seeds. You learned what plants were edible around the land, and if you had skills from the Old World, you took up something like blacksmithing. When someone stole your cattle from you, this was a serious matter, for you and your family may then starve to death. Cattle were your food and currency.

Communication with the outside world took days, even months. When tragedy hit you, you may have endured it alone. You avoided at all cost anything that could cause you to loose your meager possessions or your health. The law was the gun you carried. There were no police or courts or jails. There were no newspapers to keep you informed about what others were doing.

Such were the life and times of Peter Gottfredson.

I give special acknowledgment to my dear friend and brother, David E. Gottfredson, for giving to me his valued copy of the book, which inspired me to have it re-published. David helped support the project financially, for which I will be forever grateful.

Special recognition goes to my dear friend Dr. Ken Molen who also supported me in the project, and without his help the project would not have happened.

And last but not least, I acknowledge my dear friends Alvin & Julie Begay of the Navajo Indian Tribe, who taught me to love and respect the Navajo people. May Al rest in peace. Al died of cancer in the 1980s, and before he passed he came to me in Arizona to say goodbye. Though I was not allowed to attend his funeral on the reservation because of my race, I will forever remember him as my friend of friends.

Phillip B. Gottfredson
Great-grandson of Peter Gottfredson

Preface

In collecting and compiling this history of Indian depredations in Utah, it has been my purpose to obtain my information first handed, as far as possible. I was personally acquainted with conditions in Sanpete and Sevier Valleys during the years 1863 to 1872. It fell to my lot to be herd-boy in Thistle Valley, which was then a favorite haunt of the Indians, and they often told us that we were trespassers on their domain. In 1865, when the Black Hawk war broke out, I had left Sanpete to locate in Sevier Valley, which was then most exposed to Indian raids because of having been settled but one year when the war broke out and that valley afforded the handiest and most convenient outlets into the Indian stronghold in the mountains and country lying to the east, which was then unsettled by white people and but little known to them.

I have also made it a point to obtain information from reliable histories and individual diaries and records, and by interviewing persons who were actually in the places and took part in the affairs as recorded. And finally I obtained much information from newspaper files and documents in the Church Historian's Office.

It is half a century and more since the raids and assaults recorded in this book took place, most of the persons who took active parts in the same have responded to the last earthly call, and what information we get first handed must of necessity be obtained now or never. I have often querried; why should those

conditions be forgotten, and why has so little interest
been taken in keeping memorandas and records of
events and conditions of those early and trying
times. I have written several times over much of the
information I have gathered in order to make cor-
rections and supply additional information. I have
been more than twenty years compiling this history,
and have not left a stone unturned in my endeavors
to obtain correct data on all the important events
which properly belong to this history.

My aim has been to give credit where such was
due, but to get in the names of all who took part or
were enrolled in the different Militia Companies
participating in the Indian Wars would be too great
a task, and yet, they are all deserving of mention.

It has not been my purpose to single out any
one as a particular hero ahead of all others, but to
record conditions and facts as they existed and occurred.

I sincerely thank all who have assisted me,
especially the Indian War Veterans and the Church
Historians for their willing and interested assist-
asce. I will make special mention of Assistant
Church Historian Andrew Jenson, who has given
me important assistance in obtaining correct dates
and information, and preparing my manuscript for
the printers, and hope my little book will fill an
important place in the history of our fair State.

—*The Compiler.*

Introduction

It has always been the policy of the Mormon people to court the friendship of the American Indian and treat him kindly.

President Brigham Young said, "It is cheaper to feed them than fight them." In the early rise of the Church, Missionaries were sent out to preach to them. The Prophet Joseph Smith visited and preached to them. As early as October 1830, Oliver Cowdry, Parley P. Pratt, Peter Whittmer, Jr. and Ziba Peterson were called by revelation to preach the gospel to the Lamanites (Indians). In 1835 elders Brigham Young, John P. Greene and Amos Orton were appointed to preach the gospel to them and when the people were driven from their homes in Missouri and Illnois and wended their way into the unknown west, the various Indian tribes in Iowa, Nebraska and on the western plains received them kindly, as a rule, believing they were outcasts, driven from their homes and the graves of their fore-fathers, as they themselves had been. In the year 1858, I with my parents came from Omaha where we had lived for some two years, was then twelve years of age,

After spending one year in Salt Lake City, herding cows in the summer time, I with my parents and two brothers and one sister went to Sanpete and were pioneers of Mount Pleasant, and in the year 1864 were also pioneers of Richfield in Sevier County.

The Indians at that time were generally friendly towards the settlers, although, a few years previous

they had committed depredations upon the settlements in Utah, Tooele and a few other Counites. Not
however the whole Ute nation, but turbulent spirits
in large numbers under the leadership of the great
War Chief Walker or Wah-ker, (which means in the
American language, yellow, or brass.) and later in
1856, by a renegade Goshute Chief named Tintic and
his band, who claimed the country on the west side
of the Utah Lake in Cedar, Tintic and Skull Valleys. The Indians were numerous in those days. I
was herd boy and spent much of my time with my
companions at the Indian camps. I had a companion
by the name Conderset Rowe who could talk the Indian language nearly as well as the Indians, it seemed that he enjoyed the companionship of the young
Indians as much as he did the whites, which drew
me into their company more than I otherwise would
have been.

It was the inherent nature of the Indian to steal,
and this brings to my mind an incident told of an Indian who brought a worn out axe to a black smith to
be fixed, the blacksmith said, I can't fix it, it hasn't
any steel in it. "Oh yes, said the Indian, it is all steel,
me steal it last night."

Indians could not be depended upon as to their
lasting friendship, mostly on account of their thieving propensity, so it was necessary for the settlers
to build forts for protection. At Mount Pleasant a
fort was built the first summer, of large sand stones
that were dug out of the ground, and picked up near
the site, it was twenty six rods square, the walls
were four feet thick at the bottom eighteen inches
on top and twelve feet high, with rooms built against
the wall sixteen feet square, with a port hole through

fort wall in middle of each room, about seven feet from the ground, the holes were about two feet wide inside, four inches on outside and eighteen inches high, there were heavy double wooden gates in the middle of north and south sides of the fort, and there were some rows of houses in the inside. The creek ran through the fort from east to west. Similar forts were built in most all the new settlements.

As the settlements became more populous, towns were surveyed with blocks generally twenty six rods square with six rod streets which made 100 blocks to a square mile, or section of land.

CONTENTS

Chapter I.

Chapter II.

CONTENTS 11

PETER GOTTFREDSON
The Compiler

CHAPTER I.

1847---1864

FROM THRILLING EXPERIENCES,
By Solomon F. Kimball.

The first winter spent by the pioneers in Salt Lake Valley was a quiet one. The surrounding tribes of Indians were on their good behavior, as far as the new comers were concerned, although at war with each other. The victorious parties during such wars scalped all the warriors whom they captured or killed. Their custom was to hang these scalps on their scalp-poles, which they took great pride in exhibitng. The brave that could show the greatest number was considered the greatest Indian of them all.

The young women and children were held as slaves, and sometimes treated in the most cruel manner. The red men were not long in learning that the Saints were a tender-hearted people, and could not witness such scenes without sympathizing to the uttermost with those who were being tortured. Among the first accounts given by the pioneers of this barbaric treatment is one found in Mary Ellen Kimball's journal of 1847, of which the following is a brief extract:

A number of Indians were camped near the Hot Springs, north of the Fort. They had with them a little girl who had been captured from another tribe, and they offered to trade her for a rifle. Fire-arms were scarce with the pioneers, and besides it was not good policy to arm these cruel savages who might at any time turn on those who had armed them. The

Indians finally began to torture the little one, at the
same time declaring that they would kill her, unless
the rifle was forthcoming. One of our pioneer boys,
Charles Decker, whose heart was wrung by witnessing such cruelty, very reluctantly parted with his
only gun. He took the little girl home, and gave her
to his sister, Clara D. Young. They named her Sally,
and she lived in the family of President Brigham
Young until she had grown to womanhood. Afterwards she married a noble and friendly Pauvante
chief named Kanosh. She made him a good wife
and did much towards civilizing him. He joined the
"Mormon" Church and died a faithful Latter-day
Saint. That winter several pappooses were purchased under similar circcumstances.

John R. Young referring to the same incident
relates the following:

Elder John R. Young writes: "Soon after we
moved on to our city lot in the fall of 1847, a band
of Indians camped near us. Early one morning we
were excited at hearing their shrill, blood curdling
war whoop, mingled with occasionally sharp cries of
pain. Father sent me to the fort for help. Charley
Decker and Barney Ward (the interpreter) and
others hurried to the camp.

It was Wanship's band. Some of his braves
had just returned from the war path. In a fight
with "Little Wolf's" band, they lost two men, but
had succeeded in taking two girls prisoners. One
of these they had killed and were torturing the other.
To save her life Charley Decker bought her and took
her to our house to be washed and clothed.

She was the saddest looking piece of humanity
I have ever seen. They had shingled her head with

butcher knives and fire brands. All the fleshy parts
of her body, legs and arms had been hacked with
knives, then fire brands had been stuck into the
wounds. She was gaunt with hunger and smeared
from head to foot with blood and ashes.

After being scrubbed and clothed, she was given
to Pres. Brigham Young and became as one of his
family. They named her Sally, and her memory has
ben perpetuated by the "Courtship of Kanosh, a
Pioneer Indian Love Story," written by my gifted
cousin, Susa Young Gates.

But Susa gave us only the courtship, while the
ending of Sally's life, as told to me by a man from
Kanosh, was as tragic as her childhood days had
been thrilling. After she married Kanosh, several
years of her life passed pleasantly in the white man's
house which he built for her. Then her Indian husband took to himself another wife, who became jealous of Sally and perhaps hated her also for her
white man's ways.

One day when they were in a secluded place digging segoes, the new wife murdered Sally and buried
the body in a gully.

When Kanosh missed her, he took her track and
followed it as faithfully as a blood hound could have
done, and was not long in finding the grave. In his
grief he seized the murderess and would have burned
her at the stake but white men interfered.

In due time the Indian woman confessed her
guilt and, in harmony with Indian justice, offered to
expiate her crime by starving herself to death.

The offer was accepted, and on a lone hill in
sight of the village, a "wick-i-up" was constructed
of dry timber. Taking a jug of water, the woman

walked silently toward her living grave. Like the rejected swan, alone, unloved, in low tones she sang her own sad requiem, until her voice was hushed in death. One night when the evening beacon fire was not seen by the villagers, a runner was dispatched to fire the wick-i-up and retribution was complete.

Sally's funeral had taken place only a few days previous. Over a hundred vehicles followed the remains to its last resting place, and beautiful floral wreaths covered the casket; for Sally had been widely loved among the white settlers for her gentle ways. —*Young's Manuscript page 45, copied at Historian's Office by H. H. Jenson.*

1849. FEB. 28th, FIRST BATTLE WITH INDIANS IN UTAH, AT BATTLE CREEK.

Copied from records in the L. D. S. Historian's Office.

A report having reached Salt Lake City that some renegade Indians were molesting the settlers, a company of thirty or forty men under Captain John Scott left Salt Lake City Feb. 28, 1849, in pursuit of some Indians who had been stealing and killing cattle and running off horses from Willow Creek (Draper) and other places. The company proceeded to Utah Valley and met Little Chief and his band of Timpanogos Utes on the Provo River who told the military boys where the thieving Indians were encamped. The company left the Provo river in the night, taking with them as guide Little Chief's son who led them over the Provo Bench toward the creek (Battle Creek) north of the base of the mountains, whence from an eminence they discovered the fires of the Indians who were encamped on the creek which ran in the midst of willows and dense brush-wood in a deep ravine. The company was divided into four smaller bodies and posted north, south, east and west of the Indians, who, when they awoke in the morning, found themselves besieged. The savages packed up their baggage and ineffectually tried every way to escape. They then commenced to fight by shooting arrows and firing guns. This small predatory band of Indians consisted of two lodges under Kone and Blue-Shirt and numbered seventeen souls in all, including four men. The squaws and children were secured and fed and warmed. After a desultory fight of three or four hours, the four men who took every advantage of the brush for cover were killed. None of the brethren were injured. The skins of fifteen cattle, which the Indians had killed were found near by. During the fight Stick-in-the-Head and his band of Timpanogos Utes came up ready for a fight and took position on an elevation, whence they vainly called to the besieged and urged them to come that way. The company returned to Great Salt Lake City March 6th. The squaws and children of the slain were taken to the City, and after being fed went to their friends among the other Indians. From this circumstance the creek on which the fight took place was named Battle Creek. The fight referred to was the first battle which the "Mormon" Pioneers fought with the Indians in the Territory of Utah.

—*From Journal History at the Historian's Office.*

EXTRACT FROM THE JOURNAL OF JUDGE
GEORGE W. BEAN.

(Almost a life-long Indian interpreter.)

Early in the spring of 1849 a move was made to commence a settlement at Provo, among the powerful tribe of Timpanodes, (*Timpanogos*) John S. and Isaac Higbee and Alex Williams gathered up a company of about thirty families, James Bean among the rest. They reached the river Provo the 1st of April. About three miles out they were met by a young brave *Angatewats* by name, who placed himself on horseback across the trail in front of the foremost wagon and forbad them from proceeding farther. Interpreter Dimic B. Huntington, who was with the Company, pleaded for them to try the emigrants a while and see if they could not live in peace together, and after about an hour's delay they were allowed to proceed in peace. They located on the south side of the river, near the lower crossing. They built their houses in a paralellogram, about 20 by 30 rods, enclosing an ancient mound near the center. Most of the houses were built of cottonwood logs, in solid continuous line, and where vacancies occurred, the space was filled in with pickets, about 12 feet long, set in the ground close together, for protection in case of attack from hostile Indians. They had a general stock corral on the East side of the fort outside, beside several private corrals behind the respective houses, with gates or back door openings, the farming was conducted on the east, south and west of the fort, mostly on the west side towards the lake. They got along pretty well with the natives the fore part of the season, although some of the worst Indians of this western region belonged to this tribe, and they soon found that Provo was the great annual gathering place for all the Ute bands of the valleys for two hundred miles, east and south, on account of the wonderful supply of fish, moving up the stream from the lake to their spawning grounds every spring, indeed so great were the number of suckers and mullet passing continuously up stream that often the river would be full from bank to bank as thick as they could swim for hours and sometimes days together, and fish would be taken in all ways and places. The Indians could feast from morning until night for weeks together, free of all cost, except a little labor catching the *Pahgar* (suckers), or *Mpahger* (speckled trout, good fish). At the time of their arrival at Provo the Timpanodes were governed by a chief called by the whites, Little Chief, but in about a month after this, he led a party of warriors to attack Wanship's band, north of Salt Lake City, and was killed in a battle up at Ogden hole, or north Ogden, then Opecarry (*Stick-in-the-Head*). There was also Old Elk, (*Pareyarts*), Old Battiste, *Tintic,* his brother, *Portsorvic, Angatewats* and other noted ones here, Old *Sawiet, old Petnich,* Walker and his brother, and old *Uinta* and his sons, Tabby, *Graspero.* and *Nicquia,* old *Antero,* and some times Kanosh. These with their bands had been accustomed to meet at Provo, and have a great good time, horse racing, trading, gambling and eating fish, for several weeks every year. There were some additions made to the population at Provo during the summer, and in the fall when Indian troubles broke out, they were situated in the fort.

The Indians were anxious for traders to bring
guns, ammunition and various merchandise to barter
for their skins and furs, horses and such things as
they had, sometimes buffalo robes, as those Ute Indians were an enterprising race, generally going
once a year to the eastern plains, to kill buffalo, and
for many winters had made incursions into Southern
California, robbing the ranchers of thousands of
horses. The cause of these raids being based on the
bad treatment of some of Chief Walker's party
many years ago, by certain ranchers, taking their
buffalo robes, Indian children and confiscating their
property without compensation. The settlers no
doubt acted under law of trade and intercourse, but
which was not understood by those tribes of the
Utah band. In this way Walker's band of Utes had
accumulated many horses. Some of the men here
started up a traffic with the natives, notably Alex
Williams, the guides James B. Porter and D. B.
Huntington, their interpreter. After a while came
trouble.

The first serious outbreak was occasioned by
three of our people, namely: Richard A. Ivie, Y.
Rufus Stoddard and Gerome Zabriskie, who met an
Indian called Bishop Whitney, in the field and
claimed a shirt the Indian had on. The Indian refused to give it up. Ivie claimed it as his and tried
to take it, was resisted and in the scuffle that in-
sued, the Indian was killed, and his body weighted
with rock, was sunk in the river. so reported by
the Indians, who found the body after 24 hours
search.

This killing of the Old Bishop, so called, occurred about the 1st of August, 1849, and immediately

caused great excitement amongst the Indians, especially the Timpanodes, located here. They first demanded the murderers, which, of course, was refused by the whites. They then required compensation in cattle and horses, but nothing was ever given, and shortly after this cattle and horses were found with arrows sticking in them, several persons were shot at while in the woods and other places. Meanwhile the people prepared for defense. Peter W. Conover was chosen Captain of Militia with R. T. Thomas and G. T. Willis, lieutenants, Miles Weaver, adjutant, Joseph Clark, sergeant. Guards were posted at night and armed herdsmen on horseback, kept the stock by day. The leading Indians ordered the people off their lands. They made serious threats in case of failure to leave and stock was stolen from time to time.

About September 1st a bastion was constructed on the mound in the fort, of heavy posts, 30 feet square, with log railings, and a six pounder iron cannon placed on the pfatlorm of the bastion, which was sufficiently elevated to protect the fort and stockyards from attack, which was considered liable to occur at any time.

About this time a large company of gold seekers enroute westward by way of southern California, made their camp alongside the fort and they having plenty of arms and ammunition, were a great aid, they stayed four or five weeks and had stock which was cared for together for mutual protection.

Our militia company continued to practice almost daily, and through the liberality of the emigrant camp powder was supplied for the cannon.

After the California emigrants had passed, the Indians got very troublesome, and were sometimes aggravated by our people, so that, towards Christmas, open war seemed inevitable. The measles got among our people and from there to the natives, having taken some prisoners, from them the disease spread through the tribe.

With the aid of the measles and about 100 men from Salt Lake County the Indians were finally driven off into the mountains and far away valleys.

During a three days fight near here, the Indians being behind a breatwork of logs and earth banks, Joseph Higbee was killed and Alex Williams, Albert Miles, Alex Stevens and Sam Casus (?) were severely wounded and Isham Flyn, John Nowlin and one or two others slightly wounded.

SETTLING OF UTAH VALLEY. COPIED FROM WHITNEY'S HISTORY OF UTAH. TROUBLE AT FORT UTAH (PROVO).

It was with reluctance that the Timpanogos Indians who met the Higbee colony in March, 1848, permitted the first white settlement on Provo River, and that, too, in spite of the invitation previously extended to the colonists by the chiefs, Sowiette and Walker, to settle among their tribes and teach them how to become civilized. It has also been stated that soon after Fort Utah was founded, Walker, according to Colonel Bridger and Mr. Vasquez began stirring up the Indians against the "Mormon" settlers. In this movement Walker was aided by another chief named Elk,—variously styled Big Elk, Old Elk, etc.,—like himself a hater of the whites, and apparently quite as fond of fighting. It was with Big Elk and his band that the Provo settlers, in their first regular battle with the savages, had immediately to deal.

It was believed by Governor Young that Colonel Bridger and other mountaineers were at the bottom of much of the ill-feeling manifested by the red men, and they were incited to attack the "Mormon" settlements. The Governor, (Brigham Young), however, seemed to have confidence in Mr. Vasquez, who had opened a small store in Salt Lake City, and whose interests to that extent were identified with those of the settlers.

The Indians, at first so friendly with the Utah Valley colonists, began their depredations in that vicinity in the spring of 1849. Grain was stolen from the fields, cattle and horses from the herds, and now and then an arrow from an Indian bow would fall uncomfortably near some settler as he was out gathering fuel in the river bottoms.

THE FIRST INDIAN WAR.

The first fight with the Indians took place on Battle Creek, near the present site of Pleasant Grove, it occurred early in the spring of 1849. There, Colonel John Scott, with thirty or forty men, after a sharp skirmish defeated the savages under Chief Kone— also Roman Nose—and drove them up Battle Creek Canyon. Five Indians were killed, but none of Colonel Scott's men were hurt. He had been sent south to recover some stolen horses taken from Orr's herd in Utah Valley, and several cattle stolen from Ezra T. Benson's herd in Tooele. Battle Creek derived its name from this initial encounter between the Indians and Deseret Militia.

For some reason the authorities at Salt Lake City did not altogether approve the conduct of this campaign. No doubt they regretted the necessity for a military expedition against the savages, and deplored the fatalities attending it, not only from humanitarian considerations, but fearing probably that it would precipitate a general war, and unify all the savage bands of the vicinity against a handful of settlers at Fort Utah. "Shed no blood" was a standing general order to the "Mormon" militia in those days, and the troops were expected to adhere to it wherever possible. Yet blood had now been shed and the Indians were doubtless exasperated. This may or may not have been the reason that Colonel Scott was found fault with. That would materially depend upon the nature of the orders he had received from his superiors, and his ability under subsequent circumstances to carry out those orders. It is a fact, however, that the Colonel fell under some censure at the time, and because of it declined to take part in succeeding Indian campaigns.

It is said that the Utah Indians never sought revenge for any of their number killed while stealing or making an attack. Colonel George A. Smith is authority for this statement.

But the Battle Creek skirmish, which was not strictly an affair of that kind, could not but have the effect of straining the relations between the settlers and their savage neighbors, and extinguishing in the hearts of the latter that spark of friendship which yet remained.

They continued their petty depredations and became bolder and more insolent daily. The settlers at Fort Utah would occassionally fire their cannon to warn the redskins that they were not unmindful of their misdeeds, and were prepared to maintain their rights. But the Indians were not to be awed by sound and smoke. Their nefarious practices went on. They were evidently provoking a conflict. Stock continued to be taken from the herds, and all efforts to recover stolen property were stoutly resisted. Finally the Indians began firing on the settlers as they issued from their fort, and at last the stockade was virtually in a state of siege.

No longer was it arrows alone that fell around them. Bullets whizzed past their ears. The Indians were now well supplied with fire-arms and ammunition, obtained in exchange for horses, mostly from California emigrants who had passed through the country.

Captain Howard Stansbury's party, during the fall, had been surveying around Utah Lake, where they also were much annoyed by the savages.

As winter came on, they suspended their labors and returned to Salt Lake City, feeling satisfied that in the existing state of affairs in Utah Valley it would be both difficult and dangerous for them to continue operations in the spring, exposed, as they would be, to attacks from the savages, either in open field or deadly ambush.

The subsequent sad fate of Lieutenant John W. Gunnsion and his party on the Sevier showed that these apprehensions were well grounded.

FEB. 9th. BATTLE AT FORT UTAH.

As for the inhabitants of Fort Utah, they patiently bore their annoyances and losses until nearly spring, 1850, when affairs became so serious that they felt compelled to appeal for aid to Governor Brigham Young and the Legislature, still in session at Salt Lake City. Captain Peter W. Conover, in charge of military affairs at the fort, and Miles Weaver carried the message of their anxious fellow settlers to headquarters.

Governor Young, on receiving the message, found himself in a somewhat peculiar position. That the beleaguered settlers must be relieved, and at once was evident, not only for their own sakes, but for that of other settlements already forming or in prospect in the south. But how best to relieve them was the question. The thought of more fighting and bloodshed was most repugnant to him. Not for worlds would the "Mormon" leader have the sons of Laman think that he and his people came among them for that purpose. "Feed them and not fight them," was his life-long motto and policy toward the red men. Besides, how would the authorities at Washington, by whom the petition of Deseret for statehood was then being considered, regard the opening of a warfare by the "Mormons" upon these dusky "Wards of the Government." Deem not this a trifling consideration, reader. A people like the "Mormons, liable to be misinterpreted, had to be cautious and circumspect in their public acts and policies, where other communities, whose loyalty and good intents were unquestioned, might have risked all with impunity.

Fortunately, there was a government officer on the grounds, a brave and honorable man,—Captain Howard Stansbury. It being evident—all conciliatory efforts having failed—that force must be employed to put an end to the aggressions of the savages, the Captain was asked by Governor Young and other officials for an expression of opinion as to what view the Government would probably take of it. "I did not hesitate to say to them," says Stansbury, "that in my judgment the contemplated expedition against these savage marauders was a measure not only of good policy, but one of absolute necessity and self-preservation.

He therefore warmly approved of it, and not only that, but at Governor Young's request permitted Lieutenant Howland to accompany the expedition as its adjutant, and contributed arms, ammunition, tents and camp equipage for the soldiers. Dr. Blake, of the Stansbury party, acted as surgeon for the expedition.

A company of fifty minute men under Captain George D. Grant started from Salt Lake City, Feb. 7 1850, followed by fifty others, commanded by Major Andrew Lytle. Colonel Scott had been ordered to go, but declined, for which he was afterwards court-martialed. Major Lytle went in his stead.

The expedition set out early in February, 1850. The weather was extremely cold, and the snow, frozen and hard-crusted, was over a foot deep in the valleys. Progress was therefore rendered very difficult.

Captain Grant's cavalry, after marching all night, on the morning of the 8th, arrived at Provo River. Such a march was deemed necessary in order

to take the Indians unaware and secure an advanta-
geous position. The militia found the settlers in their
fort on the south side of the stream. and the Indians
strongly entrenched in the willows and timber of the
river-bottom, a mile or two above. They were protected not only by the river-bank, but by a breast-
work of cotton-wood trees which they felled. Near
by their strong-hold stood a double log house facing
the river. This house, built by James A. Bean and
sons, which at one time became the center of action
in the fight that ensued, was immediatey opposite
the Indian fortification. It had been deserted by
one of the settlers, James A. Bean, who had taken
refuge with his family at the fort. The house was
now held by the savages who, during the battle, kept
up a continuous fire from its windows and crevices,
as well as from their redoubt, upon the attacking
party.

Captain Conover, commander at the fort, united
his men with Captain Grant's, and the main forces
then proceeded to occupy a position near the deserted
building, about a half a mile south-west of the log
house mentioned. The Indians were led by Chiefs
Elk and Ope-Carry—surnamed ''Stick-in-the-Head''
—the latter, like Sowiette, rather friendly with the
whites, while Elk, as has been stated, was more
like the warlike Walker. Ope-Carry, it seems, desired peace, and had come out of the redoubt to
talk with Dimick B. Huntington, the interpreter,
when Elk and his warriors opened fire, and the battle was thus begun.

The engagement lasted two days. during which
time an almost incessant fusilade was kept up between the white assailants and the dusky defenders

of the river redoubt. Artillery was also employed
against the savages, but with little effect, as they
were right under the bank, and most of the balls
passed harmlessly over. A squaw was killed by a
chain shot, however, during the progress of the
fight. The Indians would make frequent sorties,
and after delivering their fire, return to cover.
Again, they would thrust their gun barrels through
the snow lying deep upon the banks above them,
and momentarily raising their heads high enough
to take aim, discharge their broad-side at the besiegers. They fought so stubbornly that all efforts
to dislodge them for a time proved futile. They
killed Joseph Higbee, son of Isaac Higbee—then
president of the settlement—and wounded several
others of the attacking force.

Finally. in the afternoon of the second day,
(Feb. 9th) Captain Grant, whose care had been to
expose his men as little as possible, determined to
capture the log-house at all hazards. He therefore
ordered Lieutenant William H. Kimball, with fifteen
picked men, to charge upon the house and take it.
Among those who participated in this charge—
the one daring exploit of the campaign—were Robert T. Burton, Lot Smith, James Ferguson, John R.
Murdock, Ephraim K. Hanks, A. J. Pendleton, Orson K. Whitney, Barney Ward, Henry Johnson and
Isham Flyn. Kimball and his men proceded up the
river until directly opposite the log-house, which
now intervened between them and the stream. They
turned to the left, facing the rear of the house, and
the leader gave the word of charge. Dashing forward
through a ravine that for some moments hid them
from view, the horsemen emerged upon the flat and

were within a few rods of the house, in the act of
crossing a small slough. when a roaring volley from
the log citadel met them. Isham Flyn was wounded
and the charge was momentarily checked. Several
swept on, however, and the Indians hastily vacating
the house, fled to their entrenchments.

The first two troopers to gain the house were
Lot Smith and Robert T. Burton, who, riding around
to the front of the building, entered the passage between the two compartments. Bullets whizzed past
them, splintering the wood-work all around, but both
they and their horses were soon under shelter. Their
companions, a moment later, gathered to the rear
of the house, and none too soon, for the Indians,
recovering from their surprise, began pouring their
volleys into the ranks of cavalry and upon the captured building. Half the horses were instantly
killed and their riders escaped by miracle. Between
the volleys, Lieutenant Kimball, Ephraim K. Hanks
and others, darting around the corner of the house,
gained the inside, while others waited until an opening had been made in the rear.

To support the cavalry charge, Captain Grant
ordered forward a small detachment of infantry.
These men, ten in number, were a portion of Captain
Conover's command, and were led by Jabez B. Nowlin. On reaching the log-house, with saw and ax they
effected an entrance at the rear. Some, however,
went around the corner into the passage, and were
fired upon by the savages; Nowlin being wounded
in the nose.

The services of a surgeon was now in demand.
Seeing that something was wrong, Captain Grant
requested Hiram B. Clawson, General Wells' aide,

who had accompanied the expedition, to ride to the house and ascertain what was needed. He did so, performing the hazardous feat successfully, though bullets sung past him as he rode. His friends at the house, seeing him coming, redoubled their volleys and drew most of the Indians fire in their direction. Returning, Colonel Clawson reported that surgical aid was at once required for the wounded. He and his cousin, Steven Kinsey, a surgeon, then rode back to the building. Returning, the two were again fired upon, one bullet just missing Clawson's head and piercing Kinsey's hat. Later another ball came nigh hitting Clawson and went through Kinsey's trousers. Both, however, escaped unhurt.

Meantime, Lieutenant Howland, with something of the integrity of a Cortez, had conceived the idea of a movable battery, to operate against the Indian redoubt. His idea was at once acted upon. A barricade of planks, in the shape of a V, was constructed and placed upon runners, blankets being hung loosely on the inside to stop the force of the balls that penetrated the timber. The outside was covered with brush and boughs to conceal the true character of the improvised battery. This pointed barricade, behind which quite a number of men could take shelter and deliver their fire without being much exposed, was pushed towards the Indian stronghold. Like Macbeth, when Birnam Wood, or what he took to be a forest, came toward Dunsinane, the Indians were thoroughly alarmed at the approach of this strange object, and divining its purpose made up their minds to retreat. Accordingly, that evening, they opened a furious fire upon the position held by the troops, and under cover of the darkness withdrew. The log-house had previously been vacated by Kimball's men, a circumstance which enabled the Indians to depart unobserved, after helping themselves to a supply of horse-beef from the dead cavalry animals lying near.

General Wells, who had been sent for to take charge of further operations, arrived next morning, Feb. 10th, but on preparing to attack the Indians it was discovered that they had gone. One party, the smaller band, had retreated in the direction of Rock Canyon, a rough and difficult gorge a little north-east of Provo, while the main party had fled southward in the direction of Spanish Fork. A dead squaw—the one killed by a cannon shot—was found in the Indian encampment; also two or three warriors, dead or dying. Elk, the chief, subsequently died of wounds received during the siege. His being wounded had probably disheartened the savages and caused the retreat quite as much as Lieutenant Howland's battery. The lieutenant had returned to Salt Lake City after the second day's skirmish. Some of the Indians, more friendly than their fellows, had deserted their ranks before the fighting began, taking refuge with the white families in the fort.

Detailing certain men to garrison the stockade, and others to pursue the Rock Canyon refugees, General Wells, with the main body of the cavalry, set out upon the trail of the Indians who had gone southward. At Spanish Fork and Pe-teet-neet (now Payson)—short skirmishes occurred, and eventually, on Feb. 11th the Indians were overtaken near Table Mountain, at the south end of Utah Lake. Another battle ensued, and the Indians were practically annihilated. Most of the fighting took place on the ice, which was very slippery, making it extremely difficult for the horses to keep their feet. The Indians, being shot at, would fall, as if dead, and then, as their pursuers drew near, rise up and fire.

They killed several horses in this manner, but none of the cavalrymen were hurt.

Night came down. and a bitter night it was. The soldiers were forced to take refuge in the wicki-ups vacated by the Indians on the bleak mountain side. As these primitive shelters swarmed with vermin the result may readily be imagined.

On returning to Fort Utah, General Wells found that Major Lytle and Captain Lamereux, joining their forces, had pursued the other band of Indians up Rock Canyon. The fate of these savages was similar to that of their fellows at Table Mountain. The total Indian loss was about forty, more than half the number of warriors engaged Efforts were made to civilize the squaws and papooses who were captured. but as a rule without avail They lived with the whites during the winter. but in the spring again sought their native mountains.

A treaty of peace was entered into between the settlers and the Indians, and the latter now agreed to be friendly and molest their white neighbors no more.

CHIEF WALKER PLANS TO MASSACRE THE PEOPLE.

In the summer of 1850, Walker, it is said, laid a plan to massacre the people at Fort Utah. It was in revenge for a slight that he imagined he had received from Governor Young. The Ute chief had visited the

"Mormon" leader to obtain his permission to engage
in a campaign against the Shoshones, in which Walker wished some of the young men of Provo to join.
Governor Young would not listen to such a thing,
and again advised the warlike chief to cease fighting and bloodshed. Walker returned to Utah Valley in a rage. Gathering his band, he was about to
fall upon the fort, when Sowiette, the white man's
friend, again interposed to thwart him. He not only
warned the inmates, who flew to arms, but told Walker that he with his band would help the fort against
him. Walker again gave way, and for several years
warred elsewhere, not molesting the "Mormon" settlements.

The late Bishop Henson Walker of Pleasant
Grove, Utah County, Utah, related an incident that
occurred at the battle at Provo, in which he formed
a conspicuous figure. He said: "I shot at an Indian sixteen times from behind a log. To do him justice, he was equally active. There we were, both
under cover blazing away at each other, when neither
showed even a part of his body. But I had the last
shot. He stuck out too much of his head and never
got back."

Copied from "Deseret News" Vol. 1:

One white man by the name of Baker was killed
by Indians on the 29th of May, 1850, between Utah
and Sanpete Valleys.

The following summer a successful expedition
was undertaken by a company of volunteer (cavalry)
under Captain George D. Grant, against the Goshute
Indians, a band of renegades who for some time
had been stealing stock and committing murders in
Tooele Valley and the surrounding region. Their

headquarters were in Skull Valley. Captain William McBride with a company of infantry had preceded the cavalry to that point, but finding it impossible to operate successfully against the Indians with his troops, had requested that a force of mounted men be sent to his assistance. The Indian camp was among the Cedar Mountains, on the western edge of a desert, twenty miles wide and very difficult to cross, owing to an utter lack of water. A first effort to surprise and chastise the savages proved futile, as they had learned of the coming of the troops and laughed and jeered at them from the rocky heights where they were entrenched. A second march of the cavalry across the desert, during the night, when the Indians supposed the pursuit had been abandoned, was completely successful. The savages were surprised in their wickiups just at daybreak, and the males almost annihilated. Tons of "jerked beef," manufactured from the stolen cattle of the settlers, were found stored in the Indians' stronghold. Among those who participated in this expedition, which gave many years of peace to the western settlements, were George D. Grant, William H. Kimball, Robert T. Burton, Nathaniel V. Jones, Rodney Badger, James M. Barlow, John Wakely, Charles Westover and Jesse Turpin.

COPIED FROM TULLIDGE'S HISTORIES, VOL. II, P. 83.

"The pioneers of Tooele County had their complement of trouble with the Indians, in common with the early settlers in Utah. "With them," writes the Historian Edward W. Tullidge for several years, the loss of cattle and horses was frequent and often

severe. Scouting after the enemy, standing guard
and forting up formed an important factor of their
lives. Many incidents of interest will remain un-
written, as only a few of the most important events
can now be gathered up and placed on record.

In the spring of 1851, some emigrants on their
way to California were assisting Ezra T. Benson
to put up a saw-mill at Richville, (now known as
the Mill), when a party of the surrounding Indians
stole their horses. One of them Mr. Custer, with
Harrison Severe, Thomas Lee and other "Mormon"
settlers, followed them, as they supposed, to the west
side of Rush Lake; but evidently mistook the route
the marauders had taken. However, they there found
a band of Indians with their families, took them
prisoners and started for Tooele, but without dis-
arming the men. On the way the Indians and consequently the guard became separated into small
squads. It appears that Mr. Custer was a little in
the rear and south of the town of Tooele when the
two or three Indians with him made a break in the
darkness, for it was in the evening, and in the melee
Custer was shot. Those ahead of him soon learned
the fact by his horse coming up with them riderless.
Some men went back and found his body on a rock
where he had fallen. The blood-stained rock was a
witness of the event for many years. His body
was taken to Salt Lake City for burial. This was
the first bloodshed connected with Indian difficulties in the County. Harrison Severe, and perhaps
others, succeeded in getting five Indian warriors into Tooele City to a military camp prepared by Captain Wright for their reception. O. P. Rockwell,
commonly known as Porter Rockwell, was sent from

headquarters and took direction of affairs in this Indian trouble. Considering it best to make another effort to obtain the stolen horses, he took a party of men, and with them the five Indian prisoners and went through the mountains west of Grantsville into Skull Valley. The prisoners were evidently in sympathy with their thieving brethern and professed to know nothing of those who had stolen the horses. Their assertions received no credit from the whites. The party formed camp, went on a scout, and left Harrison Severe to guard the Indians for some twenty-four hours, rather a precarious business for one man under the circumstances.

Rockwell and his men, not finding any trace of the stolen horses, deemed it unwise to turn the thieves in their power loose to commit more depredations and perhaps shed the blood of some useful citizen, and they were sacrificed to the natural instincts of self-defense.

Soon after the above events the Indians stole about one hundred head of cattle from a herd kept by Mr. Charles White near Black Rock, at the south end of the Salt Lake, drove them past the present site of Grantsville, through Skull Valley into the mountains west. Some of the cattle being too fat to drive, died by the way; the remainder were killed and the meat dried and stored in cedar trees. These Indians were first pursued by fourteen men from Salt Lake City under Captain Wm. McBride. They got track of the stolen cattle in the region of Skull Valley, but found the Indians too numerous for their numbers and they sent an express to Salt Lake City for assistance. General James Ferguson and Colonels Geo. D. Grant and Wm. H. Kimball came out from Salt Lake City with forty men, were joined by ten more from Tooele City, and with these went after the marauders. After considerable scouting and several attempts to surprise bands of Indians, while on the march early one morning a camp was discovered in a canyon up the side of a mountain. It was approached as near as possible wihout being discovered, when the command was given to make a rush upon it, every man to do the best he could. The best mounted were upon the Indians before they could get away, and nine of the warriors were killed. Several expeditions from Salt Lake City afterwards assisted in the defense of the settlements, but there being no records of these events it is now difficult to write them.

Mr. Harrison Severe, one of the first pioneers of the County, had ever advocated a kindly policy towards the Indians who were not known to be guilty of crime. The following circumstance shows the wisdom of such a policy, and that the dispised Indian is sometimes capable of gratitude. In the Autumn of 1852 he went into the mountains with a wagon and two yoke of oxen for timber. Near his home was the wicki-up of a friendly Indian whose life he had once saved from the vengeance of his irate people. This Indian closely followed him into the mountains where three or four thieving savages were watching the coming of Mr. Severe, and had already plotted to kill him and take his oxen. As he was unarmed they easily took him prisoner, and were proceeding to carry out their bloody purpose, when the friendly Indian appeared on the ground, placed an arrow in his bow and informed them that before dispatching Mr. Severe they would be obliged to kill him. A parley ensued and the robbers were imbued with a more kindly feeling. One of them went home with Mr. Severe, and the latter sent a messenger into Salt Lake City for an interpreter. On his arrival a personal treaty was made between Mr. Severe and the Indians, after which he always went wherever he wished in safety, regardless of the difficulties the Indians might have with others. The last raid made by Indians on the the animals of the citizens of Tooele Valley was, doubtless, brought about by some thieving white person.

Not far from Tooele City an Indian Chief known as Naraquits had a son, about sixteen years old, who sickened and died; with him, in accordance with the custom of his people, he buried a rifle and some buckskins for his use. After an absence of several weeks he returned to visit the resting place of his son to find that some sacrilegious white man had robbed the grave. It was but natural that his vengeance should be aroused. Shortly after this some one hundred horses, mostly belonging to Naylor and Bringhurst, were driven off. It afterwards transpired that they were taken to Fort Bridger and sold to U. S. Soldiers, who at the time were stationed there.

In 1864 General Connor's Command was used to protect the Overland Mail Coach on the road from Stockton west, where the Indians had committed some depredations. Detachments guarded all stations and a guard of two or three men were killed at what was then known as Bunt Station, near where the town of Clifton now stands. At one time thirty men were stationed at Government Creek for sixty days. A little west of the creek Captain A. Smith

attacked a band of Indians and killed nine of them.
The outbreak ended as usual with such affairs. The
barbarians wasted away, and a miserable remnant
was glad to make peace on any terms." (Tullidge's
Histories, Col. II, pp. 3-85.)

DEATH OF SQUASH-HEAD.

The following was written by J. C. Lemmon at
Ferron, Aug. 6, 1906:

"James Lemmon was killed by an Indian called
Squash-head about the middle of May, 1851. Mother
was helping father to plant beans, when a neighbor
came to borrow a wash-tub and board; the man had
a little girl with him. After giving the man the tub,
she returned to help father in the lot and did not
notice that James followed them and that in crossing the ditch by the fence he fell in and was swept
down by the stream in the opposite direction. The
child must have gone down the ditch about a quarter
of a mile when Squash-head happened along and
found the child and made off with him. When the
alarm was given, all turned out to hunt, but no
trace of the child could be found. Some time afterwards, however, the Indian commenced to brag about
it, in consequence of which he was arrested and
taken to Provo. He broke away, but was caught
again by Joseph Kelly between Spanish Fork and
Springville and lodged in a house belonging to Bishop Johnson. While Alex Williams was guarding
him he told how he killed the child. He had tortured
the little one by taking off its toes and fingers, and
finally finished his brutal work by taking him
by the heels and smashing the back of its head on a

rock. The child was twenty months and six days old at the time of its death. Williams then killed Squash--head by cutting his throat with a case-knife which he had brought in with the Indian's breakfast. At the time of the tragedy the child's parents lived at Mountainville (now called Alpine), Utah County. "

The writer was a brother of the child who was killed. Geo. McKenzie, assistant-adjutant general of the Utah County War Veterans, said, after read ing the above that it was written by some one who did not fully understand the whole matter.

Don C. Johnson says: "Squash Head killed himself in the absence of Alex Williams and that it happened in Bishop Johnson's house."

CAUSE AND ORIGIN OF THE WALKER WAR.
By Geo. McKenzie.

Having been requested by State commander J. M. Westwood of the Utah Indian War Veterans Association to write up the cause of the "Walker War," having been a resident of Springville at the time, and being well acquainted with James Ivie, who was the principal actor in the drama that caused the war, I submit the following as told to me by Ivie at the time, and on several occasions since the war. Walker, the war chief of the Ute nation, with his braves and their families were camped on Spring creek about one mile north of the present town of Springville, (Utah Co., Utah) all at peace with the white settlers, spending their time fishing and hunting, and trading and begging from the people. James Ivie, at that time had built a cabin, and was living in it with his wife and one child about half a mile north and west of where the Indians were camped. In the forenoon of July 17, 1853, an Indian and squaw came into Ivie's cabin. The squaw had three large trout which-she wanted to trade to Mrs. Ivie for some flour. Flour being very scarce at that time, Mrs. Ivie called her husband in to get his views on the trade of that kind, he being at work digging a well. When he saw the trout, he said "They look mighty good to me," and suggested that Mrs. Ivie might give three pints of flour for them, if the squaw would trade that way. He then went out of the cabin to resume his work. Just after Ivie left two more Indians came into the cabin, one of whom seemed to be the husband or had some kind of claim on the squaw who had closed the trade with Mrs. Ivie. When this Indian saw the three trout, and the small amount of flour received in exchange, he became enraged and began beating the squaw, knocking her down, kicking and stamping her in a brutal manner. While this assault was being committed, Mrs. Ivie ran and called her husband, Mr. Ivie came to the cabin, and while the Indian was still beating the squaw he took hold of the Indian and pulled him away, the squaw lying prostrate on the floor. Ivie tried to push the Indian out of the cabin. When the Indian came, he left his gun standing by the door, and as Ivie pushed him out he grabbed his gun and tried to get in position to shoot Ivie. Ivie got hold of the muzzle of the gun, and in the struggle the gun was broken. The Indian retaining the stock and Ivie the barrel. When the gun broke, Ivie dealt the Indian a hard blow on the head with the barrel of the gun. The Indian fell

to the ground, apparently dead, but did not expire
until some hours later. The other Indian who came
to the cabin the same time as his companian drew his
bow and arrow and shot Ivie, the arrow passing
through the shoulder of Ivie's buckskin hunting
shirt. At this Ivie struck the Indian a violent blow
and he fell unconscious by the side of the prostrate
body of the other Indian. Just as Ivie got through
with this second Indian, the squaw that he had been
trying to protect came out of the cabin door with a
stick of wood in her hand which she had picked up by
the side of the fire in the cabin. With it she struck
Ivie a blow in the face cutting a deep gash in his upper lip, and the scar showed plainly from that time
until his death. Ivie again used the gun barrel to defend himself and struck the squaw. She fell unconscious by the side of the prostrate bodies of the two
Indians. At this stage in the drama Joseph Kelly
one of the foremost settlers of Springville, came
upon the scene, and while looking at the three Indians lying apparently dead he was told by Ivie what
had taken place. Kelly took a bucket of water that
stood in the cabin and poured it on the Indians, trying to restore them. He then sent the Indian who
first came to the cabin with the squaw for another
bucket of water to try to restore the Indians to life;
this Indian having taken no part in the trouble.

Kelly told Ivie to take his wife and child and
go into town before the Indian camp was notified of
the trouble, which he did.

The Indian that Kelly sent after the water went
to the Indian camp and told of what had taken place
at the Ivie cabin. The news of the trouble soon spread

through the camp and the settlement of whites. Intense exictement reigned, both in the Indian camp and the settlement.

Bishop Aaron Johnson, who was chief magistrate in all civil and military affairs at Springville, took immediate steps to protect the settlement. He ordered Caldwell's cavalry and Parry's infantry to be mustered in and be ready for action at call. All the other male citizens over sixteen years of age were enrolled as a home guard. Johnson with his interpreter, Wm. Smith, tried everything in their power to settle the trouble with Chief Walker, by offering ponies, beef, flour, and blankets, but Walker refused to settle unless Ivie was given up to be tried by the Indians, which Johnson refused to do.

The next day (July 18th) Walker broke camp and went to Payson; joined his brother Arrapene another Indian chief, and together they went into Payson canyon, killing Alexander Keele who was on guard at the outskirts of Payson, saying, that, the war would last until the white people were all exterminated. The Indians then went into the mountains east of Sanpete Valley and left their families in a place of safety.

The Indians returning in war paint, raided the settlements of Utah, Juab, Sanpete, Millard and Iron Counties during the summer and fall. The last engagement was at the south end of Utah Lake generally spoken of as the Goshen Valley battle, which lasted about three hours; the troops taking the Indian camp. Nine Indians were killed; some of the troops and horses were shot, but none mortally.

Some Indians and their families came down

Hobble Creek canyon to Springville a short time after, saying that the war was over.

A short time after Caldwell's cavalry and Parry's infantry were released from duty, having served a period of ninety-one days; from July 18th to October 15, 1853.

The treaty of peace was signed by Walker in May, 1854, at his camp on Meadow Creek, Juab Co.

—Signed Lieut. Geo. McKenzie.

Walker died Jan. 29, 1855, at Meadow Creek, Millard County, Utah and was buried by his tribe with the highest honor that could be given him as the most noted war-chief of the nation.

His brother Arrapeen succeeded him as chief.

FURTHER PARTICULARS OF THE WALKER WAR GIVEN BY JOHN W. BERRY OF PALMYRA, UTAH COUNTY.

"On the 19th of July 1853 the Indians killed Alexander Keele at Payson and commenced what is called the Walker War. On the 20th of July, Colonel Conover, from Provo, in command of a company of militia known as the Nauvoo Legion, called at Palmyra and asked for volunteers to join his company and defend the settlements not provided with sufficient guards. Major Stephen Markham, John W. Berry and fifteen others went with him as far south as Manti. Colonel Conover, wishing to send a message to President Brigham Young, at Salt Lake City, to ask for his advice, appointed Clark Roberts, of Provo, and John W. Berry as messengers to the President.

These messengers left Manti at 4 o'clock P. M. on the 23rd of July 1853, and arrived at Summit

Creek, (now Santaquin) about 10 A. M. on the following day. On their arrival they found the inhabitants had all moved to Payson for safety and that the town was in the possession of the Indians. While riding along through the streets of the deserted settlement, with no thought of the Indians being in full possession of the same, they were fired on by twenty one Indians, from a house in which they were concealed. Clark Roberts was shot through the right shoulder and John W. Berry in the left wrist. Six or seven Indians pursued the two white men on horseback to Spring Lake, where the Payson cow herd was stationed under a guard, consisting of five or six men. The Indians seeing this guard gave up the chase and started back into the mountains. The wounded men went on to Payson, where their wounds were dressed, and in the afternoon they were conveyed to their homes. When the messengers arrived at Palmyra, the citizens were camped in the school house.

On July 23rd, 1853, W. S. Berry and Charles Price, who were on guard discovered Indians attempting to steal cattle, and the savages commenced firing upon the guards, Charles Price was hit in the right thigh by a bullet, which made a very severe flesh wound. For fear of further Indian hostilities the people from the upper settlement all moved to Palmyra where they spent the winter of 1853-54. Indians stole about fifty or sixty head of cattle, among which were a number of oxen, and took them up Spanish Fork Canyon to the Warm Springs, where they camped all winter and fed upon the stolen stock.

In February, 1854, Captain Hancock of Payson,

captured two Indians, one of them being the son
of Chief Peteetneet. He held the chief's son a prisoner, and sent the other Indian to the tribe with the
message that he would hold the chief's son a prisoner until an interview was obtained with the chief.
On the following morning the chief came and held
a consultation with the citizens, after which he agreed
to terms of peace, which in a short time ended the
Walker War. Governor Brigham Young advised the
brethern to erect Peteetneet a home in the fort line
and have him make his home among them. This was
considered wise counsel, and accordingly the house
was built; the chief moved into it and remained until
the settlement was broken up.

Silas Hillman of Palmyra, Utah County, makes
the following statement which is published in Tullidge's Quarterly Magazine, Vol. 3, page 154.

It was feared the Indians would attack Sanpete
County settlements as they appeared to be heading
that way. The settlements in that county were
sparse and some were small, and the inhabitants
knew nothing of the Indians being hostile. Therefore, a council of war was decided to follow the Indians and get to Sanpete as soon as possible.
We started next morning. I took command
of the cavalry company, of Palmyra, being
lieutenant of said company; the captain staying at
home left me in command. This was on the 21st of
July, 1853. "When we arrived in Sanpete Valley,
the main body of troops kept straight on for Manti
City, but I, with my company, was detailed to go
around to the Allred settlement, afterwards called
Springtown. We saw some fresh signs of Indians,
but no Indians. We found the families gathered to-

gether and a board fort put up around them—a rather flimsy fort to stop bullets. We camped with them that night, during which one or two Indians were seen skulking around. Our boys shot at them, but I do not think they hit them; it raised the alarm however, and every man was at his post ready for a fight, but no Indians came.

We advised the few settlers of Springtown to move down to Manti City, but they said they could take care of themselves.

We had been ordered to make for the main army to report what we had discovered of the situation of affairs in that section of the country, therefore, the next morning we took up our line of march for Manti, where we arrived the same day in the afternoon, joined the main army consisting of about two hundred men under command of Colonel Markham and Conover.

"We stopped at Manti seven or eight days, during which time companies were scouting the country in every direction in search of Indians. One of our companies ran across a camp of thirty or forty Indians and had a brush with them. Some of the Indians were killed; the balance retreated.

Another party of the Indians came down the canyon to the mill, a short distance above Manti, in the night. After this discovery was made, a strong guard was kept up in the mouth of the canyon. One night I had command of a company doing guard service and Captain Chidester had charge of another in the mill below us, where the road came down the canyon. It was a very steep place, and a thick undergrowth of young pines grew close to the road. We concealed ourselves along the road in this under-

growth and watched all night for Indians, having
planned to let the Indians pass us; and when they
should reach the mill Captain Chidester's company
was to attack them and drive them back for us to
attack them. Thus they would have been attacked
both in the front and rear; but we got no chance to
put our plans into action, for the Indians never came.

"After we had been away about twelve days, we
received orders from the Lieutenant-General to return home. The first night after we left we encamped at the springs north of Nephi City. That night
the Indians tried to drive off our horses, which were
feeding, but our guard being strong around the
horses prevented the Indians from getting them,
and fired pretty lively for a short time; the balance
of the guard with the camp surrounded the horses
and drove them into a corral, which had been left
standing when the inhabitants evacuated the settlement and took shelter in the city of Nephi. The next
morning we saw some blood, but no dead Indians.
Next day we reached Palmyra. During the summer
and fall we had to keep up a vigilant watch against
the Indians. While we were in Sanpete, Indians
were lurking around Palmyra. One man by the name
of Price was shot in the knee; also one of our men
(John W. Berry), sent home with an express, was
shot at Summit Creek through the hand. The Indians drove off the Allred settlement's stock, and
during the season killed several men in Sanpete.
One man was also killed at Summit Creek.

We had another expedition, Sept 26th, of a
couple of days after Indians at Salt Greek, in Goshen Valley. We came to an Indian camp just at day
break and took the savages by surprise. As they

begged for peace, we told them if they would give up their arms and go to the settlements, we would not hurt them. We dallied with them for some time, as they did not like to give up their arms, that being the last thing an Indian will part with. But at last Colonel Markham gave them five minutes to decide. Not complying with his order the colonel gave the order for our company to attack. The Indians returned the fire very lively for some time, but our men pressed them so hard that they soon silenced the firing of the Indians. Those of them that were not killed retreated into a cane swamp and got away. Casualties on our side were small, considering the smartness of fire of the Indians. One man (Bishop Charles Hancock) was slightly wounded in the head, and one horse shot in the hip. The Indians being in the cane and in the swamp dragged their dead in there; Consequently we could not tell how many were killed.

After peace was made they told us we only wounded two or three; but they reported at Nephi that we killed nineteen or twenty of them.

They made a haul of sixty or seventy head of cattle from our place late in the fall and during the fore part of the winter, while the cattle were running two or three miles up the creek from Palmyra; the owners thought it was so late in the fall that there was no danger of Indians disturbing them; but they nevertheless, came down from the canyon over to Palmyra and took some out of our corrals, and took all they could find up the creek and got away with them to Uintah Valley. After peace was made they returned what they had not killed and eaten.

THE WALKER WAR CONTINUED. TREACHERY OF THE INDIANS.

From Whitney's History of Utah, Vol. 1, p. 514.

"On July 18th, 1853, Walker, with a number of warriors, rode down to Fort Payson, whose inhabitants, thinking no evil, received the red men kindly, and as usual gave them food. The Indians made no hostile movement until they started back to camp in the evening, when they shot and killed Alexander Keele, who was standing guard near the fort. Knowing well what would follow, Arapeen hastened back to his brother and told him what had been done.

Walker immediately ordered his followers to pack their wigwams and retreat up Payson Canyon, which they did. Several families of settlers were then living in the canyon. Upon these the savages fired as they passed, but were evidently in too great a hurry, fearing pursuit, to do serious execution.

The people of Payson on their part, expecting a general attack from the Indians, at once flew to arms. They also sent messengers to Provo to apprise the military authorities there of what had occurred, and request immediate reinforcement. Colonel Peter W. Conover, who still commanded the militia in Utah County, hastily gathered about a hundred and fifty men, and proceeded at once to Payson. He arrived there July 20th. Troops from Spanish Fork and Springville were already on the ground.

A council of war convened, consisting of Colonel Conover and his associate officers, and it was decided to follow in the tracks of the savages, who, it was feared, intended to attack the Sanpete settlements. Leaving the infantry to garrison the Payson fort, the

cavalry, under Colonel Conover and Lieutenant
Markham, at once set out for Manti. These movements were doubtless in accordance with orders from
headquarters. General Daniel H. Wells, at Salt Lake
City, having been apprised of the situation, had dispatched Lieutenant-Colonel William H. Kimball with
a hundred mounted men to join Colonel Conover at
Payson.

Meantime, simultaneous attacks had been made
by Indians at various points.

At Springville, in a second assault upon that settlement, William Jolley was shot and wounded in the
arm. At Nephi, in Juab County, cattle were stolen
and the guard fired upon, while similar depredations
were committed at Pleasant Creek and Manti in Sanpete County. (This was July 19th.)

On July 20th the Guard at Nephi, Juab County,
was fired upon by Indians.

Colonel Conover, on reaching Sanpete, left some
of his men at each settlement to protect it against
the Indians, who were now raiding and running off
stock in all directions. Arriving at Manti and secur-
ing that place against attack, Conover's command
divided and companies were sent out to scour the
surrounding country in quest of redskins. One of
these detachments, under Lieutenant-Colonel Jabez
Nowlin,—who it will be remembered was wounded
in the two days' fight at Provo,—came upon a band
of twenty or thirty Indians near Pleasant Creek on
the 23rd of July. Being hailed by an interpreter and
asked if they were friends or foes, the savages
admitted that they were enemies, and without waiting to be attacked fired upon the troopers. Nowlin
then ordered a charge, and the Indians, after the

first fire, broke and fled, leaving six or seven of their number dead upon the field. Nowlin's company sustained no loss.

Colonel Conover now dispatched messengers to request further orders from General Wells. The messengers sent were Clark Roberts of Provo, and John W. Berry of Spanish Fork. Leaving Manti in the afternoon on the 23rd, they reached Summit Creek—Santaquin—in Utah County, next morning. They found the place deserted, the settlers, fearing attack and massacre, having sought safety at Payson. As the messengers rode through the town they were fired upon by twenty-one Indians concealed in some houses. Berry was shot in the left wrist, and Roberts through the shoulder. Putting spurs to their horses they rode at full speed toward Payson, hotly pursued by the Indians, from whom, however, they succeeded in escaping.''

COLONEL GEORGE A. SMITH GIVEN COMMAND OF THE MILITIA.

On the 25th of July, Colonel George A. Smith was given command of all the militia in the Territory south of Salt Lake, with instructions to take prompt and thorough measures for the defense and safety of the various settlements. The policy he was directed by Governor Young to pursue was to gather all the inhabitants into forts, corralling their stock and surrounding it with armed guards. No acts of retaliation or offensive warfare upon the red men were to be permitted; but on the contrary a conciliatory course towards them was to be maintained. At the same time vigilant watch was to be kept, and such Indians as were caught attempting to steal or kill, were to be summarily punished. These instructions Colonel Smith executed with his usual fidelity, and though it entailed much labor upon the settlers to put themselves in a proper state of defense, the wisdom of the policy, evident at the outset, was speedily confirmed. Those who failed to follow the instructions suffered heavily from the raids of the Indians.

ATTACK ON WILLOW CREEK, (MONA).
ISAAC DUFFIN WOUNDED.

August 10th.—Lieutenant R. Burns and a company of ten men, encamped at a small settlement on Willow Creek—Mona—in Juab County, were attacked by Indians, and during the fight that followed, Isaac Duffin was slightly wounded in the knee. Two of the soldiers had their horses killed, and one Indian was sent to the "happy hunting grounds." About this time Colonel Conover was ordered back from Sanpete to guard the settlements of Utah County and assist in putting them in better condition of defense.

AT PARLEY'S PARK, TWO MEN KILLED,
ONE WOUNDED.

On the 17th of August, four men—John Dixon, John Quayle, John Hoagland and John Knight,— were hauling lumber from Snyder's saw-mill in Parley's Park, when they were fired upon by Indians in ambush and two of them instantly killed. These were John Quayle and John Dixon. Hoagland was wounded in the arm, but was able to help Knight detach two of their horses, upon which they rode with all speed to Salt Lake City. Barely escaping with their lives; they left their wagon, four horses, two mules, and the dead bodies of their companions behind them. Their savage assailants did not linger long in the neighborhood of the massacre, not even long enough to scalp or otherwise mutilate the dead, according to their custom. Taking the animals they hastily decamped, and though followed by an armed party from Salt Lake City, as soon as the news of the killing reached there, they were nowhere to be found, though diligently sought for in all the surrounding region. Another John Dickson, the spelling of whose name slightly differs from that of the other man killed in Parley's Canyon, had been shot by Indians near Snyder's Mill a short time before.

The situation now became so serious that traveling from settlement to settlement, unless accompanied by a strong guard, was extremely perilous.

Though the Utah Indians had taken the initiative, other tribes or parts of tribes were also beginning to engage in the war, shooting and stealing stock in various section of the Territory. Governor Young, on the 19th of August, issued a proclamation forbidding the sale of fire-arms and ammunition to the Utah Indians and calling upon the officers of the militia in the several districts to hold their commands in readiness to march at any moment against the murderous marauders.

Colonel George A. Smith returned to Salt Lake City from Iron County on the 22nd of August. He reported that the southern settlements generally were in an excellent state of defense, and that the inhabitants were on the alert in relation to the sava-

ges. He had been assisted in his labors by Apostle
Franklin D. Richards, who was traveling through
southern Utah on public business, and returned north
with Colonel Smith. Two days later Lieutenant-
Colonel William H. Kimball, who had also rendered
important service in Iron County, came back from
the south. He and his men had been followed closely
and watched by Indians for several days, but heed-
ing the Governor's instructions they had not taken
the offensive, and the savages, seeing that they were
prepared, did not attack them.

As a means of defense and an example to other
settlements during the Indian troubles of 1853, the
authorities at Salt Lake City decided to build a
"Spanish Wall" around the town. The project was
first mentioned by President Young in a meeting of
the Bishops held at the Council House in the latter
part of August. The City Council then took up the
matter and the same month a committee consisting
of Albert Carrington, Parley P. Pratt and Franklin
D. Richards submitted a report to the council sug-
gesting the line of the proposed wall around the city.
It was to stand twelve feet high and be six feet
through the base, tapering to a thickness, half way
up, of two-and-a-half feet, and preserving the same
thickness to the summit. Gates and bastions were to
be placed at suitable intervals, and the wall, which
was to be built entirely of earth, was to be about nine
miles long. It was never completed, but fragments
of the portion finished may yet be seen on the northern outskirts of the city, a reminder of the early days
that witnessed its erection. Subsequently many of
the outlying settlements of the Territory built similar walls for their protection.

WILLIAM HATTON KILLED WHILE STANDING GUARD AT FILLMORE.

Still the Indian war went on. At Fillmore, on the 13th day of September, William Hatton, while standing guard, was shot and killed by the savages—Pah-vants—who, catching from the Utes the infection of the hour, had begun stealing and killing in that locality.

COL. MARKHAM'S BRUSH AT GOSHEN.
C. B. HANCOCK WOUNDED.

On September 26th, Colonel Steven Markham and his men had a brush with the redskins near Goshen, Utah County, in which C. B. Hancock was wounded, and a number of Indians killed. Six days later, in another skirmish at Nephi, eight more savages were slain and two or three captured.

THE GUNNISON MASSACRE.
Copied from (Lights and Shadows of Mormonism) by J. F. Gibbs.

"The attention of the traveler on the road from Deseret, Millard County, Utah to Nevada, will very likely be drawn toward a cedar post that occupies an unusual position a few rods north of the Sevier River, and a hundred feet from the east side of a shallow lake. The place, which covers about ten acres is about six miles west of Deseret, Millard County, Utah, with no habitation within several miles. The rough bark has been removed from the post, otherwise there is nothing in its appearance to attract attention except its isolated position. Yet, the spot over which that solitary post stands sentinel is historic and tragic—it is the burial place of a small party of employees of the United States, where, over forty years ago, Captain Gunnison and a portion of his military escort fell easy victims to a band of revengeful Indians.

"The memorable spot is situated nearly midway in the Pahvant valley, about thirty miles west of the Canyon range, and twenty-five miles east of the House mountains.

"Except where narrowed in by encroaching mountains, the valley stretches out in an almost unbroken plain to the great Salt Lake, one hundred and fifty miles distant to the north.

"About two miles to the south, the monotony of the desert-like plain is relieved by a basaltic mesa, a dark volcanic mass which rises abruptly from the level country to a height of perhaps two hundred feet, the surface of which was swept by the waves of ancient Lake Bonneville, until it is nearly as smooth as the surrounding plain.

"Dotting the valley in the vicinity are numerous shallow lakes, formed by the overflow of the Sevier River whose sinuous trails across the valley is indicated by patches of scrub willows.

"The small lake first mentioned, is separated from the river by a small strip of ground occupied by grass and willows which abound in the immediate vicinity, both sides of the river(which is only four to six rods wide) being fringed with them. Rising gradually from the lake towards the north and east, the ground is three to five feet higher than the surface of the water, and is covered with a stunted growth of grease wood and shadscale, (the local name given to a low-growing thorny shrub). Patches of saline

land glisten in the sunlight, and under the transform-
ations wrought by the western mirage are often mistaken for bodies of water.

"At the time of the massacre the present lake
was marshy ground covered with flags, rushes and a
rank growth of grass which extended well out towards the higher ground, thus forming an inviting,
but dangerous nook. At the present time nothing remains of the willows on the east and west sides of
the dead swamps.

In other respects the place and its surroundings
have nearly the same appearance as on that fateful
afternoon when Captain Gunnison went into camp
for the last time.

"The scene of the tragedy has been thus min-
utely described to enable the reader to more clearly
understand why the Captain whose reputation for
courage has never been questioned—and his little
band of brave companions failed to make even a sem-
blance of resistance, and because no description of
the place has heretofore appeared in print. Captain Gunnison's brother, when the locality was described to him several years ago in Salt Lake City,
said he had always imagined the place to be in, or
near, the mouth of the canyon from which the river
debouched upon the plain.

"In the year of the massacre, 1853, Fillmore,
was the capital of Utah, and the nearest settlement
to the scene of the tragedy, being distant thirty-five
miles southeasterly. A few of the old settlers yet remain who remember the occurrence. Among the old-
timers is Byron Warner, now residing at Oasis, and
who is not only familiar with the incidents of the

tragedy, and well acquainted with the Indians who participated therein, but with the circumstances of which the Gunnison massacre was the unhappy result.

"And it is to Mr. Warner that the writer is most deeply indebted for that part of the account of the unfortunate occurrence.

"Mr. Warner's statement has been corroborated by Daniel Thompson, now residing at Scipio, and who in company with Mr. Warner and others, helped to bury the dead. But three of the Indians that were present and took an active part in the bloody deed yet linger on this side of the "happy hunting grounds." One of them is old Mareer, who, with his squaw Mary, and old Sam, another of the surviving reds, is living in a wickiup on some otherwise vacant ground southwest of Deseret. By the aid of two rough maps placed before Mareer on two separate days, and with the assistance of some small coins and other presents of tobacco, etc, and after assuring the old fellow that the Mericats (Americans) wouldn't be mad, the story of the attack was drawn from him.

"That his story is perfectly truthful is proved by the fact that at the second interview a new map was spread before him and the relative positions of the white men and Indians were accurately indicated as compared with the first map, and no amount of cross-questioning could shake his clear and vivid description of the attack and its blood-curdling details.

"Early in October, 1853, a company of Missouri emigrants, en route to California, passed through Fillmore and camped on Meadow Creek, eight miles to the southwest.

"A small band of Pahvant Indians were also

camped further up towards the mountains on the same creek as the emigrant train.

"Anson Call was at that time bishop of Fillmore, and when the emigrants passed through, told them they would find a few of the reds camped on Meadow Creek, that they were friendly, and the company need have no apprehension of danger, and asked that the Indians be not molested.

"The train had hardly gone into camp when Moshoquop—(the Pahvant war chief—and his father, Mareer) and several others of the band, arrived at the camp of the strangers and offered to "swap" buckskins for tobacco and other articles.

"The emigrants were unnecessarily suspicious of the bows and arrows carried by the Indians, for they surrounded the reds and attempted to disarm them. The Indians resisted what they regarded as an unwarranted intrusion of their rights. One of them "jabbed" an arrow into the breast of one of the emigrants, which so enraged them that, whipping out their revolvers, they opened fire on the Indians. In the melee, the father of Moshoquop was shot in the side and died the next day. Two of the other Indians were wounded, one in the shoulder and the other in the arm. Of the white men all escaped injury except the one who received the slight wound in the breast form the arrow thrust.

"A few days after his father's death, Moshoquop and a band of about twenty Indians moved northwesterly to the vicinity of the lakes near the present site of Desert for the purpose, as Mareer said, of hunting ducks, and crossing the Sevier River, camped a little to the northwest of the site of the present residence of David Crafts at Ingersol, and about twelve miles northeast of Sevier Lake, and six miles west of the place where Gunnison and his party were afterwards murdered.

There were six wicki-ups, or tepees, and among the band were many Indians whose names are familiar to the old residents of Millard County. They are: Moshoquop, Pants (the brother of Moshoquop), Mareer and his brother Jim, Carboorits, Nunkiboolits, Tomwants and his son Koonants, Skipoke, "Doctor Jacob," Wahbits, Moab, Sam, (Toady), Hunkootoop, Boquobits, and an unusually tricky red, Jimmy Knights, well known to the early stockraisers by his thieving propensities and the boldness he exhibited in killing their stock.

There were also in the band two Snake Valley Indians, a Ute buck from Nephi, one whose name cannot be learned, and the father of Mareer; in all, a band of twenty-three warriors.

During the year 1853, Captain Gunnison, with a small military escort under command of Captain R. M. Morris, had been exploring for a railroad route through the Rocky Mountains; in the latter part of October, Gunnison and his escort entered Pahvant valley from the north and camped on Pioneer creek, six mies north of Fillmore. Gunnison, with a few of his party, went into the small settlement of Fillmore for supplies. The captain lost no time in hunting up Mr. Call, with whom he was acquainted, a warm friendship having existed between them for several years, and from him learned of the killing of Moshoquop's father by the emigrants a few days previous. Mr. Call also warned the captain of probable danger, as the Indians, with threats of revenge, had left their camp at Meadow Creek, Gunnison expressed sorrow

Portrait of General Daniel H. Wells, Commander of Nauvoo Legion and Utah Militia.

BRIG. GEN. WM. BYRAM PACE,
Commander Utah Militia led the battle
at Gravelly Ford, June 11th, 1866.

COL. LYMAN S. WOOD

Division Adjutant Interpreter, Springville, Utah.

MAJOR-GENERAL AARON JOHNSON,

2nd Division Utah Militia 1866-7.

COL. JOHN R. WINDER

GENERAL ERASTUS
SNOW

ELDER ORSON HYDE, Apostle
Spring City, Sanpete County.

COL. GEO. A. SMITH

COL.
HEBER P. KIMBALL

WILLIAM JEX
Spanish Fork, exploring Fish Lake Country
1873.

SOLOMON F. KIMBALL
Heber P. Kimball's Cavalry Company,
writer of history.

over the unfortunate affair, and said the Indians would very likely carry out their threats at the first opportunity. Being so near the Sevier Lake—the dead sea of Millard County—Gunnison resolved to explore it and then to go on to Salt Lake City and establish winter quarters.

Breaking camp on pioneer creek, the party proceeded a few miles north to the present site of Holden where they left the territorial road and bore northwesterly. Passing the southern termination of the Canyon range, the party continued on over the desert to the Sevier River and camped on a large bottom surrounded by high, precipitous banks, known at the present time as Gunnison's Bend, and situated about five miles northeast of Deseret.

On the morning of October 25th Captain Gunnison started on his last and fatal mission of exploration. Accompanying him were R. A. Kern, artist and topographer; F. Creutzfeldts, botanist; Wm. Potter, a Mormon guide and interpreter from Manti, Sanpete County, Utah; a man who served as cook; a corporal and six men.

The provisions and camp outfit were packed on an improvised cart, the tongue and front wheels of a wagon which was well adapted to the purpose. Captain Morris and a part of the escort were to continue in camp until the return of the Gunnison party. Meanwhile some of Morris's men were to examine the northwestern part of the valley as to the feasibility of a wagon road through to the Great Salt Lake.

Following down the north side of the river in a southwesterly direction, the Gunnison party arrived in the vicinity of the upper lakes, where some of the

men began shooting at wild fowl which fairly swarmed in that vicinity. The firing was most unfortunate, as the reports of firearms reached the ears of
Sam and Toady, two of Moshoquop's dusky band,
who were hunting ducks along the river and sloughs.
The Indians watched the little party until they went
into camp on the ground now marked by the cedar
post, when they hastened to the Indian camp and
reported the presence of strangers.

Wm. Potter, the guide advised the Captain to make
camp further to the north on open and higher ground.
His familiarity with the traits of the Indians led him
to be suspicious of the surroundings, but his prudent
advise was overruled. There is something in the
nature of men that impels them, when camping near
a spring or stream of water, to get as near to it as
practicable.

The horses were "picketed" along the margin of
the swamp to the north and northwest, and after the
usual camp duties were over, and the last of the
stories of exciting Western life had been told, the
little party spread their blankets on the ground and
retired for the night with no apprehension of the
terrible fate that awaited them. On receiving the
news of the white men, Moshoquop determined to
avenge the death of his father. Calling his band of
warriors together, he told them his purpose and explained in detail the plan of attack which was to begin
at the firing of a signal gun. Each warrior was instructed as to the position he would occupy in the
deadly cordon that was to be drawn around the slum-
bering explorers. It was about midnight when the
line of march began. In single file they moved silently and swiftly forward, and as the dusky line glided

in a sinuous course to avoid clumps of stunted grease-wood and willows it resembled the lithe movements of a huge serpent.

The reds followed up the north bank of the river until they reached the western margin of the swamp which separated them from their victims, where the band divided. Moshoquop, Pants, Mareer, Nunkiboolits and several others continued on up the river bank. Stealthily creeping through the willows and tall grass, the Indians took their pre-arranged stations to the south and east of the Gunnison party and not over one hundred feet distant.

The white men had beaten quite a distinct trail from their camp to the river. Carboorits skulked in the grass a few yards west of the trail on the bank of the river, while Pants crept to a position on the margin of the swamp, and not over thirty yards distant from the smouldering camp-fire; each savage being concealed in the rank grass and willows.

The other portion of the band skirted the west side of the swamp, and bending easterly, cautiously crept to the north of the low lying ridge which is not more than five feet higher than the marsh. Each Indian took the position previously assigned him, and before the faintest streak of dawn appeared, the doomed explorers were nearly surrounded by the wily savages who occupied the east, north and south sides of the camp, while the marsh cut off escape on the west. The first sign of activity on the part of the white men occurred just before sunrise. The cook was the first to arise, and in a few minutes the cheery gleam of the camp-fire shot upward, warning the men that no time was to be wasted in preparing for the morning meal. The iron tripod had been placed over the fire, the camp kettle hung in its position, the cook had begun mixing bread. Prof Creutzfeldt was standing near the camp-fire warming himself, Captain Gunnison had walked out to the river, about seventy-five feet south from the camp-fire, and while in a sitting position, was bathing his hands and face. The sun had just risen from behind the distant canyon range when Pants stealthily rose from his place of concealment near the edge of the swamp, a sharp report rang out on the crisp air and the cook fell dead beside his camp-fire.

Carboorits had been watching the captain and waiting for the deadly signal. Startled by the report, Gunnison sprang to his feet and the bullet from Carboorits' gun sped past him. Quickly pulling his six-shooter, the captain opened fire on his copper-colored assailant, who ducked and dodged to escape injury. The signal gun was followed by the rapid firing of nearly a dozen guns intermingled by the piercing war-whoop of the savages.

The surprise was complete, and the dazed officers and men thought only of escape. Amid the shower of whizzing arrows which followed the emptying of the guns, the men ran toward the open ground to the north and northeast, and in the desperate race for life, threw aside their arms and divested themselves of coats and everything that might impede their flight.

A few of the men fled in the direction of the horses. One of the soldiers, as he was about to mount, caught sight of an Indian as he was adjusting an arrow to his bow. With exceptional coolness the

man quickly lowered his gun on the savage and fired.
The Indian dropped, and the soldier rode away believing he had killed him. (Old Mareer says the
wily redskin fell as the gun fired, and escaped without injury, and that not an Indian was wounded),
Two others of the escort succeeded in mounting, one
of them escaped on horesback, the other was thrown
from his horse a short distance east of the camp, but
had the good sense to remain quiet for several hours
while the reds were passing to and fro, sheltered only
by the stunted greasewood. The fourth man that
escaped ran southeasterly, evaded his pursuers, and
plunged into the river, swam to the south bank,
where, within the friendly shadow of the willows, he
continued his flight to the camp of Captain Morris.

The Indians who had taken positions to the north
made no sign until the fleeing men were nearly onto
them, when they sprang to their feet and with fierce
yells poured a volley of arrows into the panic-strick-
en men, who, no doubt, were congratulating themselves on their escape.

Captain Gunnison, after emptying his revolver
at Carboorits, turned in the direction of the horses
and had reached a point about seventy-five yards
distant from the camp when he fell, stricken down
by nearly a score of arrows. Temporarily screened
by grass and willows, he lay helpless while the cries
of his comrades and the discordant war-cries of
the savages resounded in his ears. Some two or three
hours later he was discovered by a party of the reds,
among whom was Mareer, and who described in pan-
tomime the last act of the terrible tragedy. Gunnison was lying on his side, and when the Indians appeared, slowly and painfully raised himself to a sit-

ting posture. He made no sound, but reached out his arms in an appealing manner towards his assailants.

Gunnison, in his several years of exploring in the west, had endeavored to impress upon the red men that he was their friend. In his conduct towards them he was uniformly kind and upright, and it was this fact that probably prompted the captain to extend his arms, possibly, with the hope of mercy.

Mareer said he did not know, until he saw the captain partly rise from the ground, that he was with the party. Moshoquop was not present or he might, possibly, have given Gunnison a chance to recover from his wounds. As it was, the Indians hesitated, the captain's mute appeal seemed to stir some latent feeling, or strike a stranger cord in their savage natures. But while standing there undecided "Jimmy Knights," the renegade Indian, came up, discharged his gun into Captain Gunnison's body which settled slowly back upon the sward, and one of the bravest and best spirits joined his comrades in the mysterious beyond.

During the afternoon of the day of the tragedy, one of the fugitives staggered into the camp of Captain Morris and told the story of the attack, and stated that all but himself were slain. In a few minutes the two who had escaped on horses arrived and corroborated the story of the massacre.

Hurriedly mounting, the Morris party rode down the river. Darkness coming on, they dismounted in the vicinty of their lifeless comrades, and holding their horses by the bridles, kept vigil throughout the long night which was rendered more dismal by the howling of the wolves which had begun the work of mutilating the bodies of the slain. In the dim light of the early morning, one of the survivors guided Captain Morris to the camp ground, the bodies were identified and their positions mentally recorded.

The dreary night had been a severe strain on the men, and the spectacle of the mutilated bodies of their friends was so terrible and suggestive as to completely unnerve them. The stampede that ensued was more like that of men pursued by the bullets and yells of those who had made the previous morning memorable by their savagery than a company of armed men leaving behind them the forms of their stricken comrades. Overcoats, knapsacks, carbines, revolvers and ammunition marked the trail of their frenzied flight and added to the booty previously secured by the Indians.

The news of the massacre reached Fillmore, and Bishop Anson Call sent Daniel Thompson, William and Culbert King, to Salt Lake City with a dispatch announcing the deplorable event.

Meanwhile, Captain Morris and remnant of his command had reached Salt Lake City, and sent the corporal who, twenty-four hours after the massacre, went over the ground and helped to identify the remains, down to Fillmore. On his arrival, some ten days after the tragedy, Bishop Call selected George Black, Daniel Thompson, John King, Lewis Bartholomew, Byron Warner, and as Mr. Warner believes Nelson Crandall, now of Springville, Chief Kanosh and Narrient of the Pahvant tribe to go with them to the scene of the massacre.

Messrs Warner and Thompson describe the sight as the most pitiable they ever saw. About twelve days had elapsed between the morning of the massacre and the arrival of the burial party. The coyotes had so mutilated the dead that nothing remained of the small party of explorers but glistening skeletons. In some instances a leg, arm or foot could not be found. The remains of Potter were nearly intact. Those of Captain Gunnison were more readily recognized by the iron gray hair which clung to his temples. The remains of Prof. Creutzfeldt were found near those of the cook, who was the first to perish. A steel-pointed arrow had pierced the body of Creutzfeldt and the barb was found imbedded in his backbone. Some of the men had reached a distance of about one third of a mile to the north east before being killed.

Immediately after the arrival of the Fillmore party, Kanosh sent Narrient down the river in search of Moshoquop and his band, and gave orders to come in if they could be found.

In those days not a member of the Pahvant tribe dared to disobey the intrepid chief, and as Mr. Call and his party were rounding up the top of the common grave, Moshoquop and his band came in sight across the swamp on their ponies. Circling the marsh they came on whipping, kicking and leaning from side to side and yelling like demons. The reds were in their war paint, and with their long black hair streaming behind, presented a wild appearance.

The corporal, who was not acquainted with the absolute power wielded by the Indian chiefs, thought another massacre would be perpetrated, and trembled like an aspen. Mr. Warner, who is a very nervy man, and accustomed to the ways of the Indians, says his sensations were anything but agreeable.

However, when within a few rods of the scene of their murderous work, a motion from Kanosh caused them to be quiet, when he upbraided them for their devilish work.

Moshoquop then told the partial story of the massacre, and endeavored to exonerate himself by relating the circumstances of his father's death at the hands of the white men. Mr. Warner asserts that during the recital, tears streamed from Moshoquop's eyes and that his appearance was a mixture of fiend incarnate and savage affection.

The remains of Captain Gunnison and Wm. Potter were wrapped in blankets and taken to Fillmore where the captain was buried; those of Potter were sent to Manti for interment.

Of the three surviving Indians, Carboorits, who shot at the Captain, has lost his eyesight, and is ending his days in darkness on the Indian farm near the town of Kanosh. Mareer and Sam, as previously stated, are living near Deseret. Mareer is fast hastening to the grave, and Sam is a muttering imbecile.

Moshoquop died two years ago in Deseret. He was of medium stature, compactly built, and as lithe and wiry as a pather. His forehead was high and retreating, his bearing reserved and dignified, his face, while indicating strength and a fearless nature, was frank and not unkind. In spite of the terrible deed he planned and carried out so relentlessly, he was better than the average Indian. While his part in the Gunnison tragedy cannot be justified by revenge for the death of his father, it is somewhat palliated by reflecting that his nature—like that of all other

Indians—was the result of generations of trasmission of ideas and customs incident to the environment of the red men.

FOUR MEN KILLED AT UINTAH SPRINGS, SANPETE COUNTY.

On September 30th, 1853, a party of four men, William Reed, James Nelson, William Luke and Thomas Clark, started from Manti, Sanpete County, with ox teams loaded with wheat for Salt Lake City. It was arranged that they were to camp the first night on the Sanpitch River, near where Moroni is now located, and wait there until a company with horse teams under the leadership of Isaac Morley should overtake them; then they were to travel slowly together through Salt Creek Canyon; but contrary to arrangements they went on to Uintah Springs (now Fountain Green) and camped for the night. Early on the morning of October 1st their camp was attacked by Indians and all four men were killed.

The savages had time in this instance to complete their fiendish work, mutilating the bodies of their victims to such a degree that when found they could scarcely be recognized.

When Morley's company came along they found three of the bodies of the murdered men, but the body of Clark had been covered up in the wagon with wheat that the Indians had emptied out of the sacks which they had taken away with them.

SKIRMISH AT NEPHI, JUAB COUNTY.
EIGHT INDIANS KILLED.

The company went on to Nephi at the mouth of Salt Creek Canyon, and on the morning of the 2nd of October encountered a camp of Indians and had a skirmish, in which eight Indians were killed and one squaw and two boys taken prisoners.

When they reported in Utah County, a possee of about twenty men from Springville, Spanish Fork and Payson was organized under command of James T. Guyman. They went to the Uintah Springs and found the remains of Thomas Clark under the wheat in the wagon. He had been scalped, his head crushed and his body cut open and his heart taken out. The posse went on to Manti and reported. They were accompanied by George Peacock from Springville who returned with the posse. At Manti they learned of the killing of William Mills and John Warner near Manti on the 4th.

On their return the company stopped and buried the remains of Clark which was by then badly decomposed. It was said that George Peacock, who was a relative of Clark, got the body and buried it at Manti.

The particulars here given were obtained from Samuel T. Curtis of Salem, Utah County, who was one of the posse.

WM. MILLS AND JOHN E. WARNER
KILLED AT MANTI, SANPETE COUNTY.

On October 4, 1853, William Mills and John Warner were killed by Indians, near Manti. The following particulars are copied from a sketch written by Eunice Warner Snow, wife of John E. Warner one of the men killed at Manti, October 4th:

"On the 4th of October, 1853, my husband was killed by the Indians in the edge of Manti Canyon while attending the grist mill. Mr. Warner, my husband, owned one third of the mill at the time he was killed, and it fell to his lot to attend the mill and grind the wheat for the people of Manti. The mill was situated about a mile from town. He had taken a number of men with him as a guard until the day he was killed. On that day it seemed there was no one who was willing to go with him. A man by the name of William Mills offered to go, as he needed some wood. He said he would take his oxen and cart and while Mr. Warner was grinding a grist, he would go into the mountains close to the mill and get some wood. Mr. Warner would not let him go out alone, so they both went out a short distance from the mill, but before they went, my husband filled the hopper with wheat. He had taken his gun with him every day and had killed two rabbits the day before. I was cooking them for his supper when word came that he had been killed. We heard the report of the guns that killed the two men, but paid no attention to it as we had heard similar shooting before when my husband killed the two rabbits.

The men were killed in the morning, as we thought. Soon after dinner a young man went up to the mill for some flour. There was no one to be found around the mill, which was running at full speed, but had no wheat in the hopper. He knew something was wrong and came to town as fast as he could and told the condition in which he found the mill. They soon found a number of men to go in search of Warner and Mills and found their bodies a short distance from the mill. The cattle had also been killed with poisoned arrows. The Indians had been in ambush waiting for an opportunity to do their work. Both men were stripped naked, except that my husband had his garments left on him. I was not allowed to see him as he was so badly disfigured in the face. The Indians, after they had tried to make peace with our people told that Mr. Warner had fought desperately and killed one Indian.

Soon after the killing an Indian came to our house carrying my husband's gun, and one day two Indians came to our door, one of whom had my husband's neck tie on his black neck; the other had his pocket rule, which he always carried with him, and also his pen knife. This knife was a useful one, as it contained a number of articles, such as a button hook, an ear spoon, etc. Two or three articles they had broken up. They were showing these things to my father and mother at the table as we happened to be eating dinner at the time. I grabbed a butcher knife which was lying on the table and started for them. My father seeing me rise from the table, caught me in his arms and carried me out of the room. It was more than I could stand to see the black imps with my husband's things. This happened a short time before the birth of my son, who was born six months after my husband was killed.

Another serious trouble came of which I will
make mention; Soon after my son was born, Chief
Walker came to our house one day. He said he intended, when I got around again, to have me for his
wife. He told my father and mother his intentions.
They did not let me known anything about it until
he came several times to see me; when they told me
it almost frightened me to death. I was obliged to
keep in hiding from him for about six weeks, in fact
until the good news came one mornng that Walker
was dead. He died very suddenly."

ATTACK AT SANTAQUIN, UTAH COUNTY.
FERNEE L. TINDRELL KILLED.

On October 14, 1853, Indians attacked the infant
settlement of Summit (now Santaquin), Utah Co.,
of which occurrence Albert Jones, of Provo, Utah
County, wrote the following:

The settlers of Santaquin had been driven from
their homes, and had made their temporary residence
at Payson, that being a more populous town and
able by its numbers to defend itself against the Indians who were then on the war-path under the
lead of their chief Wah-ker. Crops had been planted
at Santaquin that spring and a small party owning
land there had come from Payson in the morning of
Oct. 14, 1853 to harvest their potatoes. Among the
number were Jonathan S. Page, Fernee L. Tindrel,
Sybrannus Calkins, (a Mormon battalion boy) and
John Sheffield, then a lad of about fifteen years.
These harvesting parties came and returned to Payson the same day.

On the morning of this day one of the boys going over the hills with some companions espied a

wolf and could not resist taking a shot at the brute,
although that was contrary to orders in those days,
as the firing of a gun was the signal agreed upon announcing the approach of Indians. The older people
were alarmed on the instant, but upon finding out
the cause of the shot, reprimanded the boys and returned to their several patches of potatoes, working
with a will to secure them for their winter's use.

About 2 p. m. firing was heard again, but the men
had grown careless, thinking it was the boys shooting again. However, as the shooting continued, the
parties became alarmed, and Jonathan S. Page and
Sybranus Calkins, who were working together,
looked up from their work and saw a number of Indians in the distance firing at Furnee L. Tindrel and
the boy John Sheffield. They saw Tindrel run quite
a distance and then fall, but lost sight of the boy
entirely.

"The Indians," said Captain Jonathan S. Page,
who narrated this incident of the early Indian wars,
"came straight on towards us, firing at us as they
came. We prepared to take off a wagon box for
breast works and fight them, but so many of them
came in view through the oak brush and corn that we
decided to leave and run to the main body of harvesters. We had two yoke of oxen with us, one yoke
chained to a wagon got so excited and sagged back
on the chain, so that we could not unhook it.

We started off driving a yoke of Calkin's cattle
before us, but they were so heavy and moved so slow,
that we abandoned them, and away we ran. The Indian war-whoop was ringing in our ears, and the bullets whistling around us. I was young and a good
runner, and with that horrid war-cry to urge me on, I

cleared the three foot sage brush in our path like a deer. Calkins who had been exposed in his service in the battalion, could not keep near me—and called out, "Page you ain't going to leave me?"

I slackened speed until he came up. The bullets and arrows were whistling and screaming around us again.

We renewed our pace, the Indians pressing close behind us, until we came to a thicket of large oak brush, into which we rushed for shelter; the Indians soon approached above us on a ridge—not a rag on them. Their red bodies shone and glistened in the sun. They must have been greased. They danced about the ridge, waving the scalp of poor Tindrel, and shouting their terrible war-cry. The thrilling effect is felt when imitated in our sham battle in the celebration of the twenty-fourth of July, but in the position we were in at the time, its terrifying effect had full force and our hair stood on end. As we dashed into the thickest oak brush we saw Abel Butterfield (a man noted for his great size and strength) on another ridge. We called to him that the Indians were upon him and that he had better run for safety. It seemed to daze him, as we looked out from our hiding places, we could see the old man (we always called him old) walking up and down on top of the slope opposite the Indians, waving his arms, and calling with his stentorian voice for the boys of Payson and the boys of Spring Creek to come on. This ruse, no doubt, had its effect, for the Indians did not advance farther.

They continued to cry to us to come out of the brush and attack them. They dared not come near us. I had a Kentucky rifle that carried a ball about as big as a pea, while Calkins had an old time Taylor rifle. After some time the Indians withdrew and went to the wagon and the cattle we had left. There were two other yoke of cattle there belonging to James Holman. The Indians shot and killed the oxen chained to the wagon and drove off the others with them.

Luke Holman and Levi Colvin came up to the thicket where we had hid. There were now five of us, and we followed on after the Indians in hopes of getting the cattle back. The Indians saw us coming and divided their party, some continuing on with the cattle, while the rest made southward, toward Santaquin canyon. Here I found a good opportunity to count them, and made out thirty-nine. We thought they might have had horses at the mouth of the canyon, and concluded we had better turn back for fear they would cut us off from the main body of harvesters. We then went back to the rest of the people, who numbered about nine.

Levi Colvin had a pair of horses there, and Jonathan Davis mounted one of them and rode down to Payson to give the alarm; soon about forty men in wagons and on horseback were hastening to our relief, in charge of Col. W. C. McClellan.

Robert E. Collet (later of Pleasant Grove) also ran into Payson on foot, following down the creek northward, and arrived there soon after the horsemen got in.

Levi Colvin and myself, before the relief party came, went up through the brush and found the body of Tindrel; he was scalped, and all his clothes were off, except his shirt. He was shot seven times. Two bullet holes and five arrows were found in his body.

The reason they had not taken off his shirt, was that one of his arms was pinned to his body with an arrow. One arrow had gone through the body, entering the back and protruding at the breast bone; one bullet passed through him close to the heart, and he must have run seventy-five yards at least, after receiving this shot, before he fell.

The horror that filled my soul at seeing the scalped and naked body of my friend, who but a few hours ago had been full of life, is indescribable. Shot down by cruel and relentless Indians, he laid there stripped, dead and mutilated, under the bright October sun. We left him there, and returned to the position occupied by the party of harvesters.

The company from Payson under the command of Col. W. C. McClellan soon came on the ground. We took up the body of Brother Fernee L. Tindrel and sorrowfully wended our way back to Payson, where we interred his body in the cementery with military honors. I being one of the party that fired the salute above the grave.

Young John Sheffield had hid in the brush and escaped unhurt. He came to us when he saw the arrival of the relief parties from Payson.

The leading Indian of this party of marauders was a Ute known by the name of Showan, the brother of Santaquin, who lived in Thistle for many years and owned a ranch there and is now on the Indian reservation.   —Albert Jones.''

CHASE'S SAWMILL IN SANPETE COUNTY BURNED BY INDIANS.

November 6th—Chase's sawmill in Sanpete County, was burned by Indians. Three days later,

November 9th—The Indians burned six houses in Summit Creek (Santaquin) Utah County, which had been vacated during the summer.

THE ALLRED SETTLEMENT, (SPRING CITY) BURNED BY INDIANS.

1854, Jan. 6th—Allred's settlement (Spring City) Sanpete County, which had been deserted the previous summer because of Indian troubles, was burned to the ground by Indians.

April.—A number of Elders was called on a mission to the Indians in southern Utah. This more directly resulted in opening up that part of Utah south of the rim of the great basin to settlement.

TREATY WITH CHIEF WALKER AND KANOSH. END OF UTE WAR.

In May, 1854, after a "talk" with President Brigham Young, the Indian chief Walker (Surrounded by his braves) and Kanosh, chief of the Pahvant Indians, entered into a formal treaty of peace at Chicken Creek, Juab County. This ended the Ute war, during which nineteen white persons and many Indians had been killed.

During the war a number of the smaller settlements had been broken up, and their inhabitants moved to larger towns.

WILLIAM AND WARREN WEEKS KILLED IN CEDAR VALLEY.

August 8th William and Warren Weeks, sons of Bishop Allen Weeks, were killed by Indians in Cedar Valley.

CHIEF WALKER DIED AT MEADOW CREEK, MILLARD COUNTY

1855, January 29th.—Walker, the Utah Chief, who had so long been a terror to the whites, died at Meadow Creek, in Millard County, and was succeeded by his brother Arapeen. Walker prior to his death, became convinced that the "Mormons" were his friends, and among his final words was an injunction to his tribe to live at peace with the settlers and not molest them.

According to the cruel custom then in vogue among the savages, an Indian boy and girl and thirteen horses were buried alive with Walker, being secured near the corpse of the Chief at the bottom of a deep pit or walled enclosure, and left to suffer until death brought relief, It was said that two Indians passed by the place, and the boy begged to be let out, but they passed on. The boy said that Walker was beginning to stink.

THE ELK MOUNTAIN MISSION, AND ABANDONMENT.

An Indian Mission known in the history of the Church as the Elk Mountain Mission was established for the purpose of educating a tribe of Indians who occupied the region of country in south-eastern Utah in the vicinity of the Elk Mountains (now the La Salle Mountains). Their main rendezvous was in a little Valley on the Grand River where the settlement of Moab is now situated. Those who went on this mission were called at a general Conference of the Church held in Great Salt Lake City in April, 1855.

Forty-one men were called, namely Alfred N. Billings, Robert Brown, John Clark, Oliver B. Huntington, James Ivie, John Lehi, Levi G. Metcalf, John McEwan, Joseph L. Rawlins, Moses Draper, Alma Fairchild, Wm. Freeman, Wm. R. Holden, James W. Hunt, Lot E. Huntington, Charles A. Huntington, Steven R. Moore, Byron Pace, Ethen Pettit, Christopher C. Perkins, Wm. W. Sterrit, Wm. P. Jones, Ephraim Wright, Clinton Williams, Thomas Wilson, Andrew Jackson Allred, Edward Edwards, Archibald W. Buchanan, William P. Fairchild, John Crawford, John Lowry, Jr. William G. Petty, Peter Stubbs, John Shelby, Shelton B. Cutler, Martin Behunin, Wm. Behunin, D. Johnson, John Lewis, Richard and William Hamblin. Elder Alfred N. Billings was appointed president of the mission by President Brigham Young. The company after being partly organized for traveling, left Manti, Sanpete County, Monday May 21, 1855. It consisted of 41 men, 15 wagons, 65 oxen, 16 cows, 13 horses, 2 bulls, 1 calf, 2 pigs, 4 dogs, and 12 chickens, besides implements, seed grain, etc., and provisions. After a hard journey they arrived on Grand River on the evening on June 11th. On the 12th they crossed the river, came to some land that was cultivated by Indians who were friendly and wanted the white people to settle among them. By July they had built a stockade corral of logs, set three feet in the ground and six feet above, and had put in their grain, etc. and they started work on a stone fort. The fort was finished July 19th.

One of the settlers writes: Sunday September 22nd we changed herd-ground, feeling apprehensive of mischief intended by some Indians as they were

very saucy and impudent. On inquiring why we
had changed herd-ground, the boys began loading
their guns, which caused the Indians to cool down,
the Indians went off a short distance to consult together. Soon three of them started for the field in the
direction of the cattle, and in a few minutes James
W. Hunt started with a lariat to get his horse. Charles, a son of Suit-Sub-Soc-Its or St. John, followed
him on horse-back; he kept telling him to go ahead of
him, asking what he was afraid of, Hunt kept turning his head occasionally towards him, as though
being apprehensive of danger, they got nearly a
mile from the fort when Charles told him to look at
the stock. He did so, raising himself on tip-toe.
That instant Charles shot him, then shouted to another Indian, not far off, to run and take the horses.
The ball entered Hunt's back, ranging downward
about one and a half inches from the back bone, on
the left side, and four inches from the small of the
back. This happened about half past twelve o'clock.
Ephraim Wight and Sheldon B. Cutler were herding
the stock.   The Indians left and went across the
river, Cutler came to the fort on horse-back and
told what had happened.   President Billings jumped
on behind him.   Peter Stubbs followed, and while
John Clark and another followed with water and returned to the fort, Clinton Williams started on
horse back after the stock.   The boys carried Hunt
in a blanket; but before they got within one fourth
of a mile of the fort, the Indians re-crossed the river
and came charging towards the boys and stock, raising a war whoop. Wm. M. Sterrett, Sheldon B. Cutler and Clark A. Huntington acted as rear guard to
the boys who were carrying Hunt and fired upon

the Indians who had fired some eight or ten guns before our boys commenced shooting. President Billings was wounded by a ball passing through the
fore finger of his right hand. The bullets whistled
briskly all around. The men arrived safely with
the wounded man and the horses and cattle were
taken inside the corral, except those the Indians had
driven off. Every man was engaged. Soon one of
the Indians set fire to our hay stacks which were adjoining the north end of the corral; they were entirely consumed, as also the corn, and it took five or six
men steady to carry water to save the corral logs, so
as to keep what stock we had on the inside. The
firing was kept up by the Indians till after dark. We
succeeded in saving the corral, although some of the
logs were nearly consumed. Seven Indians were seen
to leave, Charles at their head, going to the mountains. The day previous (Saturday) two of the boys,
Edward Edwards and William Behunin went hunting, expecting to return Sunday afternoon, Captain
Capsium, a Tampa Ute, came down to the corner of
the fort and corral and talked to Clark A. Huntington for some time when a few more Indians came.
They said we had killed two or three of them and
wounded as many, and they would not be satisfied
till they had killed two more "Mormons." They at
first denied having killed the two boys who were out
hunting and wanted bread. We gave them all we
had. The Indians had turned the water off from us,
They finally acknowledged killing the two boys out
hunting. Hunt expired the following day.

Early in the morning of Monday, Sept. 24th the
Indians came to the fort and said they were glad
that three Mormons had been killed; they had killed

the two boys as they were coming down the mountain. Thus three of our boys were killed. Three Indians had also been killed and three others wounded who would die. It was now thought best to move out right away, or we should all die, as the Indians had sent runners out into the mountains for help. We packed up and without breakfast left about eleven o'clock in the morning, leaving fifteen head of horses twenty-four head of cattle with a calf, besides six head which we gave the Indians. When we got to the north side of Grand river, a brother of St. John and uncle to Charles, the leader, came to us. Clark A. Huntington told him all that had taken place, and what we had left behind. He said it was too bad, but he was only one against many. He said we should have our cattle, and he would see that the bodies of the boys who had been killed were taken care of and buried. Together with his sons he went to the fort and talked to the Indians. He had some difficulty with them, when they began shooting the cattle. The friendly Indians who succeeded in driving away fifteen head of cattle, delivered to us eight cows and kept seven that were wounded. They butchered three head and brought us a little of the meat.

We arrived in Manti, Sunday Sept. 30th, between 4 and 5 o'clock p. m. John McEwan who was left behind the last morning driving his pony which was tired, some three miles from where we started, got bewildered and lost his way. The trail being dim and not very easy to follow, left all he had except his gun, and traveled eating nothing from Saturday night the 27 till Wednesday forenoon the 3rd of October about eleven o'clock a. m. when he was met by three men, viz: Nathaniel Beach, John Lowry, jr. both of Manti and Lyman A. Woods of Provo, and two Indians belonging to Arrapeen's band who left Manti on Tuesday night at half past ten o'clock in pursuit of him. They arrived at Manti Thursday morning 7:30 o'clock.

THE SALMON RIVER MISSION.

On May 19, 1855, a company was organized on the west side of Bear River, Utah, for the purpose of colonizing the Great Northwest. The company consisted of twenty-seven men with thirteen wagons, twenty-six yoke of cattle, a few cows and implements of industry. The personel of the company was:

Thomas S. Smith, Farmington, Davis County, Utah; Ezra J. Barnard, Farmington, Davis County, Utah; Isaac Shepherd, Farmington, Davis County, Utah; Baldwin H. Watts, South Weber, Utah; Geo. R. Grant, Kaysville, Davis County, Utah; Charles Dalton, Centerville, Davis County, Utah; Israel J. Clark, Centerville, Davis County, Utah; Wm. H. Batchelor, Salt Lake City, Utah; Ira Ames, Salt Lake City, Utah; William Bunbridge, Salt Lake City, Utah; Thomas Butterfield, West Jordan, Salt Lake County, Utah; William Burges, Provo, Utah; Abraham Zundel, Willard, Box Elder, Utah; Everett Lish, Willard, Box Elder, Utah; Francillo Durfee, Ogden, Utah; David Moore, Ogden, Utah; Benjamin F. Cummings, Ogden, Utah; Gilbert R. Belknap; Ogden, Utah; Joseph Parry, Ogden, Utah; Nathaniel Leavitt, Ogden, Utah; Pleasant Green Taylor, Ogden, Utah; Charles McGeary, Ogden, Utah; John Gallagher.

Ogden, Utah; John W. Browning, Ogden, Utah; David H. Stevens, Ogden, Utah; William Birch, Ogden, Utah; Geo. Hill, Ogden, Utah.

The following officers were elected:

Thomas S. Smith, President; Francillo Durfee, Captain; David Moore, Secretary; B. F. Cummings, Captain of the guard.

Thus organized, on the 20th day of May, the company commenced their journey. They traveled up Malad valley and crossed the Bannock divide, then they went down Bannock Creek, crossed Portneuf River, and Ross' Fork and Blackfoot River, thence until they reached Snake River, which they crossed at a point five miles above Fort Hall and near Ross' Butte, and traveled on the west side of the river until they reached a point three miles above Eagle Rock. On leaving Snake River they passed Market Lake on the north and camped on Muddy Lake. Leaving Muddy Lake the company traveled thirty miles across a desert when they reached Spring Creek, (Birch Creek). Traveling northward they followed little Lost River sixty miles until they arrived at the top of Salmon range of mountains. They journeyed down this creek called Salmon River (now Limhi), until they reached a point twenty miles above where it empties into Salmon River. They arrived at this point June 15th, which was three hundred and thirty-three miles from Ogden, according to the odometer constructed by Col. David Moore. Here they built a stockade fort and named it "Fort Limhi." It was about twenty rods square. The wall was built of logs sixteen feet long, standing on end close together. It had one gate on the east side and one on the west. They built

their houses of logs, on one side of the fort. Bastions were built at each corner of the fort.

The country through which they traveled was a
dreary waste, very forbidding, and covered thick-
ly with wild sage, and at that time was but little
known to white people. It was eastern Oregon, (now
in Idaho.)

On their arrival they found a large number of
Indians consisting of Bannocks, Sho-shones and Nez-
Perses, who were on their annual fishing trip.
Through their interpreter, Geo. W. Hill, the Indians
were made to understand that the colony had come
there to settle, that they were their friends, that they
were there to help them, to teach them how to till
the ground, how to build houses and live like white
people. The Indians gave the colonists a friendly
welcome.

In the afternoon of the same day on which they
arrived, the colony commenced to build their irri-
ation canal. David Moore and B. F. Cummings,
surveyed the ditch with a bottle filled with water
for a level and steel square for a straight edge. A
part of the company commenced work on the water
ditch, while others were engaged in herding cattle
The water for irrigation was brought from a creek
on the east side of the valley, about forty rods above
the fort, where the dam was built, to flood the land
before it could be ploughed.

About the 22nd of June the colony planted peas,
potatoes, turnips, etc. This was the first irrigation
that was done in the Great Northwest. Bancroft
gives this credit to these first settlers. The crops
of the first year were a failure, being destroyed by
heavy frost on the night of the 4th of September.

The same year the grasshoppers appeared in countless numbers and deposited their eggs.

There being no saw mill, the lumber for the windows, doors, and floors, was manufactured with a whip-saw. Every day and night a strong guard was placed over the cattle; and men were forced to go heavily armed.

Prior to the loss of the crops it was discovered that the supplies on hand would run out and the seed remaining would be insufficient for next year's sowing. So, early in August, about one half of the colony returned to Utah for supplies and to carry the mail. They returned on the 19th of November, 1855, bringing the mail from Utah. Some of them also brought their families. Francillo Durfree brought his wife and daughter; C. M. McGeary, his wife; I J. Clark, his wife and three children. These women and children were the first white females to settle in the Great Northwest. Louisa, daughter of Col. G. Moore subsequently became the wife of Lewis W. Shurtliff, who is now a member of Congress.

(This marriage took place January 4th, 1858, being the first white couple married in this north country.)

About the first of August, Lewis W. Shurtliff and John Leavitt started from Salt Lake with mail and supplies.

By the first of December, 1855, President Smith, ascertained that their food supplies would be exhausted before the first of March, 1856. He called for volunteers to go to Utah for supplies and also to carry mail. The following eight responded: viz: George W. Hill, Joseph Parry, Abraham Zundel,

Wm. Burch, Isaac Shepherd, Thomas Butterfield and William Batchelor.

They left fort Limhi on the 4th of December with an outfit consisting of eight men, six yoke of oxen and three wagons; one wagon they were compelled to leave by the wayside. They arrived in Ogden on December 26th in good health, but "Mighty hungry" and suffering more or less from frost bites.

On March 28th, 1856, they left Ogden on their return to Limhi with the mail from Utah and their supplies, bringing with them the following new colonists:

Alexander Hill, John Freece, Sylvanus Collett, Thomas Abbot, Wal. McIntyre, William Perkins, Thos. Carlos, Thos. Day, Clifton, S. Browning, Jos. Harker, Jacob Miller, Geo. McBride, H. A. Cleveland, Thomas Bingham, William Shaw, John Murdock, Pardon Webb, James Walker, R. B. Margetts, Henry Nebeker, William B. Lake, Hathron C. Hadlock. The party reached Fort Limhi May 15th, 1856, in charge of Joseph Parry. During the summer '56 Messrs. Moore, Cummings and Parry commenced the erection of a grist mill; Mr. Burges having brought the mill stones with him from Utah and Mr. Moore brought the mill irons. The mill was completed in 1859. In 1856 the colony commenced to build another irrigation ditch, which they finished in 1857. and it is still in operation by Mr. J. B. Sharkey.

An addition was made to the colony by the arrival of M. D. Hammond, H. V. Shurtliff, E. Robinson and Owen Dix who brought the mail from Utah. They came during the summer of 1856. In August L. W. Shurtliff and Nathaniel Leavitt carried the mail from Limhi to Utah, and had a narrow escape from death by Indians, near where Bailey Lake was subsequently shot and killed. During this summer Lot Smith and John Clawson arrived from Utah with the mail, and returned with the mail from Limhi to Utah.

Early in the spring of 1856, the colony sowed a large acreage of wheat which gave promise of an abundant harvest; but the grasshoppers hatched out in myriads and destroyed the fruits of their toil and blighted their hopes for this year. Before them was indeed a fruitful field, but when they left, behind them was a desolation. The land was cleaned of every vestige of vegetation. This forced the colony for the third time to resort to Utah for fresh supplies of provisions and for seed grain for the ensuing year.

David Moore, Pleasant G. Taylor and others were sent with the mail to Utah and to bring back supplies. At the commencement of winter, Hill, Parry and Lychonius Barnard were also sent with the mail from Limhi. The two companies returned with the mail and supplies for the colony, May, 1857. (It should have been stated in the summer of 1856, a body of troops, fifty or more arrived at the colony in search of Indians who had commited depredations on white settlers in Oregon. They stayed about one week and then left.

In May, 1857, the colony had a pleasant visit from President Brigham Young and a large company of others, including Heber C. Kimball, Gen. Daniel H. Wells and prominent citizens of Utah. They expressed themselves much pleased with the colony and the President said he would send them more aid to strengthen the colony. He advised them to build a

Spanish wall for their better protection, which they did at the south end of the fort. The wall is still standing. This same year, they raised about 2,000 bushels of wheat besides other grain and vegetables. This was the first grain raised in Idaho by irrigation.

In fulfillment of this promise the President sent the following persons to strengthen the settlers at Limhi: John L. Dalton, James Wilcox, Jane Hadlock, Oliver Robinson, James Miller, Chas. F. Middleton, Henry Smith and wife, Jesse Smith and wife, William S. Smith and wife, William Marler, Frederick A. Miller, Reuben Collett, Fountain Welch, Orson Rose, Andrew Quigley, William Perry and wife, William Taylor, Levi Taylor, James Allred, Martin H. Harris, Jonathan Bowen and wife, Joseph Bowen, Steven Cheen and wife, Henry Harman and wife, and James McBride. They arrived at Fort Limhi Oct. 27th, 1857.

Arrangements were at once made for building a new fort about two miles below Limhi, thereby increasing the acreage and strength of the colony, and also giving more room for new arrivals. A number of log houses were erected on the plan of those of the upper fort. Milton Harmon was appointed to preside over this little community. Everything went along peacefully and all were taking hold of needed work, to prepare for winter.

November 28th, President Smith and L. W. Shurtliff started with the mail for Salt Lake City, but were compelled to return, arriving on the 11th of December, and reported that the snow was too deep and they found it impractical to cross the mountains.

The threshing of the wheat (which was done by oxen) and the cleaning occupied all winter. The cleaning was done by a fanning mill, which was constructed by David Moore and others at the fort. Feb. 28th, 1858, Col. Smith saw the Indians in a hostile attitude; he saddled his horse and called on the men to follow him, and then started to head off the cattle which the red skins were stealing. Many of the men started to follow him, but Col. Moore, fearing that the fort would be left exposed to the foes, organized a company of ten to follow Col. Smith and detained the rest to defend the fort. The Indians fired on all of the colonists. Geo. McBride and James Miller were killed, and Col. Smith and four others were wounded. Col. Moore detailed men to bring in the dead and wounded. The foresight of David Moore saved the fort, for it was discovered afterwards that the Indians expected that the colonists would pursue them, when, having some of their tribe in ambush, they would take possession, kill the men and carry off the women and children.

An express was sent by B. H. Watts and Ezra Barnard to President Young, informing him of what had occurred. He immediately sent out one hundred and fifty mounted men and twenty wagons with provisions, under the command of Col. Cunningham, to relieve the colony and escort them to Utah.

The fort was vacated March 28th, 1858. The men were sent forward as a van guard. The Indians followed them two hundred miles. They waylaid them. They killed, stripped and scalped Bailey Lake. When the colony left the fort snow was on the ground in many places, and the men had to help the teams with lariats. On April 11th, 1858, at 3

JESSE KNIGHT

Sergeant in Captain Alva A. Green's cavalry company, American Fork. One of
our comrades whom fortune has favored. Now prominent mine owner and
capitalist. What is more legitimate than to cause the earth to yield her fruits
and treasures in abundance.

BRIG. GENERAL ALBERT KING THURBER
Indian Interpreter and Explorer.

o'clock p. m. they arrived in Ogden. Before leaving Limhi the colony cached their wheat, about two thousand bushels, in different places.

This ended the first mission to colonize the great Northwest to introduce the system of irrigation and endeavor to civilize the aborigines, after two years and nine months most incessant labor, toil and sacrifices. It cost three lives of colonists, and five others were wounded. It also cost them hundreds of thousands of dollars in time, horses, cattle, crops and other property.

THE SALMON RIVER MISSION ABANDONED.

Since the fort was vacated the land fell into other hands, and a government reservation was established a little distance above this point, and now appears on the maps as "Fort Limhi" and "Limhi Valley Indian Reservation."

The names of Crandle Dunn and Amos Wright of Box Elder Co., and James Hill of Mill Creek, Salt Lake County, have been inadvertently omitted from the body of this report. They should be in as they were in the Salmon River Mission.

ANOTHER ACCOUNT.

An account of an expedition that was sent out from Utah by Governor Young to relieve a colony of settlers that had located on Salmon River, Oregon:

In 1855 President Brigham Young and the leaders of the Church called a company of men with their families to go North into Oregon and explore the country and establish a settlement to open up the country for other settlers. This company crossed the mountains to Snake river and followed the river up

to Market Lake. From here they turned Northwest
onto the head waters of the Salmon river and built
a fort which was named Fort Limhi from which Limhi County, Idaho, was afterwards named. This colony got along alright until the winter of 1857 and
spring of 1858, when through the influence of one
John Powel, a mountaineer who was very bitter
against the Mormons, the Indians made a raid on
the colony. A battle was fought and the colonists
lost all their stock, except some animals they were
using at the time. Two men were killed and four
others wounded. The names of those killed were
George McBride and James T. Miller of Farmington
Davis County, Utah. Those wounded were Thomas
S. Smith, the Captain of the company, O. L. Robinson, Andrew Quigley and Fountain Welch all of
Farmington. The last mentioned never fully recovered from their wounds.

This left the colony in a helpless condition, and
over four hundred miles from any assistance. After
some consideration they saw there was only one
chance for them to get help, and that was for some
one or two persons to risk their lives and go out by
night and attempt to get by the Indians. George W.
Hill and Baldwin Watts undertook this task. After
three weeks travel and suffering from hunger and
cold they got through to Salt Lake City and reported
the condition of the colony to Governor Young, who
immediately called out three companies of the Utah
militia consisting of fifty men in each company. One
company being from Davis County with Horton D.
Haight as captain, one company from Weber County
and the other from Lehi, Utah County, Abram
Hatch, Captain. Colonel Cunningham of Salt Lake

County was placed in command.

We were called out on the fourth of March, 1858, and started on the 10th. Some of the men were poorly clad and suffered with the cold. Every man had to furnish himself, except what neighbors were pleased to donate to help him. We reached the fort on March 27th, seventeen days after starting and found the colonists alright.

The commanding officer concluded to send an express of ten men on the return to report the condition of things, which was opposed by all the other officers, but he was obdurate and would not yield. The men were selected and I was one of the party. We started on the 29th of March. When we got to Market Lake, we met a party of Indians who had the horse that George McBride was riding when he was killed. The boys seemed determined to get this horse and after some dickering they succeeded, but the Indians seemed quite sulky. Just as we were ready to start someone told the captain that they had seen a cowhide close to the Indian camp. The captain foolishly accused the Indians of stealing cattle which made the chief angry and he raised his spear and would have killed the captain, had not Brother Watts raised his gun in his face, shouted at him which made him drop his spear. The chief gave a war-whoop and in a few seconds we were entirely surrounded by the Indians and it looked as though we would all be killed on the spot, but brother Watts talked to them in their own language for about ten minutes. Finally he went up to the captain and gave him a push and called him a squaw. This saved our lives for they turned away and left us. This was on the first of April. Again on the 4th of April, the Indians

ambushed us in Bannock Canyon about thirty miles
southwest of where Pocatello now stands. We fought
them from two o'clock p. m. until after sun down
when they pulled off and left us. We had one man
killed—Bailey Lake of Ogden—three saddle horses
shot and we lost all our pack animals with our supplies and one extra horse,—nineteen head in all.
Our loss was not less than $1,500.00. We were one
hundred miles from any settlement and two men were
without horses to ride. We traveled this distance in
forty-eight hours without food or rest.

The names of those in this party were Franklin
Cummings, George W. Hill, Baldwin H. Watts, Bai-
ley Lake, who was killed, Thomas Bingham, George
Barber, Thomas Blocksom, John B. Blanchard, J.
T. Workman and one other whose name I have for-
gotten.

The last of the company arrived on April 20th
and we were honorably discharged after having been
out forty days.

(Signed) F. A. Miller,
Parker, Fremont County, Idaho.
July 2nd, 1906.

THE TINTIC WAR.

In the year 1856, the Indians, a part of the Utes,
again became hostile, and a sufficient number of
them went on the war path to make it expensive,
and annoying to the settlers. The Indians were
stealing cattle and horses in Utah and Cedar Valleys
and a sub-chief of the Utes named Tintic was the
ring-leader of the hostiles, some of whom dwelt in a
valley subsequently called Tintic, and others in Cedar Valley; both of these valleys lies west of Utah

Lake. The Indians killed two herdsmen,—Henry
Moren and Washington Carson, Feb. 21, 1856. When
these two men did not return when expected
a search was instituted by the citizens.

A POSSE WENT IN PURSUIT OF CHIEF TINTIC AND BAND.

Deputy Marshal Thomas S. Johnson came to
Provo and enlisted a posse of about ten men who,
armed with writs of arrest, issued by Judge Drum-
mond, in Utah County, set out for Cedar Valley to
apprehend the murderers. The posse started from
Provo and went by way of Lehi where they camped
the first night. Colonel Conover accompanied the
posse as far as Lehi, at which point he left for Salt
Lake City to seek advice from Governor Brigham
Young who at that time was also superintendent of
Indian affairs. The posse proceeded into Cedar
Valley, and while Johnson with part of the men
went to the north settlement, ten men were detached
to go to the south fort, afterwards known as Camp
Floyd. One division of the posse was under command of Deputy Marshal George Parish. The posse
stayed at Cedar Fort during the night, and on the
following morning sent interpreter John Clark to
the Indian camp, about a mile southwest of the fort
to talk to Chief Tintic and his followers. He went
to the chief's tent, where several Indians were present. Tintic treated the matter with contempt, and
spoke vilely of President Young. The Indians were
talking of keeping Clark there until dark, and when
he should start away, they would kill him. He
(Clark) understood them; he had on an overcoat and

carried two revolvers under it on his belt. He had walked to the camp, and as he was fast on foot (being considerable of an athlete) he intended on leaving to dodge round as he ran. Thus, if they fired at him, they would not be likely to hit him, so he said afterwards. While talking, a squaw on the outside called out, "Mommons coming." The Indians, while in conversation, had stripped and painted in their war-paints, and prepared for fight; they had their spears set up against the tent handy to get at. When the company came up, Deputy Sheriff Parish got off his horse and came into the tent, walked up to Tintic, caught him by the hair with one hand, and with revolver in the other said: "Tintic, you are my prisoner." Tintic grabbed the pistol with one hand and jumped, the pistol went off and shot him through the hand; he broke loose and went through the back of the tent; then firing commenced. Tintic's brother Battest aimed his rifle at George Parish and fired, but the gun-barrel being knocked aside the bullet missed its mark. One of Parish's friends then drew his revolver and shot Battest through the head, killing him instantly. A general fight followed in which one of the posse, George Carson was mortally wounded, one squaw and three or four Indians were also killed and several wounded. At this juncture, John Clark, the interpreter, ran back into the tent and got two guns and four or five bows and quivers of arrows, ran out, untied Tintic's and his brother's horses, jumped onto Tintic's horse and led the other. He laid down on the horse as he rode away, with bullets whistling by him, but escaped without injury. All went back to the fort. A messenger was sent to notify Deputy Marshal Tom Johnson who came immediately with the remainder of the posse. That night the Indians killed two boys, by the name of Henry Moran and William Carson who were herding sheep on the west side of Utah Lake. The next morning the posse followed the trail of the Indians who left during the night, and found them camped on the side of a mountain in the cedars on the east side of Rush Valley. A parley was held, but the Indians refused to surrender and fired upon the posse. It being late in the evening the Deputy Marshal deemed it wise to return to the fort with the intention to pursue the next day; but in the morning they found the Indian camp broken up and the Indians going in a direction where they would be overtaken by Colonel Conover's company, the posse gave up the pursuit, turned attention to the security of the settlements, and in searching for the other two, Moran and Carson and young Hunsaker, a thirteen year old boy whom the Indians had also killed; they found them where the Indians had killed them. Meantime, Governor Young had given orders to Colonel Peter W. Conover to raise a company of the Utah County Militia, pursue the Indians and recover the Hunsaker herd of stock which had been driven off after killing the herds-men. Accordingly, Col. Conover, with eighty men pursued, crossed the Utah lake on ice, and took the trail of the Indians where they crossed the mountains.

The company pursued all day and camped in Tintic Valley, just out of the mouth of a canyon. On the second day the pursuing party came so close upon the Indians in the lower end of Tintic Valley that they took fright and left the stock behind ex-

cept a few saddle horses; and the expedition returned with the stock.

Bishop Nephi Packard, to whom we are indebted
for some of this information says—"While at the
fort, the citizens brought in the bodies of Moran and
Carson, frozen stiff. Their bodies had been mutilated, and when they were thawed out with warm water
for the purpose of dressing them, it created a stench
which together with the sight of their mutilated
bodies, made him sick. They were buried there."

FROM TULLIDGE'S HISTORY, VOL. 3, PAGE 157.

By John Banks.

John Banks of Spanish Fork, one of the found-
ers of that place communicated the following additional details confirming the Tintic War, which
was supplied in Tullidge's History, Vol. 3, p. 157.

In February 1856, T. S. Johnson, a U. S. Deputy
Marshal, came to Palmyra in pursuit of Indians
who had been committing depredations on the whites,
expecting that he would find some of them with
Peteetneet's band, but failed. He then received word
by express that the Indians had killed two of the
Hunsaker's herds-men, on the west side of Utah
lake, and that a herd-boy was missing who was supposed to be killed also, for the Indians had taken the
whole herd of cattle. Peteetneet, the chief of the
Indians on the Spanish Fork, being friendly disposed was consulted. Peteetneet was grieved at the
hostilities of Tintic and his band, and remarked that
Tintic had ears that were no good and of no use to
him. He had good council given him, but he would
not hear it, and (Peteetneet) wanted Peanitch, the

Indian guide, and three others, when they would find Tintic, to cut off his ears, as they were of no good. This talk took place just before the Marshal, with about seventy-five men left Palmyra for the west mountains. "This was a very exciting time," writes John Banks. "We camped the first night on the north end of the so-called west mountain, where we experienced an extremely cold night, without any bedding except our saddle blankets, and were not allowed to have any fire after sundown. When day dawned we learned that several of our men had frozen feet, and consequently had to return home. Among those with frozen feet was William Fairbanks of Payson, but he would not return home. Early in the morning we saddled our horses, and the order, "mount, forward march," was gvien. Fairbanks would continue the march, nothwithstanding he suffered much during the expedition. We had not gone far before we struck the trail of an Indian, which track we followed on the ice across the Utah Lake, till we came to the dugout where Hunsaker's two herdsmen had been killed in the cedars. The blood was lickered in the sand, the sight of which caused quite a sensation. Orders were given to scout. Scouters returned with an ox, which was soon killed, and a time of general sharpening of sticks to roast beef for dinner took place. Meanwhile, the officers consulted each others as to the best course to pursue, and decided that the men be divided into tens to examine the most likely places for Indians or to ascertain which way they had gone. This was soon found out, and when the signal was given that the trail had been discovered, the whole company marched up the canyon, leading to what is

now called Tintic Valley. The name of the place
originated with this expedition, said valley being
until that time unexplored by white men. We learned that the Indians had taken a southwesterly direction and as we journeyed on we had to encounter
deep snow and exceedingly cold weather. Frequently we saw cattle standing up, braced in the snow,
frozen quite stiff. In this locality we expected to get
our supply of food on our return provided we did not
overtake the Indians. We pushed forward as fast as
we could, and as we came on their camping places we
could learn how fast we were gaining ground on
them. We made three of their days travel in one
day. The third day we saw their camp fire smoke,
but we did not like the location, as it seemed like we
were marching right into the fortification of the
savages. Passing a heavy body of cedars, we found
ourselves on the edge of the great desert, where we
were pleased to discover some stock and we picked
out the best beef from seventy-five head, having had
nothing to eat that morning. Our Indian guide
informing us that it was about six miles to the Sevier
River, orders were given to march thither to water
our stock. There was no trail to follow—the Indians
having scattered in every direction. Our horses had
been without water since we left the Utah Lake. We
camped on Sevier river that night. Early next
morning we found thirty head of horses, but no Indians. We then traveled up the river in a northeasterly direction and came out at Nephi. The inhabitants rallied to a point on the north side of the herd
to save the cattle. There being a raise of land intervening between us, the one party could not see the
other for a little while. The next time they saw us

the supposed Indians were making for the settlement, and would take the town ere any of the citizens could get back. It was a time of general rejoicing with the Nephites when they found the supposed Lamanites were their friends; and, on the other hand, we rejoiced on being well treated, and having plenty of good food to eat, having had nothing to eat for seven days previous except fresh beef, without salt.—weary and tired, we appreciated the comfortable beds and happy rest afforded us that night. Next morning we, with grateful hearts, shook hands with our Nephi friends, started for home, and great was our mutual joy.

Deseret News of March 5th, 1856, published the following:

"Tintic, head chief of the disaffected band, and who was wounded in the skirmish near the south fort in Cedar Valley, is reported dead."

FOUR PERSONS MASSACRED IN SALT CREEK CANYON.

June 4th.—Jens Jorgensen and wife, Jens Terklesen and Christian E. Kjerluf were massacred by Indians in Salt Creek Canyon, June 4th, 1858 while traveling unarmed on their way to Sanpete Valley. They had camped at the head waters in the canyon. After traveling about a mile after dinner, and having reached a point about a mile and a half from the head of the canyon, some Indians came from their hiding place and attacked them; two of the men were killed in the wagon, and burned with it. One man was killed about fifty yards from the wagon, and the woman was found dead close by the wagon,

making four killed. John Ericksen, the only one
who escaped, made his way to Ephraim where he arrived about dark. An ox hitched onto a hand-cart,
and driven by one of the men, got frightened, and
ran back to Nephi.

The bodies were brought to Ephraim for burial.
These people were on their way to Ephraim where
they intended to settle.

(Most of this information was obtained from
N. O. Anderson of Glenwood Utah.)

THE BODIES OF JOSIAH CALL AND SAMUEL BROWN FOUND MURDERED AT CHICKEN CREEK, JUAB COUNTY.

On October 15th, 1858.—The remains of Josiah
Call and Samuel Brown, of Fillmore, Millard County,
were found in a state of decomposition near Chicken
Creek bridge, Juab County. They had been murdered by Indians on October 7th.

The following details of the murder are culled
from the Deseret News of Nov. 3, 1858:

On Friday last some fifteen men started again to
renew the search, they met Brother Shepherd at
Cedar Springs, who had just come in from the north.
He told them that he saw a dead body about two
miles south of Chicken Creek; accordingly they proceeded forthwith to the place and found both bodies
within about two hundred yards of each other.
Brother Brown was shot through the heart, scalped,
and his throat cut. Birds had eaten the flesh from
Brother Call's bones, with the exception of the left
leg below the knee and his left arm; but it was
evident he had been shot three times; once through

the right breast, the ball lodging in the back bone; once through the left ankle and once through the head, the ball entering the back part of the skull near the seam and coming out at the left side of the nose. It is supposed his throat was also cut, as the blood had run from where his neck lay and his right arm was entirely gone and was not be found. They were both stripped of all their clothing except their under clothes, shoes and stockings. The remains were this day interred in the cemetery of this place, the occasion being one the most solemn I ever witnessed.

MURDER OF A PEACEABLE INDIAN BY OFFICERS FROM CAMP FLOYD.

Fillmore City, Apr. 10th, 1860.

From Deseret News:

Yesterday I heard of the most outragous murder that has come to my knowledge for some time. When the company returned from the Colorado they brought an Indian with them who has been living at Cedar Springs with David Savage ever since. Some few days since, an Officer by the name of Kirk, in company with one Johnston, came to the Springs —with a writ for the Indian, whose name was John The officer served the writ by arresting the Indian, and then started with him immediately for Camp Floyd. Shortly afterwards a rumor reached our City to the effect that the Indian had been murdered on the Sevier near the bridge, and thrown into the river. Bishop Brunson and some others saddled their horses and rode to the place designated to ascertain the truth of the report; they made search and found the body in the river, a short distance below the place described. On taking the body from the water, they found it had been pierced with four bullets, two passing through near the heart. The savage custom of scalping had also been performed upon the Indian. Such laurels are easier won than worn.

March 22nd, 1860.—The Overland Mail Coach with four passengers was attacked by Indians near Eight Mile Station, Tooele County. Henry Harper, the driver, was killed and one passenger wounded. Judge Mott, Delegate to Congress from Nevada, who was in the coach took the reins, drove for his life and escaped.

MAIL STATION AT DEEP CREEK AT-TACKED, ONE MAN SHOT.

May 28th, 1860—The Indians attacked the mail station at Deep Creek, Tooele County, shot a man and stole several horses.

ATTACK ON SMITHFIELD. JOHN REED AND IRA MERRILL KILLED.

July 22nd Smithfield, Cache County, was attacked by Indians. A fight ensued: John Reed and Ira Merrill and two Indians were killed and several others wounded on both sides. The Indians sought to liberate one of their number who had been captured while stealing horses, but in the melee the guilty In dian and another were killed. Previous to this time, the Indians made a similar attempt of rescuing another at Logan, Cache Valley, Utah, but the whites rallied quickly, and in force, defeated the attempt.

COLONEL CONNOR'S COMMAND
START TO BEAR RIVER.

On the 19th of January, 1863, a miner named William Bevins made affidavit before Chief Justice John F. Kinney in Salt Lake City to the effect that about ten days previous, he and party numbering eight men, who were on their way to the Grasshopper Gold Mines in Dakota were attacked in Cache Valley by Indians and one of their number killed. He also reported that another party of ten miners enroute to Salt Lake City had been assaulted and murdered by the same Indians, in the same locality. Upon this information warrants for the arrest of three of the chiefs were issued and placed in the hands of the United States Marshal Isaac L. Gibbs, who, realizing that resistance would be offered, laid the matter before Colonel Connor. Three days later a company of Infantry with two howitzers started for the camp of the hostiles, and on Sunday evening the 25th, four companies of cavalry, under command of Colonel Connor himself followed. Marshal Gibbs accompanied the expedition, though with what purpose is not clear, as the mission and intent of the troops was to summarily punish, and not merely to arrest the savages for the various crimes and depredations of which they were accused. The Colonel in his report said he informed the Marshal that all arrangements for the expedition were already made, and that the civil process had little to do with it is evident from the Colonel's further remarks: being satisfied that they (the Indians) were part of the same band who had been murdering emigrants on the overland mail route

for the past fifteen years, and the principal actors
and leaders in the horrid massacre of the previous
summer. I determined although the weather was
unfavorable to an expedition to chastise them, if
possible. Tuesday night the 27th, the cavalry force
overtook the infantry at Mendon, Cache County; but
the infantry at once resumed the march and were
again overtaken during the following night at Franklin, twelve miles from the Indian encampment.

COLONEL CONNOR'S BATTLE AT
BEAR RIVER.

At 3 o'clock, on the morning of Jan. 29th, the
infantry was in motion and an hour later the cavalry
set out, overtaking and passing their plodding comrades about four miles south of the river. The battle
began at 6 o'clock. The Indians having detected the
efforts of the mounted troops to surround them, and
defeating it by at once engaging them. The position of the savages was one of great natural strength,
and they had improved it with considerable ingen-
uity. A narrow dry ravine with steep rocky sides
sheltered them from the fire of the soldiers, who,
advancing along the level table land through which
the gorge ran, were exposed to the murderous volleys of the concealed foe. Steps cut in the bank enabled the Indians to ascend and descend as necessity
required, and artificial copses of willows served as
additional defenses where the ravine's course left an
exposed point. The battle opened inauspiciously
for the troops who quickly saw the disadvantage at
which they were placed. Several fell killed and
wounded at first fire. The Indians gleefully not-

ing the fact, and defying the survivors to "come on." Meantime the infantry, whose advance had been checked by the swift icy waters of the Bear River until horses furnished by the cavalry had assisted them over the stream, had joined in the engagement; and a successful flanking movement soon afterwards enabled the troops to pour an infilading fire into the enemy's camp. This was the beginning of the end; for though the savages fought with fury they were now at a disadvantage and were met by a line of soldiers at either end of the ravine, as they moved towards the lower end. The colonel ordered his troops thither, disposing of the calavry so as to cut off escape. One company stood at the mouth of the gorge and visited terrible execution upon the enemy; at a single spot forty-eight corpses were afterwards counted. By ten o'clock the savages were completely routed and the slaughter was ended. Two hundred and twenty-four warriors, it is claimed, where found dead upon the field—but this number may have been exaggerated. Among them were the chiefs Bear Hunter, Sagwitch and Lehi. The first it is said falling into the fire at which he was moulding bullets, and being literally roasted. Sanpitch one of the chiefs named in Judge Kinney's warrant made his escape, as did also Pocatello, and probably fifty braves. The fighting strength of the Indians were estimated to be over three hundred. One hundred and sixty squaws and children fell into the hands of the victors, and one hundred and seventy-five ponies were captured in the camp; seventy lodges were burned; and a large quantity of grain, implements and other property believed to have been stolen from emigrants. That which was not neces-

sary for the captives was either destroyed or carried
to Camp Douglas and sold. On his side Colonel
Connor lost fourteen men and forty-nine were wounded during the engagement. Eight died within ten
days. The force in the outset numbered three hundred men. But not more than two hundred were in
the fight; the remainder were either teamsters or
men incapacitated by frozen feet. The hardships of
the journey were extreme. The snow being deep and
the cold intense. The casualties of this latter class
were seventy-nine, and the commanding officer in
his report expressed the fear that many of the victims would be crippled for life. Colonel Connor employed as his guide on this expedition the experienced Mountaineer Orrin P. Rockwell, who rendered
the command very efficient service; without which
it is believed many more of the soldiers would have
perished by being frozen. This fact accounts for
the friendly feeling that Connor always entertained
towards Rockwell.

The dead and wounded arrived at Camp Douglas on the night of the 2nd of February and on Wednesday the 4th, the survivors were again at their
quarters. Next day, the 5th, fifteen of the dead were
buried with military honors. Theirs being the con-
secrating dust of the beautiful little cemetery at the
fort. On the 6th, Lieutenant Darwin Chase who
died of his wounds on the night of the 4th, at Farmington was buried with Masonic and martial honors;
he had once been a Mormon Elder. At dress parade
on Sunday, the 8th, the colonel's complimentary order was read, and that same day the two who were
the last to die of their wounds were placed by the
side of their deceased comrades. If the battle in its

latest stage had possessed less of the elements of a massacre Colonel Conner and his command would have been more generally praised by the people; but perhaps it would not then have proved a lesson so well to be remembered by the savages. As it was, it completely broke the power of the Indians there and conveyed to them a warning that it has never been necessary to repeat. In a letter to General Wright commanding the department of the Pacific, General in Chief Halleck wrote from Washington under the date of March 29th, highly praising the courage and discretion of the colonel and his brave Californians. And in a dispatch of the same date to Colonel Connor, he and his command were congratulated on their heroic and brilliant victory. And the commander was notified that he was that day appointed a brigadier general.

ATTACK ON A PLATOON OF SOLDIERS AT PLEASANT GROVE.

April 12th. William H. Seegmiller of Richfield, Sevier County, Utah, gives the following account of a fight between a small party of soldiers from Camp Douglas and a band of Indians under chief Little Soldier at Pleasant Grove, Utah County.

Returning from San Pedro (Cal.) with Woodmansee Bros.' freight train, Sam Serine, captain, on the evening of April 12, 1863, we camped at Pleasant Grove, Utah County. We had been camped but a short time when a band of Indians, probably fifty, under the leadership of Little Soldier came to our camp and inquired if we were Americats. We answered no, and he then asked if we knew where the

Americats were camped, we told them that we did not know. They then said: 'we find them.' They passed on down the street towards the center of town. Some of Brigadier General Connor's command from Fort Douglas were in town, we saw two or three wagons with heavy canvas covers on and some mules; also teamsters and a few soldiers. Soon we heard a loud report, and learned that Connor's men had found out that the Indians were coming for them, and had shot a "Howitzer" a small cannon, at them as they were turning to go south to where the soldiere were located. We were informed that the soldiers went to Samuel Green's house on the east side of the road and asked the people to leave, which they did in a hurry. The soldiers then went into the house, pulled their cannon in with them, pulled up some of the floor and got under it leaving their wagons in the road and their mules and horses were in a corral on the west side of the street. The Indians dared not follow the troops into the house, but shot into it through the door and window, peppering the back wall with bullets. When the Indians saw they could not successfully rout the soldiers or kill them, they turned their attention to booty. But when the soldiers saw they were going to lose their horses they fired a charge of grape shot from their cannon into the corral at their animals, prefering to kill them to letting the Indians get them, they killed and maimed some, the Indians got those not hurt and loaded them with blankets and supplies, and struck for the mountains very much pleased with their success as manifested by their chatter and antics.

When the first shot was fired from the cannon it was not aimed at the Indians but over them to scare and stop them, it was loaded with a bomb which went over the Indians and corral and struck and exploded in William H. Adam's field west of town about where the railroad track now is. Some of this information is given by Wm. H. Adams, Jr., an eye witness. When the Indians left. some of the men of town went to the house where the soldiers were to learn from them what should be done, and were informed that a company of soldiers were following them. These men went in the night soon after dark and found this company camped at the Warm Springs at the point of the mountain in the south end of Salt Lake Valley. and reported. They immediately broke camp and proceeded to Pleasant Grove.

W. H. Seegmiller continues:

The following morning I went down town and found Brigadier General Connor and quite a number of his cavalry. Orrin Porter Rockwell was also with them. They had arrived during the previous night. On the day before the attack by Little Soldier and his warriors we learned at Spanish Fork that some of General Connor's soldiers, on the bench above Spanish Fork met an Indian, Pintutch, going to his wickiup from town and killed him on the edge of a ditch in the southwest corner of town, by beating him over the head with their muskets. That no doubt was the cause of Little Soldier and his band attacking General Connor's outfit at Pleasant Grove. I will ever remember the appearance of Little Soldier and his Indians. None of them wore much clothing, a breech clout and mocassins were their

uniform; their faces were painted black, all seemed
to have guns and pistols, and some had bows and
quivers of arrows. On April 13th, we arrived in
Salt Lake City. Having been invited by President
Brigham Young before starting to California to call
on him on my return. I did so on the evening of my
return. While I was conversing with the President,
Orrin Porter Rockwell called and gave President
Young an account of the affair with the Indians at
Pleasant Grove. I listened very attentively to his
recital of the matter, and he freely told the above as
I understood it.

O. Porter Rockwell while at Pleasant Grove was
taken to be slightly intoxicated. He was active in
moving among the crowd at the soldiers' camp; this
all seems very distinct even now, I thought him almost silly with drink and had little respect for him,
until this interview with President Young. On that
occasion he was well dressed in a black broadcloth
suit, wore neatly polished shoes and a black silk
hat; his language was free and grammatical. I concluded then that Rockwell lived a double live in the
interest of his friends and God's cause on the earth.
I will ever remember him with esteem.''

INDIAN OUTRAGE IN BOXELDER
COUNTY, WM. THORP KILLED.
Copied from Desert News, Vol. 12, page 364.

On the afternoon of Friday last, May 18th,
as reported by Mr. Burt, of Brigham City, six
or eight Indians of Sagwitch's band, as supposed,
made their appearance in Box Elder Canyon, or in
the Little Valley, about four miles from Brigham

City at a herd house, and made inquiry of a boy
who was there alone relative to the whereabouts of
the soldiers.   The boy replied that he did not know,
but supposed they were in Salt Lake City, for he had
not heard that any portion of General Connor's
command was moving northward. The savages told
the boy he was a liar, and designated the place where
the soldiers camped the night before.   They then
took the lad's hat and two horses that were near by
and went to the herd some distance away, where they
got eight or nine more, which they succeeded in driving off, making ten or eleven in all.   They made a
strenuous effort to drive away the entire herd of
cattle grazing in the canyon, but were prevented by
eight or ten Danishmen, who were making a farm in
the valley not far from the herd.   These men were
unarmed, but on seeng the movements of the free-
booters, they immediately took measures to defeat
their object, which, after a severe struggle with the
red men, they succeeded in accomplishing.—On being
convinced that they could not get the cattle, the Indians fled with the horses, and in their flight came
upon a man by the name of William Thorp who was
burning coal in the side canyon, whom they killed
with arrows, the party having no guns.   The body
of the murdered man was found the following day
considerably mutilated.

STAGE ATTACKED IN CEDAR VALLEY, TWO MEN KILLED.

June 10th.   The Stage Coach was attacked by
mounted Indians between Fort Critenden and the
Jordan River, Utah County.   The driver, Wood

Reynolds and another man was killed and their bodies fearfully mutilated by the savages.

TREATY AT BRIGHAM CITY, WITH SHOSHONE INDIANS.

July 30. Governor Doty and General Connor made a treaty of peace with the Shoshone Indians at Brigham City.

In August, the troops under command of Captain Smith killed twelve Indians near Shell Creek Station, Utah.

STATEMENT BY N. O. ANDERSON OF EPHRAIM.

On June 1st, 1863, I was in company with Rasmus Hansen Kleurke and James P. Larsen. We were driving a band of horses south along a steep wash known as Willow Creek Wash, we saw three Indians, who were on the west side of the wash, while we were on the east side. When we came to them I recognized one of them as Jake Arrapeen, the old chief's son with whom I was well acquainted. I was about two rods from him when he pointed his gun at me. I looked at his gun, saw that the hammer was back and that his finger was on the trigger. Speaking to James Larsen, he said "Let us run a race." Larsen answered in the negative, which did not suit him, so he pointed his gun at James. Rasmus seeing the Indian pointing his gun asked, "Is he pointing at you, boys." We answered that he was. Rasmus who was one hundred and fifty yards distant, said, "Tell him to go to H——." At that the Indian raised his gun and shot at Rasmus, the ball passing close by Jim and me as we were in line.. It passed in front of Rasmus, just over the horn of his saddle. We then all rode up to Jake and Rasmus said, "If I had my pistol here, I would shoot you, you son of a B—." While Jake was loading his gun as fast as he could, we put spurs to our horses and rode to James Sanford Allred and told him what Jake Arrapeen had done. Brother Allred told us Jake was mad and would kill some one. The Indians went up the canyon, we could see their dust, and that was the last time that I ever saw Jake Arrapeen.

My object in writing a sketch of this kind is to show that while there was not really a war on, at that time, it was plain that the Indians could not be depended upon.

HERDSMAN C. C. ROWE IN THISTLE VALLEY.
By Conderset Rowe and Peter Gottfredson.
In Thistle Valley.

From the close of the Tintic War in 1856, the Indians were comparatively peaceable till 1863. Then they became dissatisfied, thinking that the Whites were encroaching upon their rights by crowding them off their lands and hunting grounds. They would often say. "White man's horses, cows and sheep eat Indian's grass. White man burn Indian's wood, shoot Indian's buckskins, rabbits, etc." And they frequently wanted horses, cattle or sheep in payment for it. Often they would bring an order from the Bishop. or some one for a beef or a mutton, and in such cases they always wanted the best. In the summer of 1863, the Mount Pleasant dry stock and sheep were taken into Thistle Valley. at the head

of the South Fork of Spanish Fork Canyon to be
herded. Caratat Rowe, his son (Conderset Rowe)
and a hired boy (Peter Gottfredson) were caring
for horned stock. Nathan Staker and his sons, Aaron
and Joseph were herding the sheep. One day. about
dusk. in the fore part of October, 1863, an Indian
came to our camp while we were out milking. He
rode a fine cream colored horse, bare backed, having
as he said, left his saddle and gun down near the
wagon road. He was dressed in a new military
officer's uniform with gilt epaulets on the shoulders.
and said his name was Godfrey. We did not learn
to what tribe he belonged. He asked for something
to eat and we told him that as soon as we were
through milking, we would have supper. He ate sup-
with us. After eating, he asked if he could stay all
night, saying he had no blankets. We told him he
could. As Rowe and Staker had gone to Mount
Pleasant after supplies. we four boys constituted the
whole personel of the camp. The Indian told us
that the Snake Indians had killed eight men in Provo
Canyon, and said that may be at daylight they would
come and kill us and steal our cattle. He seemed
to be very uneasy and would listen attentively at
every little noise and say, "maybe Snakes." He asked to see our guns, Aaron Staker got the guns, a
rifle and a shotgun. both muzzle loaders. Then he
wanted to see our ammunition. but I had hidden it
under the bedding where Staker could not find it.
The Indian next wanted to know how much powder
we had. I showed on my hand that we had about
five inches in the powder-horn. We had only four
or five charges for our guns. Every little while
the Indian would listen and say Snakes, as I thought

to try to scare us Rowe had a wagon which he
had made himself, the wheels being cut off the big
end of a large red pine log. he worked oxen on this
primitive wagon and we could hear the wagon squeak
miles away. As Brother Rowe was coming with supplies late in the night, the Indian heard the wagon
squeek again said Snakes. Conderset replied "na
nini-montz-pege" my father is coming. This was
about ten or eleven o'clock in the night. As Rowe
drove up, the Indian took Condersets hat and put on
his own head and stood astradle of the fire. We did
not understand why. Rowe looked at the Indian and
said. "boys. he is here for no good." Conderset
told his father what the Indian said about the Indians killing eight men in Provo Canyon. Rowe
began asking the Indian questions about it. The
Indian said that it was eight sleep ya-tes, eight
days since, holding up eight fingers. Rowe said,
"You are mistaken, for if it was so, the papers would
talk about it." The Indian became uneasy and wanted to go to his saddle. Rowe said, "I will go with
you." The Indian seemed willing that he should
do so till he got his horse, when he said his horse's
back was sore, which was very common with Indian
horses. Rowe told the Indian that he would walk
for he was anxious to keep the Indian with us all
night. He also told the Indian that there would be
ten men there by morning, and ten more later, word
having reached Mount Pleasant, that the Indians
intended making a raid on Thistle Valley. Upon hearing this the Indian became more eager to go than
ever, he jumped on his horse and was gone, and we
saw no more of him. Mr. Rowe remarked that trouble was brewing, and that we would have to shift

for ourselves as best we could. About midnight, after we had conversed about what we would do in case we were attacked, we heard a yell down in the valley in the direction of the road. Rowe said: "there comes the boys." We boys fearing that it it might be Indians, planned what to do if such should be the case. It proved to be four boys from Mt. Pleasant, namely R. N. Bennet, Don C. Seely, Peter Miller and James Hansen. They told us that as they were coming up from the road, they saw a small fire up Indian Hollow, and started towards it, when they got onto a ridge and saw our fire, and came to it. We got supper for them. We looked for more men in the morning, but they did not come. We gathered the stock and sheep and drove to Mt. Pleasant. At Fairview we got supper at Gammet's. There was no further trouble with Indians that fall, but we always believed that if we had not received timely help we might have been murdered.

HERDSMEN JENS GOTTFREDSON AND OLE JENSEN IN THISTLE VALLEY.

P. Gottfredson.

My father, Jens Gottfredson, had taken the Mount Pleasant dry stock to herd in Thistle Valley, and also stock from Moroni and Fairview, as well as a part of the Mt. Pleasant sheep. An old gentleman named Ole Jensen had charge of the remainder of the sheep. Six or seven families from Fairview had settled in the Valley, about six miles from the herd house that we occupied. All went well till along in August, 1864, when the Indians became hateful to the families down the valley and demanded a lot of

horses and cattle for the land, or they wanted them
to move off, and they made some threats. The people consequently moved back to Fairview. A few
days later fifty or more Indians came up to where
we were, about a half mile south west of the pres-
en site of Indianola. The old gentleman Jensen was
northeast of the herd house, about one quarter of a
mile, taking out his sheep. An Indian rode up to
him and asked for his dinner, which he had wrapped
up in his coat. Brother Jensen refused, whereupon
the Indian grabbed his coat and dinner and jerked it
away from him, laying it across his saddle in front
of him. The old man caught the horse by the bridle
with one hand and his coat with the other, and with a
quick pull got the coat away from the Indian, nearly
pulling him off his horse. Jensen followed his sheep,
and after getting away about 75 yards, the Indian
fired at him; the bullet grazed his face and killed
two sheep in the herd.

My brother and I were a short distance west of
the herdhouse when another Indian who had seven
or eight dogs with him, came after us and made for
our sheep. We had a large brindle dog which had
been brought in with Gen'l Johnston's Army. We
sicked him after the Indian dogs and he threw them
right and left; this stopped their rush for the sheep.
The Indian then came towards me. He had, besides
a gun and bow and arrows, a large painted wagon
spoke, with a string through the small end, hung on
his wrist. I suppose he used to whip his horse with.
As he rode up to me, acting as if he wanted to hit
me with it, I kept backing away from him, but could
not move fast enough to keep out of his reach. I
asked him what he wanted, and what was the matter

with him, but he would not talk. When I saw I could not back fast enough to keep out of his way I squatted down, cocked my gun and with my finger on the trigger pointed it at his face. He jerked his horse back so quick having what we called a jaw-breaker bit, that the horse fell back on his haunches but the Indian stayed with the horse. He then began to talk. He asked what the people said who moved up from below. I said "nothing." He said, "you lie." I told him that they said the Indians wanted more horses and cattle for the land than it was worth. He said, "all right" and rode to the herdhouse where all the Indians had gathered by this time. They broke open the door and went in and took and carried away all our bedding, provisions and cooking utensils, and other things, and started towards Fairview. When near the divide, they met Lyman Peters, coming to Thistle Valley, and when they saw his head over the ridge, they pulled their guns out of their cases. Peters saw it, got off his horse, turned it between him and the Indians, laid his gun across the saddle, pointing it towards them, and asked what they wanted. They answered "navish" nothing, placed their guns back in the cases and came on. As they passed Peters, one of them made a grab for Peters' gun, but as Peters struck at the Indian with his gun, the Indian dodged and hit his own horse on the shoulder, laming him.

Peters then came down to where we were and we told him what the Indians had done. Just then one lone Indian, who had been hunting, came down through the brush on foot. When he was off about three hundred yards, Peters rested his gun on a knob on the corner of the house, cocking it and said, "Now see me make that Indian jump ten feet in the air." I told him not to shoot as that would cause trouble. He answered, "No one will ever know it." Believing that he intended to shoot I pushed the gun off the knob.

Before the Indian came up, Peters had set his gun against the house; it was a large new rifle. The Indian took hold of the gun to look at it, but Peters took the gun from the Indian saying, "You let that be." The Indian answered "You mad." Peters said, "Yes, I am mad." The Indian said: "Hombo (what) make you mad." and shoved his finger around on his body, saying "You bullets no pass." Lyman Peters took a handful of large bullets from his pocket and, showing them to the Indian, said, "Don't you think they will pass." The Indian started off, looking back over his shoulder till he got a long way off.

A week or two before this happened, a small band of Indians came to my brother and I, and said they wanted a beef. We told them the animals were not ours, and they would have to get an order from Bishop Seely. A large five year old steer belonging to Chris Wintergreen was near, and an Indian raised his gun to shoot it. My brother pulled the gun down. Another Indian struck him in the face with a lariat. making it bleed, and said "Can't you cry?" Then the Indian with the gun shot the steer; they skinned the hind parts and cut out what meat they wanted, leaving the hide and balance of meat. The Indian who struck my brother seemed to be making love to a young squaw who was riding another horse. The same Indians killed some cattle in the immediate vicinity of Fairview. In order to avoid further

trouble we had to move the stock and sheep out of
Thistle Valley. They also took a herd of sheep from
some herd boys, drove them off quite a distance,
killed one sheep and turned the balance loose. James
M. Allred happened on them just as they were roasting the mutton on the fire. He said that they drew
their guns on him. Just at that time Jehu and Elias
Cox, fathers of the boys from whom the Indians had
taken the sheep, rode up; they shot at the Indians
who went off in a hurry.

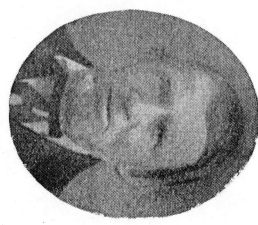

JENS GOTTFREDSON
Sergeant to Niels Mortensen, Richfield

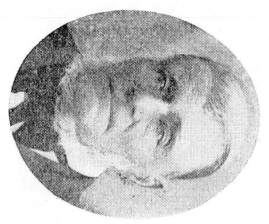

JENS K. PETERSON
Lieutenant to James Wareham Glenwood

JOHN LOWRY

Lieutenant in Wm. Bench's infantry company, Indian interpreter of experience, explorer, pioneer, colonizer.

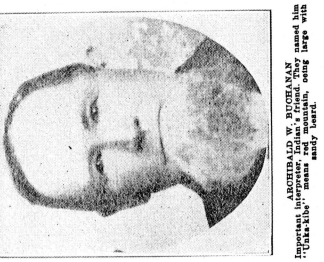

ARCHIBALD W. BUCHANAN

Important interpreter, Indian's friend. They named him "Unka-kibe", means red mountain, being large with sandy beard.

CHAPTER II.

THE BLACK HAWK WAR.
TREATY AT MANTI.
THE JOHN LOWRY AFFAIR.

Several stories are told as to how the Black Hawk war started. and these stories conflict in several essentials. It is well known that many of the Indians, were dissatisfied and unfriendly, and that during the years 1863 and 1864 they had committed several acts unfriendly towards the white people; thus they had stolen some horses and killed a number of cattle, at different places, and it needed but a pretext to open hostilities.

During the winter of 1864-65, a small band of Indians were camped near Gunnison, Sanpete Co. It is said that they had contracted small-pox, and that many of them died.

The Indians seemed to think that the white people were to blame in some way for this and were threatening to kill the whites and steal their horses and cattle. Arrangements were consequently made for a meeting between the Indians and the whites at Manti on the 9th of April, 1865, to talk over matters.

On that date a number of prominent Utes came to Manti. They met at Jerome Kempton's place, and it appeared that an understanding would be arrived at, but a young chief (Yene-wood) also known as Jake Arropeen could not be pacified; he kept talking

and making demonstrations, trying to persuade
the other Indians against making peace. John Lowry
and Archibald W. Buchanan were interpreters and
leading spokesmen on the peoples' side.

John Lowry, who was said to be under the influence of liquor, demanded of Chief Yene-woods (Jake
Arropeen) that he should keep quit and let him
(Lowry) finish talking, when some one spoke, saying,
"Look out, he is getting his arrows." Whereupon
Lowry stepped up, caught hold of the Indian and
pulled him off his horse, and he was about to abuse
him in some way, when some of the by-standers interferred. Indian Joe mounted his horse and rode
out to an Indian camp at Shumway Springs, where
he reported what had happened. This caused a big
excitement among the Indians who sent out their
runners to distant Indian camps with the information. In consequence the Indians generally broke
camp and moved into the mountains. Those at Richfield went to Salina to join those from Sanpete.

P. LUDVIGSON, BARNEY WARD AND J. P. ANDERSON KILLED.

It was reported that the Indians were going to
steal stock. Consequently. early in the morning of
the 10th, a small party of men from Manti went out
to the Indian Farm at Twelve Mile Creek to gather
the stock, which was turned out there, to bring them
home. On the way they were attacked by a number,
of Indians, who killed Peter Ludvigsen and put the
others to flight. A. W. Buchanan says that he
and Fred Cox went out to the Indian camp at
Shumway Springs to have a talk with Chief "White

Eye.'' On their arrival there they handed their bridle reins to a young Indian to hold, while they went into the chief's tent. The chief at first seemed sullen and would not talk. Buchanan told him what they had come for, and finally the chief called for his pipe. Buchanan now knew that he would get a hearing, and finally the chief said that only one Indian and one white man were mad, and that if he and Cox would go with him he would get back the stock which the Indians had taken.

The brethern named reported at Manti, but the people were not willing that they should go, believing that the Indians were treacherous and were likely to kill them; hence the venture was not made.

After the Indians had taken the stock and killed Ludvigsen, they went to Salina canyon where they were joined by Indians from Richfield, and they quickly gathered up most of the Salina cattle and drove them up Salina canyon to Soldier Fork, where they came onto Barney Ward and James P. Andersen who, not knowing that the Indians were mad, fell an easy prey to them.

It appeared that the Indians had held these two men prisoners for a time before killing them; they were both shot with many bullets and arrows and the condition in which their bodies were found suggested that they had been tortured. They were scalped and most of their clothing taken. Their bodies were not recovered until the next day. During the following night many white men arrived at Salina, from in the Sanpete settlement.

The Indian Agent in Sanpete at the time was Fred J. Keisel, since mayor of Ogden—whose prudence in withholding the supply of powder and lead

from the savages and giving it to the settlers, helped the prospect somewhat, but the situation was
very strained, and the witness to the indignity offered the Chief at Manti as already noted felt the
affront had furnished the spark to kindle the Indians' vengeance into full fury. Learning later in
the evening that a raid was contemplated upon the
cattle of the settlement, a small body of horsemen
started for the feeding grounds.

Early next day they encountered the Indians who
opened fire, killing a young man named Peter Ludvigsen. and put his comrades to flight, mutilated
his body, and then made off with a herd of stock.

Hostilities now being formally opened, the victorious bands broke for the mountains to the southeast.

Near Salina, Sevier County, on the same day
they killed and scalped two men, one being the veteran Barney Ward, and the other a Mr. Lamson,
(James P. Andersen) and drove off a large number
of stock into the adjoining canyon.

COL. ALLRED WITH 84 MEN DEFEATED
IN SALINA CANYON.

A company of cavalry was quickly mustered into
service under Colonel Reddick N. Allred and started
in pursuit, but having chased the savages ten miles
into the mountains, they were compelled April 12th
to retire before the deadly fire of the ambushed foe,
with the loss of two men killed, Jens Sorensen and
William Kearns, and two wounded.

Reinforcements having been received, another
advance was ordered two or three days later, when

the bodies of the two militia-men were recovered
and the Indians were pursued into the rugged country between Fish Lake and the Grand River. A
spirited engagement took place and the Indians
repulsed with heavy loss.

From a write-up by Joshua W. Sylvester (formerly Bishop of Elsinore, Sevier County) we obtain
the following:

"It was in the spring of 1865, when we were
busy plowing and planting, that the news came to
Gunnison, where we lived, that the Indians had
killed a man at Twelve Mile Creek, that they had
gone up Salina Canyon and killed Barney Ward and
another man, and driven off all the Salina stock.

The next morning a company of us started with
Bishop Kearns to look for a band of horses. While
we were out of town word came from Manti to raise
men and ammunition, and to proceed to Salina as
soon as possible. Not finding the horses, (as the
Indians had taken them), we were returning home,
when, about half way between Gunnison and Salina,
we met the Gunnison boys, (the sons of Bishop
Kearns with them), who said they had my bedding
with them, expecting me to go with the expedition.
I told them it was no use for me to go, as I had only
one bullet for my gun; but William Kearns said,
"Come on, you'll get some bullets." Consequently
Andrew 'Anderson and I went on while the Bishop
and others returned home. We found men gathered
at Salina from all parts of Sanpete. I began inquiring for bullets, when I was informed that Barney
Ward had been seen moulding some for his pistol
which were the size I wanted, and as he did not
have his pistol with him when he was killed, it was

thought the bullets were in his trunk. Some one went with me to get them; it was dark and we had no light. And as Ward's corpse was laid out on the trunk, or chest, we had to raise him up, while I searched for the bullets, until I found them. Firing off the bullet I had in my gun the next morning. and reloading with a good charge of powder, I started with the posse up the canyon, in order to overtake the Indians and recover the stock, as they had driven off all the stock at Salina. We followed the trail through narrow places, above precipices and under cliffs, till we came to a place where they had killed a beef. There we put on an advance guard and proceeded till we passed a very narrow place on the trail, when an Indian fired a signal gun, and immediately they all fired on us from the rocks above on the steep mountain side. We found that we were trapped. Colonel Allred then gave orders for a retreat to a ridge, in order to flank the Indians, and where we made a stand. Bullets were passing over our heads like hail, and had the Indians known how their guns were carrying they could have shot us down fast. In being shot down hill a bullet will raise, so they over-shot. However, their trap was well laid, for they had arranged to close in on the trail behind us; but an unexpected move on our part frustrated their plan. The officers found that they were getting a cross fire, and as they had worked down on the mountain, called for another retreat to the next ridge, in order to flank.

Some of our men, not understanding the order from the commanding officer, went too far, which hindered the Indians from closing the trail, but they had got so far down the mountain that they could get good shots at us while we could not see one of them. William Kearns was shot from his horse and killed while riding beside his brother Austin, who had to leave him where he fell, in order to save his own life.

The following statement is from Austin Kearns himself:

"When we made our second stand, after we had been fired upon by the Indians, I noticed one particular Indian behind a big rock. He had loaded and fired his gun three or four times, and I asked comrade Anderson, my companion, who stood near me to hold my horse while I went up the hill-side to take a shot at the Indians. I laid down, resting my gun on a root. While I lay there a ball struck near me, causing the dirt to fly in my face. When I looked up I saw my comrades were making a quick retreat down the canyon. I then returned to Anderson who handed me my reins and I mounted and followed the company. But instead of my horse following the trail, he turned in the opposite direction, jumped into a patch of oak brush, and tried to force his way through. By doing so he got fast and was unable to get out. I had matcheres (heavy leather covers) on my saddle; they spread out, holding me fast. While trying to get out the Indians were coming closer; they cross-fired in quick succession on me from three directions, and perhaps fifty or more shots were aimed at me while in that condition. At last the string in front of the horn of the saddle broke and I raised up letting the matcheres with my wool blankets slide off, freeing the horse. All my companions had gone, leaving me alone with the howling Indians who thought sure they would have my scalp. I escaped without a scratch, although bullets had been flying around me like hail, cutting the oaks all around me. It surely was an exciting time."

Mr. Sylvester continues his narrative as follows: "William Kearn's horse worked along the trail with the crowd. Therefore, when the second retreat was ordered there was no chance to flank; we were not acquainted with Indian warfare then, but this experience made us look out ever after. Had there not been a providential move at this point, there could have been a massacre equal to that of General Custer's of a later date for bullets flew everywhere and we could not see where they came from.

We saw four Indians run across the canyon to get a cross-fire on us. One of them, quite a distance up the canyon, was swinging his hands to the others on the mountain, motioning to them to work down. Some of us fired at him and he fell from his horse. This incident was followed by a lull in the firing for a few moments of which we made good use. The Indians afterwards reported that the Indian we had shot soon got well, but was afterwards killed by another Indian.

I will here relate an incident that occurred during the second retreat which was called, when we reached the top of the ridge. I was cinching my saddle when a man came up the trail, holding to the tail of another man's horse; he was nearly exhausted. A mule was seen near by that had thrown a man who was afterwards killed by the Indians. This man was Jens Sorenson of Ephraim. The animal worked its way down the trail, but stood entangled in the reins. The man on the horse called out "Get that mule."

The exhausted fellow reached the animal, but had no knife. I took my knife from my belt and ran to him, leaving it with him. I returned to my horse. The cinch of my saddle was so long that the rings met and I had a heavy pack on behind, so, when I endeavored to mount, the saddle turned with me. I wanted my knife then, but the man had gone and so had everybody else. I then had to undo a long strap, but about that time the bullets were coming toward me thick and fast. I threw the whole business down, jumped on my horse bareback and soon overtook the others. I saw the man to whom I had loaned my knife, and asked him what he had done with it. Taking it from his pocket he said, "Are you the man who let me take this knife? It saved my life." That man was Frank H. Hyde.

We marched on feeling pretty blue, and at the mouth of the canyon we met Bishop Kearns. The reader may imagine the feelings of the father and son thinking of the other son and brother who was left a corpse on the trail; it was indeed a sad scene to those who witnessed the same.

The bodies of Kearns and Sorensen laid in the canyon two days before they were rescued, then a friendly Indian (Sanpitch) went up and got them.

When the Indians found that Kearns was an old friend with whom they had frequently played and hunted, they placed the body against a rock and wove willows around it to keep off the wolves; while the man who fell near him was horribly mutilated. An Indian (the chief Sanpitch) came in the night to Bishop Kearns and reported that it was safe for the men to go after the body of his son as the Indians had gone.

STATEMENT OF GOTLIEB ENZ.

Gotlieb Enz of Richfield makes the following statement:

"I came to Richfield in November, 1864, with a few head of cattle, having lost a yoke of oxen between Gunnison and Salina. Early in April, 1865, a band of Indians were camped at Richfield by the big spring, and a man by the name of Sutton came from Provo to trade with them. He exchanged a quantity of ammunition for buckskins. About the 8th of April, 1865, I went out to hunt for my oxen, expecting to find them in the Gunnison field. Being on foot, and failing to find them there, I, surmising that they might have strayed up Salina Canyon, left Gunnison and came to Salina. I called on Elias Crane, who was living in a dugout. The Indians had left Richfield and were camped near the mouth of Salina Canyon, southeast of town, on the bench. I told the Crane family that I was going up the canyon to look for the oxen. Mrs. Crane asked me if I was not afraid of the Indians, to which I replied that I was not, as I was acquainted with them. I left my blankets there and went up the canyon about three miles into Soldier Fork. There I found one of the oxen. Having walked all day, I sat down on a rock to rest. An impression came to me that I should not stop there; the same impression came to me three different times. Consequently I got up and looked around, but saw nothing unusual. I then started down the canyon, leaving my ox there feeding on good grass; I intended to go after him the next day and drive him home. As I went down the canyon, I met two men going up to look for stock; I

passed the time of day with them, and went on. Soon
afterwards I met the Indians going up the canyon,
most of them on the main road. I saw six or eight
up on the south side of the canyon, driving up some
stock. I passed the Indians unmolested and had no
idea that they were angry. I stayed that night at
Elias Cranes'. After singing and prayers we retired.
About midnight a man carrying an express came
from Gunnison with the information, that the Indians
were on the war-path, and that the people must prepare to defend themselves. He further reported that
the Indians had killed a man near Manti. All the
people gathered at the little rock meeting house.
While there a lady said, "My husband went up the
canyon last evening to look for some stock, and has
not returned. I wonder what can have become of
him." This was Mrs. Ward. Then a young lady
also said, "My brother went up also and has not
come home." Towards morning we heard the report
of some guns, seemingly a long ways off. Thinking
something might be wrong. I, together with six or
eight other men, went up the canyon. When we arrived at the place where I left my ox the previous
day, we found the two men killed and scalped, and
most of their clothing removed from their bodies.
There were a lot of arrows sticking in them, and it
appeared that the Indians had taken them captive,
and tortured them for some time before killing them.
We left the bodies and went down to the settlement
and reported. A number of men went up with a team
and brought the bodies down. When preparing the
remains for burial, we examined them closely. The
two men had been shot with a number of bullets, and
many arrows. Some of the latter we were unable

to get out, owing to the beards on the spikes. During the day a lot of men arrived at Salina from the settlements in Sanpete and elsewhere.''

WALTER JONES OF MONROE SERIOUSLY WOUNDED.

On April 15th, 1865, Walter Jones with some others were on their way to Marysvale with teams to bring out a few families who had located there. When on the ridge (before getting into the valley), Jones reached down into the wagon to get his dinner. He accidentally pulled the gun, when something caught the hammer and discharged it, the load passing through Brother Jones' feet. The accident compelled him to use crutches for four years.

JENS LARSEN A SHEEP HERDER KILLED NEAR FAIRVIEW.

In the evening of May 25, 1865, while gathering his sheep, Jens Larsen was shot and killed about four miles north of Fairview, Sanpete County. His daughter Pauline subsequently became the wife of Jacob Dastrup of Sigurd, Sevier County.

JOHN GIVEN, WIFE AND FOUR CHILDREN MURDERED IN THISTLE VALLEY.

Between daylight and sunrise on the morning of May 26, 1865, the same murderous band attacked John Given and family who had moved up Spanish Fork Canyon into Thistle Valley and intended locating there for the summer. Besides Given and his wife, the party consisted of his son John, aged nineteen, his daughters Mary, Annie and Martha, aged respectively nine, five and three years, and two men named Leah and Brown. All were sleeping in a hut constructed of willows, Leah and Brown being in a wagon box at one end. The former was awakened by hearing the cattle running wildly down the canyon, and shortly afterwards the firing of the Indians through the brush of the hut, apprised him of the cause of the alarm. To their concealed position in the wagon box the two men owe their escape. The other occupants of the hut were speedily killed, the blood thirsty Indians completing with arrows and tomahawks the work which their first volley had begun. Quickly gathering up the flour, axes and guns of their victims, they surrounded a herd of stock, and after killing the calves, drove off between one and two hundred head of horses and cattle into the mountains.

The following details were given by Charles Brown, survivor of those who were attacked in Thistle Valley when John Given and family were massacred:

Charles Brown and Charles Wager Leah had gone into Thistle Valley from their former home, together with John Given and family and located in the meadow land north of Thistle Creek bridge, intending to make it their home. They were engaged in plowing and planting crops, and had several head of cattle and milk cows with calves.

At daylight on the morning of the 26th of May, 1865, Leah awoke on hearing stock moving past the willow shanty in which the people were all sleeping, the two young men, Leah and Browne being in a wagon box at one end of the shanty. When the Indians came to the shanty they poked their guns through the willow wall and fired, shooting Mr. Given in the region of the heart and Mrs. Given in the right cheek. Their son, John, aged nineteen, jumped up, saying, "You d—d sons of B—s." when an Indian shot him down before he could reach the door. These three were shot before the two young men left the cabin. Leah, without dressing, grabbed his gun and ran out, hiding in the willows, and Brown, who slipped on his clothing, ran out at the same time. An Indian fired at them, the ball passing between them, striking the ground about two rods ahead of them. Browne ran to the creek and waded down it, the water being up to his armpits and very cold. When down the creek some distance he got out and went down the side hill about six miles to where Dr. Joseph S. Wing and five other families from Fairview had located and reported what had happened. They all left and went to Fairview. When they came to the Given cabin they found the three grown persons lying dead on the floor of the hut with the feathers of the feather bed scattered over them, and also the three young girls, Mary, aged nine, Annie, five, and Martha, three years old, in the wagon box killed. Oscar Barton, one of the rescuers from Mount Pleasant, says: "On the morning of the killing, between daylight and sunrise, Andrew Larson of Mount Pleasant who had camped during the night with the Wing family passed the Given place on the road, and as he passed he heard calves bawling in the corral. Thinking that the people had not yet arisen, he passed on, but when he reached the herd house, about where In-

dianola railroad station is now located, he saw horsemen about half way up the valley, driving stock eastward toward the mountains. His first impression
was to unhitch one of his horses and ride up to them,
but he finally concluded to travel on in the direction
he was going.

Brother Barton further reports that one of the
men who escaped ran to North Bend (Fairview), and
reported what had happened. An express was immediately sent from Fairview to Mt. Pleasant.
Twenty armed men were soon in their saddles and
on their way to Thistle Valley. A few more men
joined this Mt. Pleasant company at North Bend, and
they all arrived at the Given cabin in Thistle Valley
before noon. Here they found Mrs. Given outside of
the cabin stripped and lying on her back with her
head towards the shanty, and John Given Jr. lying
on the floor on his back with his feet toward the door,
where he had fallen, being shot in the breast. The
three girls lay in the wagon box, each with a deep
tomahawk gash in the left side of the head. They were
all stripped, with the exception of a small waist
which the savages had left on each. The bedding
had all been taken away, together with much of the
house furnishings, guns, etc. The murdered people
were taken to Fairview for burial and Charles Brown
and Charles W. Leah, after attending the funeral,
went back to Spanish Fork by way of Salt Creek
Canyon and remained there.

Ten or twelve of the young calves which had
been left in the corral on the Given premises were
found by the brethern tomahawked across the loins
and were dragging their hind parts. The supposi-

tion was that the Indians, fearing that the calves
would be a hindrance in driving off the stock into
the mountains, had thus crippled the poor animals
to prevent them from following their mothers.
The massacre of the Given family in Thistle
Valley represents one of the most horrible deeds
committed by the Indians during the Black Hawk
war.

DAVID H. JONES KILLED NEAR FAIRVIEW

On Friday, May 29, 1865, three days after the
massacre of the Given family in Thistle Valley,
David H. Jones, a member of the Mormon Battalion
and a resident of Fairview, was killed by Indians
about three miles northwest of Fairview. This killing was supposed to be done by the same band of
Indians that had murdered the Given family.

Comrade James M. Allred says that ten persons
killed by Indians are buried in the Fairview cemetery, namely, John Given, wife and four children,
Thomas Jones, David H. Jones, Jens Larsen and
Nathan Stewart.

INDIANS KILLED AT CIRCLEVILLE

Although the Indian depredations were raging
in all directions and many murders had been committed by Black Hawk and his band the year before,
the Piute Indians still remained in Circle Valley
professing friendship, although they were mis-
trusted by many of the settlers. Some of their
actions were so suggestive that the whites felt
themselves in danger every moment, not knowing
when a break would be made by these savages on
the settlement. On Monday, April 21, 1866, an ex-

press reached Circleville with the news that two of
the pretended friendly Piutes had shot and killed a
white man who belonged to a party of militia stationed some distance up the Sevier River at Fort
Sanford. This fort, which had been built that
spring by the militia under Silas Sanford Smith and
his men was about half way between Circleville and
Panguitch. Word was immediately sent to the
people of Circleville to protect themselves against
the Indians who were camped in their valley. On
receiving this admonition, the men of Circleville settlement were called together for consultation, and
after considerable deliberation it was concluded as
the best policy to place the Indians encamped near
their settlement under arrest. Consequently, all the
able-bodied men of Circleville were mustered into
service, some on horseback and some on foot. Thus
organized they proceeded to the Indian camp, which
they surrounded after dark. They had no trouble or
occasion, however, to use force as James T. S. and
Jackson Allred went into the Indian camp and per-
suaded the savages to come to the meeting house in
Circleville to hear a letter read, which had just been
received. All the Indians complied willingly with
this request, with the exception of one young Indian
warrior who not only refused to go but commenced
to shoot at the posse, who returned the fire and killed
him; the rest of the Indians were guarded in the
meeting house that night. The letter brought in by
express was then read to the Indians who were told
that they would be retained as prisoners, awaiting
further particulars of the killing of the white man at
Fort Sanford. The Indians showed resistance, but
their bows, arrows and knives were taken from them,

and thus secured the boys took turns in guarding them through the night.

Toward evening of the next day (April 22nd), while the Indians were still being guarded in the meeting house, some of them succeeded in getting loose and immediately commenced an attack upoh the guards, knocking two of the men down. There was every reason to fear a general break on the part of the Indians, and it was decided that the settlement of Circleville would be in great danger if the Indians were allowed to escape. In the general melee and excitement which followed the Indians were killed, with the exception of a number of children, who were taken care of by the settlers.

After this sad affair there were no more attacks on Circleville on the part of the savages, but companies of militia arrived in the valley from other parts of the Territory to assist the settlers in defending themselves, and a strong guard was kept around the town after that. As there was constant danger from attacks by the Indians, the settlers had built their houses in fort style around the meeting house, a short distance east of where Bishop Peterson lives at this writing. The settlers from Marysvale moved into Circleville that summer, but as the danger from attack by Indians became greater than ever, instructions were finally given by the authorities of the Church and the men in charge of the militia of the Territory, that Circleville, as well as the other places on the Upper Sevier, should be vacated and the people moved to older and stronger settlements for safety. About forty families were at that time living at Circleville. The evacuation of the settlement took place June 20, 1866, most of them going north to Sevier and Sanpete Counties, while a few crossed the mountains on the west to Beaver and other places, leaving their fields of promising grain behind unharvested, about 700 acres of land was under cultivation at the time. About fifteen families constituted the population at Marysvale, but it is not known how much land they had under cultivation when they left their settlement, first to seek refuge in Circleville and afterwards to vacate that place again for other parts. The fields thus left with growing wheat and vegetables were afterwards harvested by people from Beaver who came over the mountains for that purpose. Circleville and Marysvale were the only two settlements in Piute Co. at that time.

ABOUT 150 HEAD OF STOCK STOLEN FROM RICHFIELD.

The following is from the pen of the author, Peter Gottfredson:

In 1865, the Richfield Canal was completed and the water turned into it and the people had got some grain planted. It was customary to drive the stock down on the river bottom to feed. One Saturday evening about one hundred and fifty head were driven down to the sand knolls, about a mile north of the Glenwood Ford. Together with two other boys I was down there all day (Sunday) watching them and fishing, and when we left after sundown the stock was all right. On Monday morning, about daylight, I went down after some oxen belonging to myself and my father to finish putting in grain. When I reached the place I could not find any of

the cattle, but by looking around I soon discovered
that the tracks led to a cattle ford, about a half a mile
north of the wagon ford, and that the stock had crossed the river. The water in the river being high, I
stripped, and carried my clothing, gun and pistol
above my head, the water reaching to my arm-pits.
When safely across I dressed and followed the
tracks. I thought at first that the cattle had been
driven east by way of Glenwood but I discovered that
they had turned south up the river bottoms between
the river and the Black Ridge, about two miles to the
place where Annabella now is located, then they
had turned up east through a wide dry wash passing
Saul's meadow,   and up the Glenwood mountain.
Judging from footprints in the sand (in the wash)
I concluded that only five Indians had been driving
the cattle and I thought I could take them away from
five Indians. I ran from one bend of the dry wash
to another, carefully going up the points of ridges
and looking ahead to see if I could discover them.
I followed in that way up the Glenwood Mountain
about four miles till I struck the trail that leads
from Glenwood to Grass Valley. There I met two
oxen that had broken away from the Indians; they
had both been shot several times mostly through the
neck. One a black Texas ox belonging to me had
two arrows sticking in its side, nearly in half their
length. I had not heard the shooting and concluded
that it was no use to follow any farther, and in fact
I began to feel somewhat timid. Surmising that the
Indians must have taken the stock in the evening,
soon after we left them.

    I drove the two oxen down by way of Saul's
Meadow, through a gulch, to the Glenwood field;

there I drove them into a corral and pulled out the arrows, after which I drove them to Richfield. When I arrived home I learned that a lot of men were out hunting for me and the stock, fearing that I had been killed somewhere in the brush. Some of the men followed the tracks of the stock the way I had gone; others were hunting for me in the river bends. Most of them stayed out all day and came home hungry and tired. When they learned that I had been home since before noon they were cross and thought that I should be punished for not coming home to report the stock gone, instead of following them. Major Higgins notified me to appear in the evening before what was called a court martial. I did so and told my story. I remember that some of the men suggested that I should stand some extra guard as a penalty for my foolishness. Major Claus Peter Andersen said, I motion we let him go; I have done such foolish tricks myself. They let me go unpunished. During the summer a company of about twelve teams went to Andersen's Canyon, south of Monroe, after timber, in care of Major Andersen; this man had been a major in General Johnston's Army, which was sent to Utah in 1857 and he had also belonged to a company of rangers in Texas previous to joining the army.

In the evening, at the campfire, I asked Major Andersen to tell us one of his fool tricks to which he consented by relating the following: On a certain occasion while I was doing military service in Texas, some Indians took five of the rangers prisoners and carried them away with them. It was in the afternoon, too late for the company to follow, but I and another man volunteered to follow the Indians. We

obtained information as to the direction the Indians
had taken before dark. We traveled in that direction
till about midnight, when we came to a creek. Here
we saw the Indian fires about a mile up the creek.
We left our horses and waded up creek to the camp.
The creek bank being about four feet high. Our
belts were hung with Colts revolvers. We laid the
pistols on the bank. We saw our comrades stripped,
tied hand and foot and lying near a fire, while some
of the savages danced around them and were amusing themselves by sticking brands of fire on their
naked bodies. After being eye-witnesses to this re-
volting scenes I and my companion opened fire with
a revolver in each hand, and as soon as two revolvers
were empty we picked up two others and repeated
the process. The Indians ran for the timber, without
having time to get their guns, leaving their prisoners.
My companion and I unbound the men, secured some
clothing, guns and horses, and got back with our
comrades the next day. It is needless to say that we
were highly interested in Major Andersen's story.
—Peter Gottfredson.

GOVERNMENT AID REFUSED. THE MILITIA
ORDERED OUT.

Colonel O. H. Irish, superintendent of Indian
affairs for Utah, had previously to this called on
Governor Doty, asking the military authorities at
Fort Douglas for assistance in repelling these Indian attacks and protecting the settlements; but he
was naively informed by the commander at the Fort
that the settlers must take care of themselves—
stating that the California Volunteers had no other

duty to perform than to protect the overland Mail
Route. Steps were accordingly taken to muster a
few companies of cavalry in the southern counties.

TREATY BY COL. O. H. IRISH AT SPANISH FORK RESERVATION.

And Superintendent Irish promptly proceeded
to conclude a treaty with such of the Indian Chiefs
as appeared friendly. The personal influence of President Young contributed materially to his success in this direction;
and at a meeting held at the Spanish Fork reservation farm on the 8th of June, at which speeches were
made by Colonel Irish, President Young and others
of the whites, and by Kanosh, Sowiette, Sanpitch and
Tabby in behalf of the Indians, the treaty was accepted and the Chiefs announced their willingness to
sign it. Next day another meeting was held, more
speeches were made and fifteen chiefs attached their
signatures to the treaty; Sanpitch, a brother of Walker and Arropeen, of earlier notoriety, alone refus-
ing to sign. He relented, however, a few days later,
probably being urged thereto by the generous presents distributed among his associates.

By the terms of this treaty the Indians promised
to move to Uintah Valley within one year from the
ratification of the agreement, giving up their title to
the lands they were then occupying. They were required to be peaceful and not go to war with other
tribes except in self-defense nor to steal from nor
molest the whites. They were to assist in cultivat-
ing the reservation lands and to send their children
to the schools established for their benefit. On its

part the United States government promised to extend its protection to them; farms were to be laid out, grist and lumber mills built, schools established, houses furnished and annuities paid to the principal chiefs; and the tribes $25,000 for the first ten years, $20,000 annually for the next twenty years, and $15,000 annually for thirty years thereafter were to be distributed.

The Indians were also to hunt, dig roots and gather berries on all unoccupied lands, to fish in their accustomed places, and erect houses for the purpose of curing their fish. On the 18th of September of the same year Colonel Irish successfully negotiated a similar treaty with Piede Indians at Pinto, Washington County.

Meanwhile the hostiles were not inactive, and notwithstanding the vigilance of the settlers and the militia, frequent raids and occasional murders were still perpetrated. Some of the smaller settlements were entirely deserted, and herds of stock which had formerly ranged freely over the mountain's grassy sides were collected in the valleys near the larger villages where they could be closely watched. Lurking in the adjacent fastnesses the Indians would swoop down in the night time or at an unexpected moment, and almost before the startled settlers were aware, or before the local home guard cauld be collected to repel the sally, the bold marauders would be safe from pursuit in the rugged country through whose passes and defiles they successfully drove their stolen cattle. The season's work yielded them as plunder two thousand head of cattle and horses, in obtaining which they had killed either by massacre or in fight, between the thirty and

forty whites, including women and children. Black
Hawk's own numbers in the beginning had not exceeded two or three score warriors; but his success
gave prestige to his name and strength to his following, so that although he lost about forty of his braves
during the campaign, his force at the end of the year
exceeded a hundred men, and when he retired for the
winter toward the Colorado River he had beef and
horses for all who wished to join him. Other raids
during the year 1865, besides those mentioned were
made near Salina, Sevier County.

On Wednesday, June 7th, 1865, President Brigham Young and party accompanied Col. O. H. Irish
to the Indian Farm where a treaty was made with
the Indians. Dimick B. Huntington and George W.
Bean were interpreters. Col. Irish referred to some
good acts performed by a few of them and bestowed
presents upon them. He then read an abstract of a
treaty which is quite liberal in its provisions, and
talked to them. He recalled his council and advice to
them. Kanosh led off on the part of the Indians.
He was a boy, but Sau-e-ett was an old man and
could speak; he couldn't, yet he kept trying and
made quite a speech before he got through. Col.
Irish talked with one tongue but others had talked
with two; they had lied to the Indians; would Col.
Irish always talk one way? Brigham Young had
always talked with one tongue, they knew him, and
he had never lied to them but had always spoken the
truth and been their friend. What did he say about
it? They did not want to sell their land and go
away; they wanted to live around the graves of their
fathers. Sanpitch followed him, and spoke rather
bitterly, manifesting a strong desire to exert his in-

fluence against the treaty. President Young then talked to them. He recalled his council and advise to them in the past, and assured them he was still their friend, and advised them to sign the treaty and accept the provisions guaranteed in it for their benefit. The effect of his advice manifested itself in a few moments, most of the chiefs being strongly inclined to act upon it at the time, but Tabby counseled waiting a little to calm their minds, so that they might act without any excitement of feeling. The Pow-wow was consequently adjourned till the next morning.

MEETING WITH THE INDIANS.

Wednesday morning a little before ten the President and Company drove down to the farm, where under a temporary bowery the Indians were to meet Commissioner Irish, to have the treaty talked over. There were present, besides Col. Irish, representing the United States Government, President Young, Elders John Taylor, W. Woodruff, Geo. A. Emith, F. D. Richards, Bishop Hunter, Mayor Smoot, Col's J. C. Little, R. T. Burton and D. J. Ross, Capt. Winder, Marshal Gibbs and a number of other gentlemen from G. S. L. City, Bp. Harrington from American Fork, Bp. Miller and Col. Pace from Provo, Bp. A. Johnson from Springville, Br. G. W. Wilkins presiding in Sp. Fork, Bp. Fairbanks from Payson, Bishop A. Moffat and Col. W. S. Snow from Manti, with a considerable number of citizens from neighboring settlements; on the part of the Indians, Sau-e-ett, Kanosh, Tabby, To-quo-ne, Sanpitch, and eleven other chiefs of lesser note, with a large crowd of Indians.

On Thursday, 8th, the President and party, including Elder George Q. Cannon, left Payson about half past nine in the morning for the farm.

INDIAN ETIQUETTE.

As the company approached the farm, a small part of Indians stationed on a rising ground, notified the main body of the fact, and in a few minutes after the party arrived the Indians came gently sauntering down on horseback, seemingly endeavoring to keep up an appearance of dignity. All the chiefs were present except Sanpitch, who had taken suddenly indisposed to attend the meeting or be a participant in signing the treaty.

After a few brief and pertinent remarks by Col. Irish, the chiefs manifested their willingness to sign, and attach their marks to the documents. Old Sau-e-ett as the oldest chief leading; Kanosh, by his manner, seemed to think that simply putting his mark to the paper was rather small business. I afterwards learned that he prided himself somewhat on his ability to write his name,—a very laudable source of pride, for, as is well known, Indians generally are in much the same condition of ignorance with regard to caligraphy, that the mailed knights of christendom mostly were who bore the banner of the cross against the Saracens to rescue Palestine from their infidel hands.

THE TALK AFTERWARDS.

Col. Irish pointed out to them that if they lived up to the conditions of the treaty, they might date the commencement of a career of prosperity from that day, encouraging them to do so.

President Young advised them to remember the good advice given them, to learn to read and write and increase in intelligence, stating in connection, that Col. Irish had done all he possibly could for them, and that he was their friend and blessed them.

Kanosh, Tabby and Sow-ok-soo-bet indulged in a short talk each, expressive of their good feeling; after which the President strongly advised them not to punish the innocent for misdeeds of the guilty, and if any of their own or other bands should commit depredations, to catch the guilty ones and deliver them up to the authorities of the whites for trial. A large amount of presents were distributed among the Indians.

PRES. YOUNG AND PARTY LEFT G. S. L. CITY FOR SANPETE.

July 7th.—President B. Young, and several of the twelve and others left G. S. L. City on a missionary trip to Sanpete County, from which they returned on the 19th, having traveled about three hundred miles and held eighteen meetings.

R. GILLISPIE AND A. ROBINSON KILLED SOUTH OF SALINA.

In July, 1865, Anthony Robinson of Monroe, Sevier County, went to mill at Manti. He stopped at Gunnison on the night of July 12th, with Joshua Sylvester; the night of the 13th he camped near the Willow Bend on the west side of the Sevier River; some men from Monroe were camping a short distance below; he left his wagon and stayed with them

that night. He had a large brindle dog, which growl-
ed several times during the night, as if something
was prowling around. Next morning (July 14th)
he started for home. He soon reached a point immediately west of the Gravely Ford, where two
washes come together, the road crossing just below
them. The Indians had made some small brush piles
on the low ridge between where the two washes came
together. There they lay with their gun-barrels
through the brush piles pointing towards the road
on the brink of the wash, where they could not be
observed. When Brother Robinson got within about
thirty feet of them, they fired, and he fell back on
his flour dead. One of the oxen was also killed,
while the other ox broke the yoke in the
middle and got away; he was found about
two weeks afterwards in a larke willow patch,
carrying half of the yoke. The Indians also
killed the dog. The people of Monroe were waiting
for Robinson's return as the town was out of flour.
When his remains were found it was discovered that
the Indians had scalped him, that they had taken
what flour they could carry away and then turned
the balance out of the sacks over his body. They had
taken the sacks and all his other things, gun, pistol,
bedding, etc., away with them. The evening previous
Jake Harris of Glenwood and Robert Gillispie of
Mount Pleasant were hunting some horses south of
Salina. As they were crossing a dry hollow, about
one half a mile north of Lost Creek, Indians fired
on them from ambush, shooting Gillispie in the back.
Harris who was walking, beside him, leading his
horse, ran to the river close by; he claimed that he
ran so close by some Indians that he could have

touched them, jumped into the river. He crossed
over and hid in the willows on the west side till
night; bare headed and with feet bleeding he then
made his way to Gunnison about 16 miles distant.

A conference had been appointed at Manti,
President Young and some of the twelve were expected to be there. On the 14th of July a company
of men from Monroe (then called Alma) and some
from Richfield, were on their way to Manti on horse
back enroute to Conference. Near the Gravely Ford
where a trail left the road making a cut-off to the
ford, they took this trail. In doing so they saw Robinson's wagon up on the road, but thought it was
some one camping. After crossing the Ford they
saw, near a large bunch of brush, a man's hat.
Lorentz Dastrup picked up the hat and handed it to
Wm. Morrison, after which they rode on, crossing
Lost Creek and the large wash. There they saw,
out in an open grassy place, a horse with the saddle
on feeding, and thought they saw a man lying
down supposedly resting. They stopped at Salina.
Some men from Glenwood returning from Sanpete,
carried the sad news of the killing of Anthony
Robinson to Glenwood and then to Richfield and
Alma, whose people turned out and brought his ef-
fects and the body of Robinson home. Joseph Millett coming from Manti reported at Glenwood and
A. W. Buchanan and Geo. Pectol took the news to
Salina. An express party under August Nielsen of
Richfield also carried the word to Salina, overtaking Judge Morrison and party, who took the sad
news to the Manti Conference where Presiden Young
and party from Salt Lake City were in attendance.
A number of men were sent back from Salina, and

before reaching Lost Creek went out to where the saddled horse had been seen feeding, and found Gillispie lying on his back dead. As they went on, they could see the tracks of Gillispie's horse from the hollow where the man was shot; the horse had been going fast to where the hat was found, about three miles distant and it proved to be Gillispie's hat. It appeared also that he had turned and gone east toward Glenn's Twist, where a road passed through to Glenwood and that when he had reached this road he had gone back and crossed the hollow where he was shot; thence he rode out to where the body was found. Here he is supposed to have dismounted and died there. He was taken to Mount Pleasant for burial.

GEN. W. S. SNOW TOOK COMMAND OF SANPETE MILITIA.

The news of this double murder aroused the martial spirit in Sanpete, and Gen'l Warren S. Snow with about one hundred men was soon on the march endeavoring to head off the hostiles in the mountains towards Fish Lake. Gen. Snow took command of the Sanpete militia July 15th.

GEN. SNOW STARTS AFTER THE INDIANS. THE SQUAW FIGHT IN GRASS VALLEY, MARINE YORK WOUNDED.

After arriving at Glenwood they stayed there all day on the 17th, and at dusk started over the mountain for Grass Valley over a rough trail, Joshua W. Sylvester says—"At daylight, on the morning of the 18th, we had a good view of the whole valley. Descending the mountain, we reached a creek, and un-saddled, resting just opposite a large cedar grove near the present site of Burrville. The picket guard was sent out and returned in a very short time. We were aroused and told that the cedars were full of Indians. The horses were soon saddled and we surrounded the grove. The first shot was fired by an Indian who lay behind a fallen log, the shot entering the breast of Marine York of Richfield. Captain Beach ordered his men to dismount and enter the cedars which was done and the Indians were soon routed. It was part of the band that had killed Robinson, as we found some of his things with them; the main gang had gone on ahead. E. C. Petersen (Chris Feuting) says that there were six Indian tents below the hill and that Colonel Ivie's company were on the outskirts of the grove and did not see many Indians; that after the fight some of his boys wanted to go back and look for dead Indians and guns, but the Colonel said: "No, let the squaws go and hunt up their pappooses. Then Ivie's company drew off. While some of the others searched the grounds. It was reported soon after the fight that only one Indian got away and a dozen or more had been killed, including some squaws and pappooses; the militia had fired into a large bushy cedar where a lot of them were concealed. It was also said that Louis Thompson of Ephraim and a man from Casper's Company came onto a bunch of squaws and pappooses, and that they were left there to guard them. One of the squaws tried to get away, and when prevented by Thompson, she picked up a stick of wood and struck him with it; he then shot her. This excited the others and they were

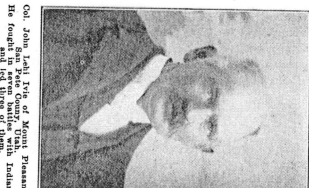

Col. John Lehi Ivie of Mount Pleasant, San Pete County, Utah. He fought in seven battles with Indians and led three of them.

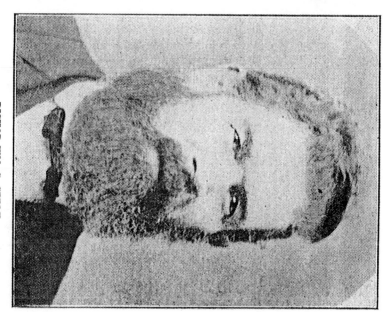

BISHOP WM. S. SEELY
Favorite with the Indians

NIELS O. ANDERSON
Prominent Indian War Veteran; Ephraim, Utah

soon dispatched. This event has been dubbed "the squaw fight." Mr. Sylvester continues: We returned through the head of Grass Valley, down Salina Canyon to Salina, where we stayed a couple of days jerking beef and getting provisions ready for a trip into the mountains.

GEN. SNOW AND COMMAND START FO GREEN RIVER.

On the evening of the 20th we started out again, and when about half a mile from town a sad accident happened; as we stopped by a large boulder to gird our saddles, Jack Harper set his gun (a Joslin) down against a rock and in some way discharged it, the ball passing through the cheek of the horse which James Mortensen was riding and lodged under Mortensen's collar bone; he still (1917) carries that ball and another with which he was shot later. The company stopped there while some of the boys took him back to Salina. After dark the company traveled to Twelve Mile Creek (now Mayfield) and camped for the night. The next day we went up Twelve Mile Canyon, crossed the mountain south of the "Nipple" and came out at the head of Salina Canyon where we camped the next night. Next day we traveled up Convulution Canyon and kept going till late at night; it was moonlight, but the sky was full of floating clouds. A short distance down the canyon was a pond of water, and when the moon shone out on the water it looked like fires being replenished at intervals with brush. The country being very rough. The men thinking it was an Indian camp stood and held their

6

horses all night, intending to surround the camp and make an attack at daybreak; but in the morning we found out our mistake and traveled down the valley where we struck the Indians' trail; they were driving a herd of cattle toward Green River. We followed, traveling day and night unt'l we reached Price River where we met Colonel Reddick N. Allred's command. Colonel Allred says in his journal: "I crossed the mountains with eighty men. We found three or four lodges of Tabby's Indians returning from a hunt, and the boys wanted to kill them, but I restrained them because they had their families with them. We formed a junction with General Snow's men on Price River and went to Green River without seeing the marauders. Returning we traveled by way of Cottonwood Creek and Huntington Creek and crossed the mountains on the rocky trail to Manti."

Mr. Sylvester continues his narrative as follows: After meeting Colonel Allred's Command it was decided to follow the trail farther. We took an inventory of our provisions and found that there was a pint of cracker crumbs to each man for three days. Two days travel brought us to Green River where we remained one day. Some of the boys swam the river and found tracks which looked as fresh as if they had been made that morning. Most of the boys wanted to follow the trail (tracks) but the officers decided that on account of jaded horses and being out of supplies we had better give up the chase, which, from what we learned afterwards, was a lucky thing for us. Thomas Caldwell, one of the company, who in after years talked with Chief Jake Arropeen, was told by that chief that he saw him (Caldwell) come to the river to get water, and could have shot him. Caldwell asked: ''Why didn't you.'' The chief answered that he did not want to; he also said that the Indians could have shot the men who swam the river. ''Why didn't you shoot them,'' asked Caldwell. Arropeen replied that they wanted all· the men to get into the river first, then the water would have been red. He said the Indians were ambushed, and as soon as the white men had got into the stream they were going to open fire. We started back the next morning, traveling two days and night without food. On the third day we were so nearly starved that the men wanted to kill a horse. The officers told them that if they did not meet supplies that day we might kill an animal.

But that evening we met the men with the packs of supplies at the mouth of Rock Canyon; we tore the sacks open and filled our pockets and shirt bosoms with biscuits and started up the trail; we could only go single file till we reached the top of the ridge or mountain.

The next day we all took our different routes for our homes from the top of the mountain. Our boys reached Gunnison at one o'clock in the morning singing, ''We will rally round the flag, boys.''

ATTACK ON GLENWOOD, MERRITT STALY WOUNDED.

At daybreak, on July 26, 1865, Merritt Staley, a blacksmith at Glenwood, went out after coal to start a fire in his shop. As he raised up with a basket of coal he was fired upon by Indians who lay concealed under the creek bank; one bullet went through

his right breast, one seared his lip under his nose, and
still another grazed his forehead. He placed his hat
over his breast where he was shot and shouted "Help
murder," and partly fell down the steps into the dugout where he and his family lived. Glenwood had
only been settled the previous year and only a very
few houses had as yet been built. Staley's wife got
out of bed and ran down to the house of Peter Allen,
who lived across the block, and gave the alarm, saying that her husband had been shot, and that her two
little girls were in bed and would surely be killed.
Isaac Allen, a mere boy, grabbed a gun and ran up
through the lot into the dugout. He seized the two
little girls, one in each arm, and ran with them, the
bullets flying all around him.

At the first shot, Solomon Case, who lived just
across the road cried out "Indians," he got his gun
from above the door, and opened the door to look out,
when Thomas Goff, his step-son, fourteen years old,
went outside in time to see Staley fall, as he supposed, into the cellar, and also to see his wife run
down to Allens. An Indian called out, "Sol Case,
shoot him" when a volley from the Indians on the hill
was fired at the boy Goff, bullets hitting all around
him. The boy ran back into the house, opened the
back or west door which had no hinges, but was held
in place with pegs, laid it down on the floor, ran out
and down to main street, where he met some men,
who saw an Indian on the hill squat down and shoot
at some one. Mrs. Case was in bed with a baby girl
two days old, and the nurse (Mrs. Charlotte Beal)
picked up the baby and ran down through a patch of
corn. Mrs. Case said to her husband "If you don't
take me down town I will get up and run." Mr.

Case wrapped a quilt round her, and with the corners over his shoulders carried her on his back down to the main part of the town.

The Indians kept up a constant fire from the rocks on the hill and some of the brethren went up near the hill and took shelter behind a house. Bishop Wareham who had a Sharp's rifle, remarked: "there sits a beggar on a rock," and handed his gun to George Pectol, who crawled out to a wagon box, took rest and fired; at the crack of the gun the Indian fell backwards off the rock. Another Indian said later that the shot fired by Pectol took the Indian's jaw off.

The people at Glenwood started a man with an express for Salina, but he was headed off a short distance north of town. Then Samuel Short was sent to Richfield and got through. When returning a company of men went with him to Glenwood.

In Richfield the drum beat about nine o'clock a. m. Those out on picket duty came in, and as they had their guns, they were ordered to get horses as quickly as possible and go to Salina, as the Indians were moving in that direction. Peter Gottfredson, one of them writes: There were ten of us and we were ordered to get through, if we had to fight our way. When at Cedar Ridge some Indians were seen on the east side of the river moving north, and when nearing the Willow Bend, Indians were seen passing a bunch of brush going toward the river; the road at this place passed along the river bank on the west side. No doubt, if we had followed the road, we would have been shot at but we circled up toward the west mountains, out of gun reach and came back into the road about a half mile north of the bend. There

a consultation was held, in which it was decided that
it was not safe for us to cross the river at the regular ford. Consequently a cattle ford was chosen.
When we got to town, we learned that most of the
men had gone to Manti to mill, but was expected
home the next day.

We all stood guard that night. The next day
about ten o'clock the Salina men came home; they
had camped at Willow Creek, distant about eight
miles, during the night. Soon after, five of us started home. When within about three miles of Richfield we scattered out hunting rabbits. Some one
outside of town saw us and reported that the Indians
were coming; he knew that it was Indians, for one
had on a red blanket. I had on a big red flannel
shirt which I wore instead of a coat. The drum beat
and all the people gathered at the meeting house.
When we got to town and saw no one, we wondered
what was wrong, but when we got to the public square
we saw the people at the meeting house, and when
things were explained it was learned that we were
the Indians that had been seen. Many of the men
with the best guns were out in pursuit of real Indians
who had driven away a lot of stock.

MINUTE COMPANIES ORDERED AWAY
FROM HOME.

About this time it was decided to send the minute companies away from their homes to guard the
trails and mountain passes. About the 28th of July,
Captain Niels L. Christensen with a company of men
from Richfield and Captain Isaac M. Allred with a
company from Spring City were stationed at Fort

Gunnison to guard the trails between Salina and
Twelve Mile Creek; they were ordered out for sixty
days. While there, nothing of special importance
happened, but one evening the cowherders came in
without the herd and reported that the Indians were
over the Sevier river gathering up the stock. We
were soon in the saddle and over the river. The
night being dark, we hunted for some time but finally found the herd lying down in a bend of the river
and brought the animals to town.

The Gunnison boys were stationed up the Sevier
river, in the neighborhood of Glenwood. At the end
of fifty days we were all allowed to go home.

BATTLE AT RED LAKE, SNOW, TAYLOR AND FRANSEN WOUNDED.

Nearly two months had passed since there had
been any serious outbreak. But Indians were prowling round Circleville, and it was reported that they
had a rendezvous somewhere near Fish Lake, east of
Sevier Valley.

General Warren S. Snow with 103 men went up
the River as far as Circleville; he had with him Colonel John Ivie's company of cavalry from Mount
Pleasant, and Captain N. S. Beache's company from
Manti, with some recruits from other companies;
they went to investigate the condition of affairs and
arrived in Circleville September 18, 1865. On the 19
they marched up the east fork of the Sevier to Clover
Flat, where they encamped for the night. There they
got onto the Indian's trail, which they follwed over
the plateau between Grass and Rabbit Valleys. Night
overtook them before reaching the latter valley; it

was raining and very dark; they made camp in the
head of a very rough canyon. Early next morning
(September 21st) Ezra Shoemaker and another man
went out to reconnoiter; they found the track of a
pony which had come within half a mile of camp and
turned back; they reported what they had seen. The
company then worked their way down the canyon.
When they reached the flat country, at a small lake
or pond called Red Lake, near Thousand Lake Mountain, they made a halt. General Snow and Col. Ivie
went up a black, rock ridge to ge t a view of the country and its surroundings. When near the top, Col.
Ivie saw a ramrod wiggling behind a brush only a few
paces away, and exclaimed "There they are," when
a volley was fired from ambush, one bullet hitting
and seriously wounding General Snow in the
shoulder.

The men retreated to the company, when a general battle ensued; the Indians firing from ambush
on top of the hill. The Indians over-shot—the bullets singing over the heads of the soldiers, striking in
the water, fairly making it boil. Orson Taylor of
Richfield received a serious gun-shot wound in the
side. George Frandsen of Mount Pleasant, while
concealed in a gully, trying to get a shot at an Indian he had seen, received a bullet high in the forehead, the missle plowing through his hair and fill-
ing his eyes and face with blood, but it caused no further injury. A short retreat was ordered for the purpose of getting flanking movements on the savages,
when it was noticed that one of the pack animals had
been left behind. Ezra Shoemaker of Manti and another man went back, and in the midst of a shower of
bullets from the enemy recovered the animal with

the pack. The fighting continued till night and several Indians were killed. The militia crossed back over the mountain in the night to Grass Valley and made camp. Next day they marched down King's Meadow Canyon to Glendwood, where they separated and returned to their respective homes.

ATTACK ON EPHRAIM, SEVEN SETTLERS KILLED, TWO WOUNDED.
Contributed by N. O. Anderson.

On the 17th of October, 1865, early in the morning, Peter Larsen came to me and asked me to go with him into the canyon, saying that it would be safe because a number of men had gone up; so we went up together. We had proceeded up the canyon a distance of about five miles to the forks of the three roads, above the long bridge, when we saw a man coming down the road on the run; it was Henry Green, who told us to turn back, that the Indians were up above in the canyon and from their ambush had killed some of the boys belonging to a company of six. Benjamin Black, Peter Graves, Thomas Wolsey, Wm. T. Hite and two others constituted the company. The place where they stopped to get their loads was one fourth of a mile east of the lake on Lake Hill. Peter Graves in running west came on to an Indian in the brush who had fired his gun and had not had time to re-load. Graves passed the Indian and ran down Maple creek, followed by two other Indians nearly all day. He had a dog with him and when hiding in the brush had to hold the dog's mouth to keep him from barking and revealing his whereabouts. He ran across Birch Creek and onto

the bald mountain where the Indian fired at him and
then turned back. He got home after dark. Wolsey
ran east and warned Louis Larsen and Rasmus
Jensen who then ran north and down the north side
of the canyon, being in sight of the Indians all the
time. Wm. T. Hite also ran down the canyon and
got on the dugway; he was killed on the so-called
Wire Grass Flat.

Down on the same road where the men were
killed known as the Black Stump Road, some men
were at work getting out timber, namely, Peter Isaac-
sen, James C. Jensen and Ole C. Jensen; they ran
north and joined Louis Larsen and Thomas Wolsey; they all reached home safely. Among the men
killed was Soren N. Jespersen, 50 years old. It appeared that he had been fearfully tortured while yet
alive. Being quite deaf, he did not hear the boys
when they called to him. The Indians came upon
him unawares and got between him and his wagon
where he had left his gun. Thus he was at their
mercy. When Peter Larsen and I met Henry Green,
we turned back and went down about a fourth of a
mile to the Black Spring; had we arrived there one
minute later we would have been cut off. The Indians came into the road a few rods behind us, but
we dodged behind a hill and went down the creek
road. The Indians went down the dugway and tried
to head us off, but they came in behind us and did not
see us. They went up the way we came down, expecting to meet us. We had then ran about two miles and
continued on to the grist mill where my partners
stopped. I continued on into town and gave the
alarm. Arming myself with a gun I went back to
the mill. The Indians were then out of the canyon,

making for the fields; a few of us got together and
started down also. We saw some teams coming on
the road from Manti and Indians directing their
course towards them. With these teams was my
brother-in-law Andrew H. Whitlock, who was driv-
ng a carriage slowly toward Ephraim. He had in
the rig an old doctor-Lady, Mrs. Snow of Manti
and L. C. Larsen. Mrs. Snow, on noticing the approach of the Indians, said, "The Indians are going
to hurt you." Whitlock replied that he thought the
Indians had made peace and therefore he did not increase his speed. Some Indians crossed the road
about seventy-five yards in front of them and
stopped. Whitlock now whipped up the horses, but
the Indians fired as they passed, one bullet from
their volley hitting one of the horses in the flank;
it ranged forward, but the horse kept up his speed
till he got into Charles Whitlock's yard in the center
of town, where he fell dead.

While running, L. C. Larsen got down on the
double-trees and lay low, while Whitlock stayed in
the seat. Chief Yenewoods who was well known by
the white people, rode along beside the carriage
shooting at the people till he emptied his revolver,
but did not hit any of them. With his bow, however,
he shot an arrow into Whitlock's back and then left.
Larsen got up from the wagon tongue and pulled the
arrow out of Whitlock's back. Brother Whitlock
suffered all the rest of his life from that wound.

The Indians then rode into the field west of
the town and killed Martin P. Kuhre, about 28 years
old, and wife, Hansine Kristine, 28 years old, and
Elizabeth Petersen, a grown girl, 17 years old.

Soren A. Sorensen was near by when Kuhre
fell. The Indian chief Black-Hawk rode towards
him. Sorensen states that when he met Black-Hawk
he walked up to him and rested his hand on the horn
of the Chief's saddle. Black-Hawk told Sorensen
that he was going to get some cattle. While in conversation with the chief other Indians killed Kuhre
within thirty feet of them, and his wife not more
than fifty yards distant. Kuhre fell with his two
year old son in his arms; the little boy made his
way to his dead mother where he was picked up by
Morten Benson and carried to town by John F. F.
Dorius. N. O. Anderson, who has given most of this
information, asked Sorensen how he could account
for the kindness of the Indian chief towards him.
Sorensen answered "I cannot say why, unless it was
owing to the fact that when I was home with my parents, my mother took a liking to the young Indian
Black Hawk; and when he came to our house, she
would frequently invite him to eat with us, and
would give him almost anything he asked for. The Indians did not take Sorensen's team, but gathered up
what stock they wanted, about two hundred head,
and went back the way they came. They left some of
their number stationed all the way from where they
started with the cattle and up the canyon. When
the Indians crossed the county road with the stock,
Louis Larsen and William Thorp came along and
asked me to go with them. We followed along
behind, while other citizens were scattered along
the road toward the mill, a distance of about a mile.
When we got up above the guard knoll known as the
Big Rocks, the Indians made a stand, and we had a
battle with them which lasted several hours. Wil-

liam Thorp was killed and Louis Larsen was wounded in the leg. This ended that day's tragedy; seven persons had been killed and about two hundred head of stock driven off.

I have written this according to the best of my recollection, I have also consulted those living who were in the most dangerous places and took part in the affairs.''

The following was reported by Charles Whitlock and corrected by Ezra Shoemaker:

On Saturday, Oct. 18th, a small body of men from Manti and Ephraim went up the canyon after the bodies of those who had been killed by Indians the day previous. They brought he body of Benjamin Black down to where Soren Jespersen lay. The remains of the latter were found about a rod from his wagon; his hands and feet were chopped off and also the upper part of his head. The rescuing party placed the bodies of the two men on a two-wheeled logging cart. They all went down the canyon, pulling the cart by hand. When they got down some distance, they saw some horse-men and thinking they were Indians it caused some excitement. The parties seen proved to be men from Ephraim who had come up to assist in bringing the bodies down. The two parties met on the Wire-Grass Flat where they picked up the body of Wm. T. Hite and brought the three bodies down to town.

The seven persons killed were buried in the old cemetery north of Ephraim.

The following statement of L. C. Larson of Mayfield was written to Niels O. Anderson of Ephraim, Utah, about 1916.

I was on my way from Circleville, Piute County, Utah, loaded with grain and headed for Salt Lake City to purchase fire-arms and ammunition. At Manti I met Andrew Whitlock who was there from Ephraim for a doctor lady, Maria Snow. As I had not been at Ephraim for about two years and had not met our comrade Mr. Whitlock before during this period, he asked me to ride with him from Manti to Ephraim and have Louis Thompson drive my team, to which I consented.

On stepping into Whitlock's rig, I informed Thompson that there was a gun and pistol placed under the quilt in the wagon. These I carried with me because several people had been killed by Indians during the summer, south and north.

We first saw the Indians when we were approximately two and a half miles south of Ephraim; they were first seen by us east of the road, south of the so-called guard knoll. At first sight we mistook them for some of the boys out scouting, but all at once they made a dash towards us at full speed. Upon reaching the old Willow Creek Ditch they leaped it without checking, where-upon I made the remark: "They are Indians and are riding very recklessly." Whitlock, (familiarly known as Cap,) answered, that he thought perhaps it was the Chief Sanpitch bringing the Indians down to make peace, as that had been talked of. Lady Snow speaking in the Danish language remarked that they were going to hurt us, but Whitlock replied: "If we try to run, they will head us off." The Indians crossed the road about seventy-five yards ahead of us and about thirteen of them formed a quarter circle about thirty yards from the road on the west. As we were passing them they

leveled their guns on us and fired. They wounded
one of the horses which died as soon as we stopped at
Chas. Whitlock's place at Ephraim. As soon as
they leveled their guns on us, Lady Snow placed
her head in her lap, which position she held until
we reached town. Our team was a pair of trained
racing horses, and as soon as the Indians raised their
guns on us the teams was on full speed. Chief Yene-
woods was the only one who overtook us, he was
on the left (West) side of the road and leveled his
pistol on me within three feet or less, where upon I
leaped over the dash-board onto the tongue where
I sat for a distance of a mile or more, during which
he emptied his pistol at us and also shot several arrows at us, none of which took effect, until we reached a swale with a ditch in the bottom where the team
slacked speed. Then an arrow took effect under
Whitlock's left shoulder on a slant toward the back,
six inches deep. On hearing him groan, I jumped
back into the seat and took the lines and whip saying,
"You are hit with an arrow; shall I pull it out."
He answered, "Yes, if you can." I did so, when
we had reached a point where Soren Sorensen now
lives at Ephraim. The swale referred to is the one
in Peter Graves's land, where the old county road
used to be. On account of the excitement I can not
remember if the arrow was hard to pull out of his
shoulder. However, I got it out, but Brother Whitlock still feels the effect of the wound, so he informed
me the last time I saw him.

The Indians followed us to the center of the
block north of Niels Thompson's present home,
where they turned west into the field and killed
Morten Pedersen Kuhre, his wife and sister in law,

leaving a small boy, less than three years old. This child was found crawling on his dead mother. Leaving this place the Indians went still farther west into the field, driving off the Ephraim cow-herd and several horses, after which they made their way back to the hills south of town.

RAID ON CIRCLEVILLE, FOUR PERSONS KILLED.

Indians made a raid on Circleville, Piute County November 26, 1865, killing four persons and drove off most of the stock belonging to Circleville.

Mrs. Mads Nielsen of Spring City wrote the following graphic account of this raid and of what befell her and her husband. "On the morning of the 26th of November 1865, my husband, Mads Nielsen and I left Marysvale for Circleville our home, returning from a visit to Salt Lake City. When within ten miles of home we passed another team which was driven by my Brother-in-Law, James Monsen. Being so near home we thought there would be no danger of Indians. When we reached a point about three miles from town and was driving around a hill, we saw a herd of cattle being driven toward the mouth of the canyon. I became very much frightened, believing it was Indians, and I begged my husband to turn back. But as he thought the Indians had already seen us, he suggested that by driving fast we might reach a company of men who were in pursuit of the Indians. In a few minutes the Indians left the stock and with a yell started towards us. Our horses were very tired, but we urged them on, thinking we might reach a swamp about three-

fourths of a mile ahead, but in this we did not succeed. The Indians rode up to us, and one of them
was in the act of shooting my husband, who, however,
frightened him away some distance by pointing an
old revolver at him. I suppose I am now safe in telling that the revolver was an old broken one, but of
course, we did not tell the Indian so. Mr. Redskin
now turned and shot our best horse, which of course
stopped the team. At the request of my husband, I
with my two year old brother in my arms, jumped
from the wagon, while the Indian was reloading his
gun. Willows were growing along the road, but as
they were low they did not afford much protection.
The Indian again mounted his horse and rode around
trying to get a chance to shoot my husband. At
this juncture I jumped into a slough that was near,
in which the water reached up to my neck, but I pre-
ferred drowning to being captured by the Indians.
My husband again pointed the revolver at the Indian who again turned back. My husband then took
my little brother whom I was holding up out of the
water and I climbed out of the slough. We walked a
short distance and tried to cross the swamp at another point, but were headed off by ten Indians.
Hence we got into the water again. The little boy
began to cry because the water was so cold, and we
left the slough once more. I sat down behind a
bunch of willows taking the little boy in my lap, and
my husband stood over us to give what protection
he could. The Indians did not follow us into the
the willows, but turned their attention to the wagon
and its belongings. They cut the harness from the
wounded horse, leaving the collar, and took the
wagon cover off. They emptied the flour on the

ground, cut the feather bed tick and scattered all the feathers, threw all the dishes out of the wagon, breaking all but one plate which I still have. They also took all of our clothing. While they were destroying the contents of the wagon, an old man named Froid, who had traveled in our company, arrived at the top of the hill and saw the Indians. He might have escaped all right if he had gone back himself at once, but he ran around his steers to drive them back. The Indians saw him, and followed him into the hills about a mile and killed him.

Just before my sister and her husband reached the ridge they were met by two men who had been sent out to guard the cattle. These men said that while they were sitting in a bunch of willows eating their dinner the Indians came out of the canyon and held a council close to them. One of the men had a dog with him, and he sat and held its mouth to prevent him from making a noise, and thus they escaped being discovered. These men informed my brother-in-law that the Indians had made a raid on the settlement. As they traveled on through the hills, my sister and her husband found the body of the old gentleman Froid, whom the Indians had killed. When they reached the top of the hill they could see our wagon, and the wounded horse lying by it; they thought we had been killed. We being hid in the willows could not hear my sister crying. My husband crawled out to a point where he could see them. And as he saw four persons he thought the two men were Indians and we dared not go to them. It was now getting dark and we had remained in the willows since two o'clock in the afternoon. We got out of the willows and started for the settlement without following the wagon road. We reached our home about an hour after my sister and her husband arrived.

It was late in the evening; we were both bareheaded and my clothes were frozen stiff on my body. My little brother had gone to sleep.

When we entered the house it was full of people who had gathered because it had been reported that we had been killed.

It is needless to say that our meeting was a happy one.

Mads Nielsen died in Spring City, March 9th 1899.''   —Ellen A. Nielsen

Sent to P. Gottfredson, April 15th, 1907.

At the time when the Indians took the stock at Circleville they killed Hans Christian Hansen, who was about a mile or more east of town with the stock, and Orson Barney and Ole Heilersen, two boys thirteen years old, who were out searching for cows.

DR. J. M. WHITMORE AND R. McINTYRE KILLED AT PIPE SPRINGS. BODIES OF WHITMORE AND McINTYRE FOUND. SEVEN INDIANS KILLED.

According to a statement of David Chidester of Venice, Utah:

Early in the year 1866 the Navajo Indians who were on the Arizona side of the Colorado River, being more numerous and superior than the Shevete Indians who inhabited the Utah side of the river. would often cross over and compel the less powerful tribe to do their bidding. Frequently they also captured and made slaves of some of them. On this certain occasion some of them crossed over and compelled the Shevete's who were camped in the neighborhood to assist in killing Dr. J. M. Whitmore and his hired man, Robert McIntyre, and drive away their sheep-herd and some cattle. This took place in the beginning of a big snow storm. When Dr. Whitmore and his hired man left the herd-house Whitmore had on his overcoat and carried in his pocket two twenty dollar gold pieces. The Shevete Indians secured the men's clothing, but not knowing the value of money, the gold pieces were later recovered. The Navajoes took the sheep and cattle over the river and they were never recovered. About the 20th of January, 1866, a company of armed men from St. George went in search of the murdered men. They came across two young Indians and compelled them to assist in the hunt. They acknowledged having seen the killing, but claimed they had no hand in it. There was about eighteen inches of crusted snow on the ground and the bodies were covered up. The men rode forward and back, four abreast and finally Colonel Pierce's horse stepped over the body of Dr. Whitmore and uncovered one hand which was raised above the body. When the whites informed the Indians that one of the murdered men had been found, one asked if it was the man with whiskers. When answered in the affirmative, he said: the other is over this way, they followed the Indian and then found McIntyre's body. There was a camp of Indians not far distant and Captain Pierce, with some of his men, went there and found the murdered men's clothing. The Indians refused to be taken prisoners and put up a fight, which resulted in seven of them being killed.

GENERAL SNOW ARRESTS A CAMP OF
INDIANS AT NEPHI.

On Monday, March 12th, 1866, General Warren
S. Snow of Manti arrested some Indians at a camp
a couple of miles northeast of Nephi, in Juab County.
One Indian who tried to escape, was shot down;
four others were tried in court and by order of the
chief was taken out of town and shot for complicity
in several raids. Eight others, including Chief Sanpitch, were taken to Manti and placed in jail. Early
in April the ecclesiastical and military authorities
of some of the settlements of southern Utah asked
for assistance from neighboring counties. One of
the first to respond was Iron County, which sent
twenty-four men with teams to help build a fort on
the Sevier River for the protection of the settlers.
General Daniel H. Wells recognized in the movements of the hostiles the indications of a disastrous
war and at once ordered all the available men of the
three counties, Sanpete, Sevier and Piute to be mustered into service as cavalry and infantry and organized for defense. But no vigilance was equal to
the task of defeating the designs of the sleepless foe,
the strength of whose forces was now increased to
over three hundred warriors, and the celerity of
whose movements defied every precaution.

KILLING OF JOSEPH AND ROBERT BERRY
AND WIFE AS STATED BY
J. S. ADAMS AND WIFE.

Joseph and Robert Berry and the latter's wife
Isabella were on their way from Spanish Fork, Utah

County, their former home, to Long Valley, April 2,
1866. When at Ezra Strong's place, called the
Troughs, in Kane County, they were asked to stay
a few days, while the ranch people gathered up their
stock, getting ready to leave they would go with the
Berrys to Long Valley, but as they were in a hurry
they did not stop.

Arriving at Short Creek, William Maxwell and
family who lived there, advised them to stop, as they
were also gathering their effects, and they would all
go in together. The Berry's declined and went on,
their team consisting of a good pair of horses and a
light wagon. They also had a plow and a few farm
implements with them, and such supplies as they
would need at their new home. When at the Cedar
Ridge, two or three miles from Short Creek, they
were attacked by Indians from the cedars and killed.
When the bodies were subsequently found it appeared that Joseph Berry had been wounded in the leg, as
a towel was wrapped around it. the travelers had undoubtedly turned and driven back towards Short
Creek, and had gone as far as the Big Sand Wash,
where they were again attacked. It also appeared
that one of the horses had been shot in the shoulder
with an arrow, as the collar was found with an arrow
point sticking through it about an inch and a half,
which crippled the horse so that he was unable to
pull; the other horse had cramped the wagon and
there they had all been killed and their horses taken
by the savages.

When found, Robert Berry was tied to the front
wheel of the wagon with his face out, and was shot
full of holes; Joseph was found a short distance from
the wagon.   Robert Berry's wife lay across the

wagon tongue face up and stripped; she had been outraged and horribly mutilated. The people from the troughs and Short Creek passed with their sheep, cattle and effects, without seeing them or their wagon, as they were some distance from the wagon road. When they arrived at Long Valley, they inquired as to when the Berry's got there, and were informed that they were not there. The two brothers with some others from Long Valley then went in search of them; when they found the wagon and place where they had been killed, the bodies were not there. They were murdered below Maxwell's ranch and Berryville. Each had two pistols. They also had a double barrel shot-gun. Some men who had been hunting stock had found them and taken them to Grafton and buried them there; consequently the brothers did not get to see them.

About two weeks later a number of men from St. George and vicinity under Colonel J. D. L. Pierce went to Long Valley to assist in moving the people out. When they moved there were from one to three families to each wagon. One Indian was found dead near the place where the Berrys had been killed; it appeared to be an old Indian judging from the long gray hair shown to the people as they passed.

REMOVAL FROM LONG VALLEY, REPORT BY MRS. J. D. L. PIERCE.

In the spring of 1866, Brother Erastus Snow called a council of his officers and men, to arrange for calling the outside people in, as the Navajoes had become very troublesome. Brother Snow said to Brother Pierce, "Brother John, if you will select a

man to take command, you may stay at home this
trip and put in your crops, as you have had such a
strenuous winter.'' Brother Branch was chosen for
the position and he selected Elroy Barney, Tom
Pierce, Jesse Crosby and several others to go with
him. I think about twelve men altogether—the best
young men in the country. They were to start from
the public square in St. George. Father went down
to see them off. Brother Snow of course was there
to see that all was to his liking; he did not seem satisfied and said to father, ''Brother John, this is going
to be a very critical trip and you have to move the
people out of Long Valley; I had much rather you
would go, and I want you to bring the women and
children, whether the men come or not.'' Father, an-
swering, said: ''All right, but I have no horse.''
Brother Branch got off his horse and turned it over
to father who wrote a note to me, saying ''I must go
and do my duty, you do the best you can, and God
bless you.'' With this he was gone. He had no
trouble, however, in getting the men out of Long
Valley as they were glad to have help. There were
about twenty wagons, and some cattle and horses.
They had a very serious trip, however, one small boy
was run over and killed, and they had to stop and
bury him; one babe was born on the journey. They
traveled at night to avoid the Indians. In coming
down a long, hard canyon, father stationed a part of
them at the back of the outfit, himself and the rest
in advance, always on the alert. Father's keen ear
heard the chirrup of a bird. He suspicioned Indians
and shouted for him to come out of the brush, or he
would shoot. Mr. Indian came out with a piece of
paper, saying, it was a letter. Father told him to call

to his friends and tell them to go away, or he would shoot him without any further talk; one other Indian came out. They seized both of them, tied their hands behind them and marched them in front of the company until morning, when they had reached a good road in an open country. They then bound the Indians over to keep the peace and turned them loose. These Indians were two of the meanest savages in that country at the time; the rest of the trip was uneventful.

On receiving the report of the trip Brother Snow he was pretty well acquainted with Indian history, but that move out of Long Valley was the best planned, and showed the best generalship of any he had heard of.''

RAID ON SALINA, THREE TEAMS ATTACKED, COW HERD TAKEN, HERDER KILLED.

Black Hawk with thirty mounted followers intercepted three teams from Glenwood Sevier County, April 13, 1866, about a mile north of Salina, on their way to the States after emigrants. They were Seth Wareham, Joseph Herring and John Wasden; The teamsters escaped and got to Salina, but their teams, consisting of nine yoke of oxen, were taken by the Indians and the things in their wagons either carried away or demolished.

A sheep herder from Fairview, Sanpete County named Johnson was killed in the foot hills northeast of Salina town. Emil Nielsen of Salina says, ''I was helping to herd the Salina cow-herd while the men were employed building a fort. We were on the west side of the Sevier River northwest of town distant about two miles, near the old wagon Ford. My brother, older than I, was with me. We had been talking about Indians and he said that if the Indians came after him he would run and jump into the river. We saw the Indians on the east side of the river, but did not know they were Indians; they had attacked the three teams from Glenwood just before ¡we saw them. They came over the river after the cow-herd. When we saw the Indians coming, Chris, my brother, ran to the river and was evidently killed there in the river as he was never found, but one foot with the shoe on was found down the river during the summer. An Indian came after me and shot at me with arrows; the first arrow hit my right arm, and the next went into my left side. I was running and fell. The Indian then took off my hat and shot an arrow into my head and pulled it out three times. I thought if I could make the Indians think I was dead, he might leave me, and as I did not flinch when he shot me in the head, he evidently left me for dead. I lay there from about ten o'clock in the morning till near sundown. I dared not get up, fearing that the Indians might be near and see me and come and finish me. When I got up, I went to look for my brother, but could not find him. I then waded the river, the water being above my waist, and I started for home. On the way I met a man by the name of Hansen, and when I reached the edge of town, I met my father, who picked me up and carried me home. I carried the arrow spike in my side for two weeks before it could be taken out. The old doctor lady, Maria Snow, of Manti, put poultices on the wounds and it drew out the spike. I was eleven years old.

The Indians on that occasion got away with two hundred head of stock.

Emil Nielsen was a respected citizen of Salina Utah, till December 1917, when he died at Salina.

INDIANS AT MANTI BROKE JAIL, THREE INDIANS KILLED, FIVE ESCAPE.

Chief Sanpitch, who had been so reluctant to sign the treaty drawn up and presented to his fellow chieftains at Spanish Fork on June 8th of the previous year, 1865, was quick to violate his pledge when opportunity offered and when Black Hawk's successes proved sufficient to seduce him from his allegiance, he joined in some of the depredations planned by the renegade chiefs, though not with the latter's good fortune for he was one of those taken prisoner at Nephi on April 12th. Sanpitch and the other Indian prisoners at Manti broke jail, April 14, 1866. From Wm. A. Cox of Manti we learn the following: The Indians broke out of the jail late in the evening, and five of them got away. Andrew Van Buren and an Indian by the name of Aukewakets ran over a pile of rocks and leaped over a fence. As they ran over the rock pile each stooped and picked up a good sized rock raised up ready to strike. VanBuren being a little the quickest brought the Indian to his knees, and then took an old jack knife with a broken backspring from his pocket, after which he and the Indian clutched each other by the throat. Van Buren succeeded in opening the knife with one hand and his teeth and cut the Indian's throat.

When W. A. Cox in the darkness of the night passed the end of a pile of fence posts, he thought he saw something move under the end of the posts; he kicked under and an Indian jumpem up with a loud "wah." Cox stepped back and with his revolver shot the Indian in the bowels. The Indian coming at him he fired again and shot the savage in the breast. When Warren Snow passed a shed that night an Indian came out after him. Brother Snow heard him, but it was so dark he could not see him; he struck the Indian with his gun, breaking the stock, but killed the redskin.

CHIEF SANPITCH KILLED NEAR MORONI, SANPETE COUNTY.

Five Indians, including Sanpitch, got away and made for the west mountain; a posse went in pursuit and on the 18th of the month Chief Sanpitch was found hiding in Birch Canyon, between Moroni and Fountain Green and was killed. The other four were tracked into the mountains between Fountain Green and Nephi, south of Salt Creek Canyon. On the 19th, Amasa and George Tucker and Dolph Bennett struck their tracks on the side of the mountain, where some men from Moroni joined them, and they followed the trail nearly to the top of the mountain where they overtook and killed three of them. They followed the track of the other one, whose name was Tackwitch, over the mountain and down some distance. Bennett stopped and sat down while the others followed the tracks. The Indian doubled on his tracks and came back to a point near where Bennett was seated and crawled into a patch of oak brush where he covered him-self up with leaves. Bennett saw him, and when the men missed his tracks they came back. Bennett motioned to his comrades pointing out where the Indian was hidden. At once they surrounded the place and one of the men shot and wounded the Indian who jumped up and came at Bennett with a large butcher knife. Bennett emptied his revolver at him without bringing him down or stopping him. When within a few feet Bennett threw his pistol hitting the Indian on the temple and knocking him down. The Indian had no more than struck the ground when Bennett was on top of him, wrenched the knife from his hand and cut his throat. This finished the jailbreakers.

TOWN OF SALINA VACATED AFTER LOSING MOST OF THEIR STOCK.

On account of the exposed condition of the town of Salina, and the people having lost practically all their stock that place was abandoned by its inhabitants April 21, 1866; most of them going into Sanpete County.

From Whitney's History of Utah we glean the the following: Two men who had been engaged in strengthening Fort Sanford on the Sevier in Piute County, had an engagement with two Indians belonging to Black Hawk's band, April 22, 1866. One of the latter was wounded and the other killed. Hakes received a severe gunshot wound in the shoulder. Immediately afterwards, a number of Piedes who were camped near the Fort gave up their arms and approached the settlers with overtures of peace. This offer being accepted, the settlers at another point, thinking the movement genuine and general, visited a neighboring Indian camp to induce a cessation of hostilities, only to receive a volley of arrows, slightly wounding several of their number; they returned the fire with their muskets killing two and capturing two of the Indians and putting the rest to flight.

ORGANIZATION OF THE PANGUITCH MILITIA.
SKIRMISH AT FORT SANFORD.
JOHN BUTLER WOUNDED.

Written by John Louder, of Parowan,
Iron County, Utah.

An election was held March 21st, 1865. Colonel George A. Smith was present. My name was proposed for Captain and I was elected. This position I held until Panguitch was vacated. Previous to this, I had raised an independent company of twenty-five men, called Minute Men of which I was captain. A stockade was built about six miles below Panguitch, on the east side of the Sevier River called "Fort Sanford," opposite to what is—and was known as Louder's Springs. I had gone up to the stockade on a visit, April 22nd, 1866, and while there we noticed two Indians coming up on the west side of the river. They fired at some ducks. We had orders to take in all the straggling Indians in the vicinity; and our doing so was the cause which led up to the shooting of William M. West. Mr. West took my horse while Collins R. Hakes took another, and both rode across the river to intercept the Indians and bring them to the stockade. The Indians objected, and said they were on an express from Black Hawk and they wanted to see Louder; the men told them that Louder was over at the stockade. They undertook to pass the men, when West rode in front of them, and as he did so, one of the Indians caught West's horse by the bit and held it, and the other Indian fired at West, hitting him in the shoulder. Then a skirmish ensued between Hakes and one of the Indians, but their guns failed to respond and no damage resulted; Hakes' gun was a cartridge-make, and the Indians a muzzle-loader. Later in the contest, Hakes got the advantage of his opponent and made a good Indian of him. By this time I procured another horse, and made my way across the country to the scene of the trouble, shooting at the other Indian, and wounding him in the shoulder; in this condition he escaped from me. I followed him about four miles and left him in some large boulders. Here dusk came on, and as my horse was a broncho, I decided to tie him up and continue on foot. I finally came back, got my horse and went to the fort.

The next day my father and two or three other men trailed the same Indian to a place where some other Indians had found him and helped him away. Here, however, they found his gun; the evidence showed that he had snapped as many as fifty caps at me. Noticing this, the men thought there must be some defect in the gun; one of them tested it and to their astonishment it went off alright.

The Indian killed at Louder's Spring was called Santick; name of the other Sanford Indian was Shegump. Both were on express from Black Hawk's band.

The next day after the fracus at Louder's Spring Major Silas S. Smith ordered me to go up to the Indian camp above Panguitch and take the Indians camped there prisoners, bring them to Panguitch and hold them until I received further orders. The order was issued by General George A. Smith. Accordingly I, with six men who were sent to me, and seven or eight others, marched to Panguitch. On approaching the Indian camp we thought it best to divide the party, so as not to excite the Indians. We did so, coming in at intervals. Old Doctor Bill, one of the occupants of the camp, became very excited when I asked for their guns, and began looking around for his gun, which was found sticking in some brush, in the back end of the wigwam. At this juncture another Indian came in with his gun in his hand. Coming up to me, he pretended to hand it to me, but in doing so, held the gun in such a manner that he turned the muzzle towards me. I caught the gun in my left hand and hurried off on my horse. By this time James Butler, one of my men, had been shot by Doctor Bill with an arrow in the side. The other men began firing at old Bill, severing three fingers from his hand with which he was drawing another arrow. When Butler saw me and the Red Lake Indian scuffling he came to me with the arrow sticking in his side, and with his double barrel gun shot and killed him. I then sent John L. Butler down to Panguitch after a vehicle to take James Butler, the wounded man, to town where he could have his wounds dressed. During the absence of the Butlers, the rest of the men guarded the prisoners. We kept them for a considerable length of time, until we received orders from Colonel Dame to liberate them, and they were consequently turned loose. The following day after the trouble at the camp where we arrested the In-

dians, we buried those that had been killed.
Written at Parowan April 24th, 1914, by Captain John Louder of Parowan, Iron County, Utah,
on his 79th birthday.
Copied by Peter Gottfredson.

AMBUSCADE AT MARYSVALE, A. LEWIS AND
C. CHRISTENSEN KILLED.

On the night of April 21, 1866, Walter Barney
and Sidney Wilson were on guard at the public corral at Monroe, where most of their stock was en-
closed. When on their usual rounds about midnight
they saw a dark object lying by the fence. Thinking it was an animal that had been left out they
went to put it in the corral; but when within two rods
of the object seen, two Indians jumped up and ran
away. The guard shot at them with their revolvers.
The Indians had been trying to dig out some pickets with their butcher knives in order to make an
opening to let out the stock. Leaving the town going
in a south-westerly direction they stopped at Andrew Rasmussen's corral and commenced shooting
his cows, oxen, pigs and sheep with arrows; they
carried away one sheep and dressed it at the head
of the ditch where they left a butcher knife. Early
the next morning messengers were sent to Richfield
and Glenwood with the report. A company was immediately formed of men from Glenwood, Richfield
and Monroe, with Dr. Elias Pierson of Glenwood in
command. The company numbering twenty-one
men left Monroe about midnight. The moon was
shining brightly and they could see the tracks of
the Indians in the road where they had dragged their

7

lariats, as was their custom. When the company got down to the Sevier River they saw a lot of cattle in the bottoms, and the appearances were to the effect that they had been gathered together by the Indians, convenient to be driven off. Having reached this place John Wilkenson said to Chris. Christensen, with whom he was riding, "If I were in command I would stop right here among the cattle, and hold our horses till morning; it will only be an hour or two; and if the Indians come after the stock, we would be prepared for them." Shortly before getting to the ford of the river Captain Pierson called a halt and instructed the boys to keep together and not talk loud, nor make any noise, and when in the river let their horses drink and proceed quietly up to the fort, which was about a mile distant.

When they had gone about twenty-five yards from the fort they came to a stake and rider fence with large rabbit brush along by it, where the Indians were concealed, no doubt intending to make a break on the little fort early in the morning. They permitted the boys to pass but opened fire in their back, hitting and killing Albert Lewis instantly; he fell off his horse exclaiming, "Oh my God." Christian Christensen who was riding beside Wilkensen was mortally wounded; the ball fired by the Indian struck the handle of his pistol, driving part of it and the bullet into his bowels. He exclaimed, "Oh, I am shot." Wilkinson asked if he was wounded badly. He answered, "Yes, feel." Christensen wanted to get off his horse, but Wilkenson said "Let us retreat back in the brush." The Indians fired up the line, wounding James Mortensen and John Petersen. The company rode up to the Fort, leaving

Wilkenson with the dead and wounded men. Shortly Major Allred and Peter Christensen (Christensen's brother-in-law) returned and Wilkinson and Allred then formed a chair by crossing their hands (one man holding the wrist of the other) and carried the wounded man up to the fort while Peter led the horses. Lewis was left where he fell till morning, which was not long. The Indians took the cattle and drove them up the Valley southward. The company followed and when up five or six miles they saw the Indians driving the stock up what they called Rock Canyon across the valley eastward. It was probably the east fork of the Sevier river. There, on a ridge, they met about forty men from Circleville. Next a council was held to decide whether the men should follow the Indians into the mountains and try to recover the stock, or turn back. They decided on the latter course, the Circleville people going home and the others returning to the the Vale (Marysvale). Obtaining a light wagon of James Monson, they wrapper Lewis's body in a quilt and brought it home.

Next day Major Claus Peter Andersen with three or four men secured a pair of large mules and a light wagon from John Reidhead and went after the wounded men. Christian Christensen lived 21 days. He was married to his betrothed, Nicoline Bertelsen on his death-bed.

The killed and wounded were all residents of Richfield. Both Lewis and Christensen were buried in the old Richfield cemetery.

On May 1st, 1866, President Brigham Young issued orders for the people in the outlying settlements to move together in companies of not less than one hundred and fifty in each as a means of safety and protection.

THOMAS JONES KILLED AND WM. AVERY WOUNDED AT FAIRVIEW.
PRESIDENT YOUNG ADVISES THE PEOPLE TO MOVE TOGETHER.

While on picket guard near Fairview, Sanpete County, a Thomas Jones was killed and William Avery wounded, April 29, 1866. Hyrum Wilson was with them, sitting down engaged in reading, while the others were exercising themselves by jumping. Wilson got Avery on a horse and took him to where he thought him safe and there let him down whereupon he rode to town and reported. .

Elias Cox, Wm. Zabriskie and some others went in pursuit of the Indians; they saw the murderers but did not overtake them.

Colonel Reddick Allred records the following in his journal: "The people in Sanpete had a Co-op herd of stock in Thistle Valley in charge of Noah T. Guyman who camped there in the valley together with his family. The Indians made a raid on Fairview killing one man and wounding another. Fearing for the safety of the herd and family with it, I went into the valley with a company in the night, it being so dark that we could not see the man next to us in line. Thomas Coates of Mount Pleasant piloted us safely through; we found the family and stock safe and moved all into the settlement next day and delivered them to President J. A. Allred. The following day (May 1st) President Brigham Young issued instructions to the people in Sanpete, Sevier and Piute Counties to move together, in bodies of not less than one hundred and fifty men, arm themselves well, and protect themselves and their stock. The people in the small settlements in Piute County moved to Circleville, those at Monroe and Glenwood in Sevier County to Richfied, those at Fayette, Sanpete County to Gunnison, those at Fairview, Sanpete to Mount Pleasant and those at Fountain Green and Wales to Moroni in Sanpete County.

DODGE SENDS WORD TO CALL OUT THE MILITIA.

On May 2nd, 1866, General Dodge sent a communication to Colonel Potter, Superintendent of Indian affairs to the effect that he would have to depend for the present on the militia to compell the Indians to behave. Before the message had been comunicated to him, Colonel Heath, in company with Governor Durkee had paid a visit to the Indians at Corn Creek, Millard County, and succeeded in obtaining from them renewed assurance of peace. He also visited the Uintah reservation, to which some of the Indians had by this time removed. His arrival appears to have been very timely, for Tabby and his braves were about to join the notorious Black Hawk in his raids upon the southern settlements. The visit also resulted in holding the reservation Indians to their neutrality.

Franklin H. Heath of Wisconsin had succeeded Colonel Irish as Indian Superintendent. He had acted for some time as private secretary to Governor Durkee, and was confirmed as Superintendent of Indian affairs in March, 1866. Like his predecessor, Colonel Heath was an energetic official.

The spring of 1866 found the military spirit at its highest pitch. Division, brigade and regimental musters and elections were held in almost every county in Utah and reorganization of the entire militia in Utah was effected. Among the promotions and changes occurring about this time may be mentioned the election of Brigadier-General Brigham Young, Jr. of Salt Lake County, Brigadier-General Lot Smith of Davis County, Major-General Aaron Johnson, and Brigadier-General Wm. B. Pace and Albert K. Thurber of Utah County. The interest manifested on these occasions explains the readiness with which the people responded to the call to arms and the efficiency of the service rendered in the Indian campaign of 1866.

The earliest calls upon the northern counties had not been for armed assistance to chastise the renegades and wreck vengence upon them, but for men to aid the settlers in pro tecting themselves and their stock until they could reach places of safety; but the increasing boldness of the marauders rendered decisive action necessary. The entire abandonment of the southern counties, to be followed by a general Indian war, seemed to be the only alternative. Steps were accordingly taken to place the settlements south and east of Salt Lake City in a state of defense, and troops were ordered to the scene of hostilities. By the 1st of May, 1866, several companies from Davis, Salt Lake and Utah counties were on the march, and on arriving in Sanpete county they reported to Brigadier-General Warren S. Snow. A company of cavalry from Salt Lake City under Colonel Heber P. Kimball and Major John Clark, reached Manti on the 5th of May, and was ordered to march up the

Sevier river and assist the settlers in moving into Sanpete Valley. These men displayed great energy and succeeded in delivering the exposed settlers, after which for a short time they were stationed at Fountain Green.

KIMBALL'S AND CONOVER'S COMMANDS ARRIVE AT MANTI.

Kimball's and Conover's Companies arrived at Manti, May 6th, 1866 and about the 10th a company of cavalry (A. G. Conover, captain) reached the scene of hostilities (from Utah county) and were ordered to occupy a picket post on the Se- vier river near the abandoned town of Salina, un- der command of Brigadier-General William B. Pace.

CHRISTIAN LARSEN, A HERDER KILLED ON SPANISH FORK BENCH.

On the 16th of May a party of ten Indians swoop- ed down from the mountains near Spanish Fork and killed Christian Larsen who was herding cows on the bench; they also made off with nearly two hun- dred head of horses from the vicinity. Earlier in the month a raid was made upon the horse herd of friendly Indians at Corn Creek, Millard County. The thieves were pursued for several days by Kan- osh and some members of his band, but were not overtaken.

Iron, Kane and Millard and all the counties south had their own troubles, yet each of them sent aid ino Sanpete anl Sevier counties. The most north- erly point to send such assistance was Davis Coun- ty, where early in July Brigadier-General Lot Smith mustered a company of cavalry under Captain Bigler for ninety days service; and as late as October Captain Robert W. Davis and company from Kaysville started for the Sevier. About the end of July Major-General Burton organized another company of seventy-five officers and men in Salt Lake County and hurried them southward under command of Major Andrew Burt, with William L. N. Allen as captain. These were Colonel John Sharp's regiment and were among the last to return home, reaching Salt Lake City early in November. Utah County sent its second company of cavalry in June under Captain Joseph Cluff of Provo, and two more companies in August under Captain Alva Green of American Fork and Caleb W. Haws of Provo.

Of the various companies and commanders doing duty in their own counties it is perhaps not necessary to speak in detail, though they aquitted themselves with much credit. As far south as Washington County where, under instructions of Brigadier-General Erastus Snow, a company under Captain James Andrus had taken the field and had lost in one expedition private Eliajh Everett Jr., slain by the savages; and as far north as Cache County there were the same alert and unceasing watchfulness against hostile inroads or outbreaks, and at one time during the year as many as twenty five hundred men were under arms. The number killed during the season's campaign was of whites about twenty and of Indians between forty and fifty. The settlers stock herds were reduced nearly two thousand, and rarely were any of the animals recovered.

OLD FATHER J. R. IVIE AND HENRY WRIGHT KILLED AT SCIPIO.

On the morning of June 10, 1866, a large band of Indians under Chief Black Hawk made a raid on the stock in Round Valley, Millard County. They killed old father James R. Ivie, father of Colonel J. L. Ivie, J. Ivie, and others, and mortally wounded Henry Wright, who were out looking for stock, and drove off about 500 head of cattle and horses. As it was known that they would come towards Salina, a messenger was dispatched to Fort Gunnison, where it was known that General Wm. B. Pace with a company of thirty men were stationed. But when word of the trouble at Scipio reached the camp, General Pace and a few others were on the way to Manti. A messenger was dispatched post haste, and caught up with the party at Twelve Mile Creek, just below the presnt site of Mayfield. The company returned to Gunnison through a heavy thunder storm. Salina which had been vacated in April, was reached by daylight, and here it was decided to take a few hours rest. Accordingly, the pickets were sent out, and the men began to prepare for a rest, but had not proceeded very far when one of the guards discharged his gun, which was the signal agreed upon that the enemy had been sighted.

GEN. PACE'S BATTLE AT GRAVELLY FORD.
WM. TUNBRIDGE WOUNDED.

Looking to the southwest, and just opposite the Gravelly Ford could be seen a band of Indians driving a bunch of cattle. They were evidently trying to make the ford, which if reached in time would give

them the passes to the mountains on the east, and
insure them a clean getaway with the stock. General
Pace ordered an advance, and the distance of eight
miles to the Gravelly Ford was covered under whip.
The advance guard was about two hundred yards in
the lead when the point of the mountain was reached
and they were permitted to pass, but when the company reached that place they were fired upon by
the Indians from ambush at the close range of sixty
paces.

The whites were commanded to cross-fire, and
the Indians were routed, but about this time the Indians were reinforced from the band driving the cattle on the west. A guard of Indians was left over
the cattle on the west side of the river, while Indians
to the number of sevnty-five or eighty engaged in
fighting on the east side.

The whites retreated to higher ground and made
the crest of a hill serve as breast-works for them.
While making this retreat, William Tunbridge was
wounded in the leg just as he was mounting his
mule, but when assisted in his saddle, he continued
to fight.

After reaching the higher ground, the Indians
surrounded the whites and began to close in on them
until by command the militia began to fire by plat-
toons; this manner of fighting proved very effective,
for at every fire an Indian or his horse would drop.
Then the Indians began to circle around, and when
a point of advantage was gained, they fired on the
whites. There was one particular point from which
most of the shooting was done. A wash led in the
direction of the point, and James E. Snow determined to put a stop to the practice of firing from it.

He followed the wash nearly to the mouth, and then dropped behind a large sage-brush, which he used for a rest to shoot from. He soon got range on an Indian who was trying to put one of his wounded on a horse. The horse being between Snow and the Indian, he could not see the body of the Indian, but judging from the position of his feet and legs, he decided that by shooting the horses through the body in the region of the heart the same shot would get the red man. The aim proved true, for at the report of the rifle the horse fell and the Indian was wounded. He was picked up by two of his braves and spirited away.

The wounded Indian was none other than the famous Black Hawk, though at the time it was not known. Mr. Snow had a narrow escape in this affair, for he was fully 600 yards from the rest of the whites and was closely pursued by three of the enemy. While getting away from them, Snow caught his saber between his legs and fell. Four men were dispatched to resue him and thus he was saved from the torture of the red men.

When the tide of the battle seemed turned in favor the whites, though their ammunition was by this time exhausted, a cloud of dust from the direction of Round Valley suggested to the militia that more Indian were coming; a retreat was therefore ordered. Black Hawk's good fortune again befriended him; the approaching horsemen were a company of Fill- more cavalry, seventy strong under Captain Owens. Before they effected a junction with General Pace the slippery foe were safe in their mountain fast- nesses.

A RACE FOR LIFE.

On the evening of June 10th, four soldiers, J. H. Noakes, Uel Stewart, Eliel Curtis of Springville and Moroni Manwill of Payson, were carrying dispatches from Gunnison to Glenwood, it rained on them nearly all the way and traveling was bad, consequently it was late when they arrived at Glenwood, where they found but one person, namely Artemus Millet. They stayed with him over night, as their horses were jaded; leaving the dispatches with Millett they started back to their company, and arrived at the ridge that runs down to the river at Rocky Ford, about half a mile south of the Gravelly Ford. When they got onto the ridge, they saw the Indians in the act of driving the stock across the river at the Gravelly Ford, but could not see the company of militia under Pace. Noakes said, "this is no place for us; if we go on, the Indians will get us." As they turned to go back to Glenwood, the Indians saw them, and about sixteen of them gave chase. Three of the men were mounted on good horses, but Curtis was riding a small mustang that they called Tom Thumb. The boys put spurs to their horses and made the best time possible, while the savages steadily gained on the mustang. Seeing this, the boys told Curtis to spur forward, and they would drop behind and check the reds. The boys turned in their saddles several times and fired a volley which checked the pursuers. Then they again overtook their comrade and stayed with him until their copper-colored warriors came close. Then the three again halted and checked the enemy until their friend was a sufficient distance in advance when they again swept forward. This maneuver was made several times and the ride made in safety. During the five-mile race Noakes shot one Indian off his horse and Stewart shot a horse. In the meantime news of the fight was received by General Snow at Manti. Colonel Kimball with his cavalry, then stationed at Fountain Green, was ordered to report at once at headquarters. In thirty minutes the command was in the saddle, and before daylight next morning was at Manti, where it remained most of the day under waiting orders until reinforcements should arrive from Mount Pleasant. That night a short march was made, and the combined forces now under personal command of General Snow went into camp. The impatience of the men who wanted to overtake the Indians by forced march and engage them could hardly be restrained by the cautious commander, who, taught by experience had no relish for rushing recklessly into a possible ambuscade. The march was resumed the next morning, and at noon the troops came upon the previous night's camping ground of the Indians in a canyon at the western edge of Castle Valley. A council of war was called, and though the young officers and the majority of the men were in favor of an advance at the best possible speed, the General decided that without heavy reinforcements it would be imprudent to continue the case.

GEN. WELLS AND MILITIA LEAVE GREAT SALT LAKE CITY FOR SANPETE.

GEN. WELLS TAKES COMMAND OF THE MILITIA IN SANPETE.

In the meantime Lieutenant-General Wells (leaving Salt Lake on the 11th), reached Gunnison, accompanied by a body of cavalry under Colonel John R. Winder, followed by a company of infantry from the regiment of Col. Samuel W. Richards under command of Major William W. Casper and Peter Sinclair, battalion adjutant, with Jesse West as captain and Alexander Burt, Byron Groo and others as lieutenants. The cavalry force was assigned to patrol duty along the Sevier River, and the infantry detailed to the settlements of Sanpete.

Colonel Winder was immediately assigned to duty as assistant adjutant to General Wells; the latter gave orders that the pursuit of Black Hawk should be at once resumed and another effort made to recover the stock; the trail of the savages was again struck and after passing the point where the pursuit had been abandoned, the troops found that they had been at the time within twelve miles of the enemy and the stolen cattle.

A longer march confronted them now, and one beset with many difficulties. The trail was followed over rocky ridges, up and down almost impassable gorges, across occasional streams of alkali water and into the most forbidding and desolate deserts. At the conclusion of the first day's march the men He followed the wash nearly to the mouth, and then and animals were well-nigh exhausted from the trials of the journey, all having suffered intensely from thirst. During two days more and the larger part of the two nights the toilsome march continued; and when futility of further pursuit was recognized and the condition of the troops was seen to be perilous, a retreat was again ordered, and it was none too soon; the command was scarcely able to get out of

the desert, owing to weakness of both horses and
men; of the latter there were several whose mouths
and tongues were so sore that they could scarcely
speak.

CAPTAIN A. P. DEWEY WAS ORDERED
TO ESTABLISH A POST IN THISTLE VALLEY.

A few days later, June the 21st, Captain Albert P. Dewey of Colonel Kimball's command was
ordered to establish a post in Thistle Valley in the
north end of Sanpete county—a point that was considered the key to any probable attack from that direction. His command consisted of twenty-two cavalry and thirty-five infantry, the latter under Captain Jesse West, who started from Moroni on the
21st of June.

On the evening of the 23rd of June the Indians gave indications of their presence in the vicinity of the camp in Thistle Valley, and extra pre-
cautions were taken to guard against a surprise.

Hyrum Murphy of Captain Dewey's company
states that when the company first went to Thistle
Valley, they were camped by the wagon road, near
the Warm Springs; but feed being better and more
convenient elsewhere, the camp was moved up east
about a mile and a half to a more exposed location;
and during the night of the 23rd of June an object
resembling in the dark, a small bear crawling round
camp, occasionally howling like a coyote, came close
by a bed in which slept two boys. The guard saw and
shot at it, when it ran away. It was afterwards believed to be an Indian trying to locate the horses, and
ascertain the condition of the camp.

BATTLE IN THISTLE VALLEY.

On Sunday morning, the 24th of June about nine o'clock, most of the horses were driven to feed in a cove about half a mile south east of camp. Without the knowledge of the militia, Indians were scattered through the cedars and ravines east and south of camp at that time. Charles Brown of Draper, Salt Lake County, and a companion were in the cedars near the horses picking gum, when they saw Indians. They ran for camp, and when out in the flat, Brown was shot through the back. When he fell some Indians shot him with arrows. The boys in camp seeing what had happened ran out to his assistance, and brought him into camp, where he expired. The Indians made a rush for the horses, stampeded them and ran down between the hills and camp, about half a mile west, when the Indians turned them south into the so-called Indian Hollows, where they caught some of them and rode them back to fight the troops.

They soon made a charge, but were turned back by a volley from camp. All the breast-works the troops had were four wagons on the south side of camp; two of these were loaded with wood. The Indians surrounded the camp, and closed in upon it keeping behind trees and brush. Some of them approached in a wash that ran north of camp. They shot into the camp wounding Thomas Snarr of Salt Lake.

Captain Dewey had sent out two companies of scouts, four men in each company, one company going north and the other south-west. Two of these going north were at the Warm Springs. John Hamliton and Homer Roberts who were farther north, saw the Indians take the horses and came back to camp. They were immediately sent to Mount Pleasant to report. The others were chased by the Indians but got into camp safely. The Indians who did not know that an express had been sent kept the direction to the settlements south closely guarded. The following account was obtained from Eskild C. Petersen, one of Colonel Ivie's men:

When the express arrived at Mount Pleasant, Col. John L. Ivie with his company of cavalry happened to be up Pleasant Creek Canyon and through the hills scouting, the cow-herd being in the foothills below them. About two p. m. they heard three shots down the canyon, and they gathered at the herd and was ordered to help gather the stock. Presently they heard five more shots, farther down the canyon, and they knew that to be a signal, upon which they left the stock and rode down to the mouth of the canyon, when they were informed that the Salt Lake boys were being attacked in Thistle Valley and needed help. They were ordered to get there as quickly as their horses could take them. The distance to town was about four miles and when they got there they received their orders and started for the north. When they reached Fairview, six or eight men were ready to accompany them; and they arrived in Thistle Valley about an hour before sundown. The Indians by this time had the camp surrounded, and the boys were keeping the enemy back the best they could without exposing themselves to the fire of the savages. Their ammunition, however, was nearly exhausted and the Indians had all their horses except six, and these were all wounded.

When Ivie's company reached the valley the savages intercepted them, one Indian who seemed most daring rode out in the open. The Colonel dismounted and with his Henry rifle took a shot at him; the redskin lopped over on the side of his horse. Some of the other Indians rode out and drove the horse with its limp rider back into the cedars. Another Indian had left his horse and was sneaking in the wash, when Orange Seeley and R. N. Bennett rushed up and got the horse with saddle, bridle, a long lasso and a buckskin jacket. Seely kept the horse as a trophy of war. At that time it was not known what the conditions were at camp, so the troops made haste to get there. After an exchange of a few shots the besiegers drew off with their booty.

About dusk Colonel Ivie's men hitched their horses onto the company wagons and moved them down to the wagon road more in the middle of the Valley, where they would be less exposed, in case of a night attack. The Indians had fought the boys all day and if they had not received help there is no doubt but that the Indians would have taken the camp, as the savages were receiving reinforcements during the day, Brown's body was taken to Mount Pleasant. The writer and three others arrived at the camp the following day with provisions from Mt. Pleasant and militia men arrived there during the day from all parts of Sanpete county. Colonel Kimball and his command arrived early in the morning and about the same time Major Casper came upon the scene from Moroni with General Snow of Manti in command; the pursuit of the retreating savages was hotly begun by the combined force of militia, the trail of the Indians being plainly marked by the blood from their dead and wounded, whom, in accordance with their custom, they bore away with them. The chase lasted until Soldier Summit, at the head of Spanish Fork River, was reached. Here the Indians, resorted to their old tactics of separating and scattering in all directions and further chase had to be abandoned. This was the last military event of importance in Sanpete County that season, and a few weeks afterwards the larger part of the troops from the northern counties (most of them having been in the service from sixty to ninety days) returned and were mustered out. They had conducted themselves with much patience and bravery, and had rendered invaluable service to the settlers in the threatened counties. General Wells and his officers showed good judgment in their disposition of the troops and inspired confidence throughout the entire district. It was felt that against leaders of less watchfulness and prudence the crafty Black Hawk and his braves would have been able to cause far greater losses in life and property. But with the withdrawal of the outside militia, the efforts of the local militia organizations were not relaxed. The men rendered uncomplaining service on picket guard and in occasional reconnoisances into the mountains, and the officers were vigilant and full of energy.

Their scanty crops had to be harvested, and winter's supply of fuel gathered, protection furnished their remaining flocks and herds, and winter's forage provided. All this work had to be performed by men under arms or attended by an armed escort. And it is remembered that the sleepless foe ranged over and ravaged a district three hundred miles in ex

tent, burning saw-mills, ranges and isolated ranches,
and causing the abandonment of a number of flourishing villages. The heroism of the settlers in re-
sisting by night and day the terrifying attacks of
the marauders is worthy of the warmest praise. In
nearly every part of the Territory regular guard
duty was ordered. Even in Salt Lake County, the
Lieutenant-General issued orders as early as May,
1866, to Major-General Robert T. Burton to have
patrols out for the protection of stock and to ob-
serve the movements and temper of the Indians.

In the settlements on the west side of the Jordan river, Salt Lake county there was much regular
work of this character under the organization of
increased military companies during the early summer. Utah County, populous and well prepared as
it was, did not entirely escape the ravages of the
Indians.

REPORTED BY JOEL ANDREW JOHNSON
ONE OF MAJOR CLUFF'S MEN.

Major Joseph Cluff's cavalry company consisting of twenty cavalrymen and two baggagemen left
Provo, for Sanpete and Sevier counties June 13,
1866; they went through Salt Creek Canyon and on
to Twelve Mile Creek (now Mayfield3 going as an
escort to General Wells as far as Circleville, in connection with others. When General Wells returned,
an escort of six of Major Cluff's command escorted
him to the Prickly Pear Ridge between Marysvale
and Monroe. The escort returned to Circlevalle and
stayed there while the inhabitants prepared to vacate the town. Some of the people went to Beaver

and Iron Counties and Major Cluff's command escorted those who came north as far as Fort Gunnison. They were six days making the trip and celebrated the fourth of July at Gunnison, after which they were sent back to Mayfield again where they engaged in camp and scout duty until released to return home. A part of the command went to Fish Lake with others, pursuing the Indians who stole the stock from Scipio; they were gone from home forty-four days, or from the 13th of June till the 27th of July.

While stationed at Gunnison, two of Major Cluff's command deserted, namely William Nelson and John Baum. They were seen crossing over the ridge between Gunnison and Warm Creek. General Wells was asked "Shall we follow them and bring them back." The General scatched his head, studied a while and then replied "No, let the poor devils go; they don't know what they are doing."

When the Circleville settlers left Gunnison they camped the first night on the Sanpitch river between Twelve and Nine Mile creeks. Eight of Major Cluff's command were sent to guard their camp during the night; they were posted on a ridge northeast of camp. Two of the guards held their horses in a swale out of sight all night, while the others guarded an Indian trail that led to Warm Creek (Fayette.)

BATTLE IN DIAMOND FORK, EDMUNDSON AND DIMMICK KILLED.
Copied from History of Springville.

A band of Indians came down Maple Canyon in Utah county, June 26, 1866 and made a foray into the valley as far as Roundy's pasture and drove off some fifty horses and twenty head of cattle into Maple canyon. H. M. Dougall and D. E. Deal had been the mounted videttes' the previous day and had patrolled the country between Hobble Creek and Spanish Fork Canyon, camping with the squad over night at the first bridge in the former canyon. As they rode into town early the next morning they met Bishop Johnson, who asked them if they had seen any Indians. Their reply was "No, no sign of Indians. Everything is all right." The Bishop replied, "No, everything is not all right: the Indians came down Maple canyon last night and took a herd of cattle from Markham's pasture at Spanish Fork, and some horses from Roundy's pasture. Go tell Colonel Bromley to come quickly." Bromley was summoned. The old bell spoke, the drums beat, and in twenty mintues several of the mounted minute men were on the public square, armed and ready to go. It was about 9 a. m. and a dispatch had been sent to Colonel Creer of Spanish Fork to meet the Springville squad at the mouth of Maple canyon, and all proceed under the command of Creer on the trail of the hostiles. Alma Spafford, H. O. Crandall, T. L. Mendenhall, J. A. Groesbeck, John Edmundson, Loren Dibble, D. C. Johnson and an old soldier by the name of Gillispie, and Wiley Thomas of Spanish Fork composed the posse. The other members of the minute company were in the fields and could not be reached in time. A gallop of thirty minutes brought the young troopers to the mouth of the canyon, but by the indications Creer's men had arrived first and gone up the canyon. Our boys rode rapidly after them mile after mile, until they had

crossed the divide and descended the steep trail into the head of Diamond Fork, but could see nothing
of the Spanish Fork troopers. There were three
young madcaps in the squad that day, who kept riding ahead in their anxiety to find the Indians.
When the party came within a half mile of the
spot where the skirmish took place, the three
boys who were still ahead rode up on a knoll
and gave a whoop, for a little way in advance they
could see Creer's men under a clump of trees and firing over towards the south side of the broad flat
canyon. With a yell the advance guard charged toward their white friends, followed by the boys in
the rear. Just as the three mad-caps got within a
hundred yards of the party they were suddenly fired
upon by a number of Indians, who at that moment
were in the act of flanking the Spanish Fork boys.
They had found their Indians, but instead of engaging them in a hand combat, Dibble turned to the right
and came back to the main body; Groesbeck was un-
horsed by the breaking of his saddle girth, but clung
to the halter strap as his horse circled to the left and
came back to his comrades in the rear. Edmundson
kept straight ahead and to the left of the Spanish
Forkers, until he was lost to view by the intervening
brush.

The Springville boys quickly dismounted, and
leaving their horses with one of the men, advanced
cautiously toward Creer's command. At this juncture several Indians were seen to retreat hastily
from their position on the south and disappear in
the thickets which hedged Diamond creek. The
Spanish Fork boys had been in their position for an
hour and had seen some warm work. Al Dimmick

was fatally wounded and lay upon a bed of leaves in the shade. In a few moments an Indian appeared upon the bluff and by his excited gestures seemed to be haranguing his men. Some shots were exchanged, but the effect was not known, as both sides were laying low.

Presently Colonel Creer selected five long range rifles and began volley firing at the chief, some 800 yards distant, and at about the fifth volley the Indian fell upon the neck of his horse, which ran behind the hill and out of sight. The Indians were then seen scampering over the ridge, and were variously estimated at from twenty to fifty. All was quiet for the next half hour and a careful scout was made, but no sign of the enemy was visible and it was concluded that they had drawn off with their dead and wounded and would renew the attack after night fall. Feeling sure of a night attack, a courier was sent to town for help. The man who volunteered to undertake this perilous task the the old veteran, Gillispie. It was 4 p. m. when he departed and he reached town about 7 p. m. with the news of the figh, the extreme peril of the white men and that Edmundson was ru.ss ing. The tocsin bell, in quick sharp tones brought the minute men from their quarters, and by 8 p. m. they had started under the direction of the scout to relieve their companions from their extreme peril.

In the meantime the Indian camp which had been abandoned at the beginning of the attack by the whites with all it contained, was relieved, by the Spanish Fork contingent, of the butcher knives, new hats, bridles and lariats which the enemy had left in his flight. One man had nine new army hats, and the others each had some trophy. Poor Dimmick was tenderly placed upon a litter and just after sunset the party sarted on their return, expecting at any moment to hear the crack of the deadly rifle and the piercing war-whoop. They were compelled to carry their wounded comrade, who groaned in agony at every step. At times he entreated his bearers to kill him and end his sufferings. Tireless the troops ascended the eastern slope of the mountain out of the Diamond, winding up the precipitous and hazardous mountain trail. The front and rear guards kept keenly on the alert, in order to prevent an ambush. About midnight the pass was reached and the descent upon the home side of the mountain began. Near the summit the relief party was met and not until then did the returning party realize that it was safe. Still slowly the homeward journey was continued and completed just at daybreak.

In front of the old hall they were met by Bishop Johnson who praised the boys for their good work, told them to get a few hours sleep and at the call of the bell to assemble for the purpose of returning to the scene of the fight to search for Edmundson, who had not returned. It was thought he had escaped and would perhaps reach home through some of the canyon passes. Alas! vain hopes! the poor boy lay upon the lonely hillside cold in death, with the moon shining in his upturned face.

At 7 a. m. the loud alarm bell called the weary troopers from their blankets and in a very few moments they were on the march, under the command of Captain Steele. At the mouth of Maple Canyon they found Col. Creer with his company. This morning they had deemed it advisable to wait for the

Springville contingent. Under command of Colonel Creer the party proceeded to the scene of the combat of the previous day. They found the camp intact, the enemy not having returned for his camp equipage. There were seventeen saddles by actual count, and other trappings used by native riders, but no other appearance of an enemy. The day before the hostiles had killed two or three beeves, and large flitches of juicy steaks still hung upon the rocks and brush where the thieves had placed them to sun-dry. The horses were left under the guard of a part of the troops, while the others in squads trailed the hills in every direction in search of traces of the missing man. After a toilsome search and just about sun-down his mangled body was found three-fourths of a mile north of the battle ground. He had been stripped of his shirt, his right hand was severed at the wrist, his scalp torn off and the savage foe had shot him twice through the heart, the muzzle of the weapon being held so close that the body was powder-burned. A signal gun was fired to notify the searchers that the hunt was ended, and all gathered quickly to their horses. When the boys came in they brought some stolen stock, among which was a horse belonging to Wm. Smith with blood stains upon the withers and down the front leg—the animal supposedly had been ridden by the war-chief the previous day. The dead man was placed upon this horse by Thomas Dallin and then came a discussion as to whether the company should return home via Spanish Fork Canyon, there being a good wagon road all the way, or take the trail back through Maple canyon. It was eventually decided to take the back trail and the bugle sounded the advance. At this juncture the horse with the dead rider began to buck and rear and plunge in a fearful manner and could not be quieted. It was held a moment while the body could be removed and strapped upon the back of "Old Beck" a family mare belonging to William Mendenhall and Richard Mendenhall mounted the refractory broncho and the march home-ward was commenced and was finished at 3 a. m. and the dead man was placed upon a bier in front of the old hall when the now thoroughly fatigued rough riders went to rest.

Hardly had their tired heads sank upon the pillows when the signal, (three quick flashes) was made at the mouth of Spanish Fork Canyon and seen by the guard in the tower, and the bell from its iron throat rang out, "Come! Come! Come! Quick! Quick! Quick!" a few of the tired riders rallied, also some of the citizens in wagons, drove like Jehu to the mouth of Spanish Fork Canyon and surprised the guard there by their sudden war like appearance. The guard said they had seen Indians appear some distance up the canyon and had made one light (be upon your guard); but as it had been only a flash, and fearing the lookout hadn't seen it, another handfull of brush had been thrown on the fire, which only emitted a faint flash, when a larger amount had been put upon the embers and a satisfactory blaze kindled. The watch-men had seen all three of the flashes and acted accordingly. After scouring the vicinity of the mouth of the canyon where fresh Indian signs were plainly seen, the cavalcade returned home. Thus ended three very exciting days. Some of the boys had been forty-eight hours in the saddle almost without food or sleep.

The Diamond fight was the most successful en-

gagement of the war in this: That the Indians were
thoroughly whipped, their entire camp equipage falling into the hands of the victors, who also brought
back some of the horses and all of the cattle except
those killed. A report came from DuChesne not
long afterwards, that the dusky marauders had eight
killed and wounded, and that Black Hawk was the
rider who left his blood-stains upon the captured
horse.

On the day after the return of the expedition,
Dimmick and Edmundson were buried with military honors. Thus ended the fight on the Diamond,
which was also the end of the Indian hostilities in
our vicinity.

CIRCLEVILLE IN PIUTE COUNTY ABANDONED.

Circleville in Piute Couny was abandoned,
June 28, 1866, by the settlers, some going to Millard County and others of Sanpete and the counties north.

CAPTPAIN BIGLER WITH 60 MEN ARRIVE IN MOUNT PLEASANT.

INDIANS STEAL 150 HEAD OF CATTLE NEAR EPHRAIM.

Captain Bigler with sixty men from Davis
County arrived in Mount Pleasant, July 12, 1866 to
relieve the Salt Lake troops. On Friday, July 27th,
Indians made a raid on the stock of Ephraim and
Manti and drove away one hundred and fifty head,
Captain Bigler pursued them into Castle Valley
without recovering the stock, or having an engage-
ment.—From History of Sanpete.

A CAVALRY COMPANY LEAVE ST. GEORGE.
ELIJJAH EVERT KILLED.
HISTORY OF ST. GEORGE STAKE.

Trip of a cavalry company from St. George to
Green River as reported by John S. Adams of Annabella. Dated Sept. 18th.

A company of sixty-one men from St. George
and surrounding settlements were ordered out by
General Erastus Snow as a minute company which
expected to go as far as Green River. The men from
the different places met at Gould's Ranch in Washington County, twenty-six miles east of St. George on
the 16th of August, 1866. They were inspected by
General Snow and Staff. General Snow told the
boys that if those who were called would obey their
officers, all would be well with them, if any of them
were hurt, it would be slightly; he also said, if any of
them had been hired to go, they might return home.
Continuing the journey from Gould's Ranch, August
18th the men made their first camp on Short Creek,
where they saw a herd of wild cattle. Captain
James Andrus, who was in command, detailed six
men to go after the cattle and drive them to Pipe
Springs, or Whitemore's ranch. The company went
on to the place, and that evening the detail brought
in the cattle, the horses of those driving the cattle
being well night exhausted, ten or fifteen men were
sent out to help them in and drive the animals into
the Whitmore corral; an old cow that had been tame
refused to go into the corral, and made an effort
to fight the men and horses; finally they had to push
her along, but she was shot several times before
reaching the corral. Captain Andrus killed and

dressed the cow and three other animals. We stopped there two days and jerked the meat, which is done by cutting the meat into strips and hanging it on a platform made of willows and building a fire under it, the fire helping the sun to dry it. On Tuesday, the 21st, we mustered in camp one captain, one 1st lieutenant, one bugler, four 2nd lieutenants and thirty-five privates equipped with good long range rifles and revolvers, and we were later reinforced by Lieutenant Joseph Fish with eighteen men from Parowan in Iron County who left there on the 22nd of August. Next day brought us to Skootem-pah, where it rained on us all night. Some of the men took colds which culminated into chills and fever; the next day's journey brought us to the Par-reah. Here six of the disabled men were sent back with the sore-backed horses, fourteen in number, and the spare camp equipage. These men were Elijah Everett, Charles Pinney, George Ishum, Albert Beebe, Frederick Reggus and Hyrum Pollock. They started back about two o'clock p. m. and at the same time we moved camp seven miles to Coal Point. At about 5:30 p. m. on Monday, August 21st, six miles on the way back, the party returning were waylaid by Indians crossing a deep gorge and passing up a steep ledge of rocks. The foremost man, Elijah Everett, being dismounted and leading two animals, was killed at first fire. The party were all dismounted and leading their animals up a steep acclivity at the time the attack was made. George Ishum received an arrow wound in the left shoulder. Supposing there **were a large party of the Indians, they retreated to** the opposite side of the gorge and took shelter in the cedars. When Everett was shot he exclaimed, ''Oh

boys" and expired. The boys who had been sent back
came straggling into camp one or two at a time, all
reporting that the others had been killed. On learning of this disaster, Captain Andrus took about twenty-five men and went down the Pah-reah, expecting
to head off the Indians; they came upon them about
12 o'clock ascending the point of a mountain. We
surrounded the place as quickly as possible, but
darkness came on and the Indians escaped. We remained until daylight, supposing we had some of
them driven into a small cove near where we overtook them. But in this we were mistaken; the Indians had escaped in the night. However, we got
all the horses and guns that the savages had captured
except the two that Everett had with him when he
was killed. About 10 o'clock a. m. on the 27th (Monday) we recovered Everett's body, wrapped it in a
blanket and burier it there, covering the place with
brush and and rocks. The men all stayed together
during the balance of the trip. We went up the east
fork of Pah-reah and through Potato Valley (now
Escalante). Here we gathered some wild potatoes
which we cooked and ate them; they were somewhat
like the cultivated potato, but smaller. From there
we went through Rabbit Valley, crossed the Dirty
Devil Creek (also called Fremont River) and got
within sight of Green River. We then turned back,
the country between us and the river being too rough
and broken to proceed farther. Black Hawk told Mr.
Adams later (at the time of the treaty) that when
the men turned away they were within three miles
of his (Black Hawk) main camp and the stock, that
he and his warriors were in Sanpete, and that there
were only old men and squaws left in camp. The

company expected to meet the Sanpete boys somewhere, but missed them. When starting back we
made a dry camp; we traveled all the next day and
made another dry camp. Some of our horses giving
out, six men were sent back after them on foot, expecting to catch the horses and ride them back. The
horses, however, were rested and would not be caught
consequently the men had to carry their over-coats
and guns and walk and drive the horses; it was a
rough experience; one of their number gave out and
they had a hard time to overtake their companions
in the evning. The company now went down the east
fork of the Sevier River, and passed through Circleville, which had been abandoned in the spring, after
the crops had been put in; the grain was ripe and
looked fine; we turned our horses into a field of oats
which was inclosed by a fence. From there we went
up the canyon westward and through Bear Valley,
where we killed some wild chickens. The following
day we continued the journey to Parowan where we
were entertained with a dance arranged in our honor.
Next day we continued the journey to Cedar City
where we were well cared for and from there we went
to our respective homes.

We were gone from home sixty days to the best
of my memory.

It was said that Brother Everett who was
killed had been hired to go on this expedition and
that he was one of those who were permitted to return home before starting. The personel of the company was as follows:

JOSEPH M. WESTWOOD
Commander-in-Chief Utah Indian War Veterans

Caleb W. Haw's Cavalry Company, Commander Utah County Department,
Utah Indian War Veterans.

JOHN HUBBARD NOAKES

UEL STEWART

FLOLL S. CURTIS

ORSON MORONI MANWILL

SCOUT

MUSTER ROLL OF INDIAN EXPEDITION TO REACH JUNCTION OF GRAND AND GREEN RIVERS.

James Andrus, captain, Franklin D. Woolley, Adjutant, Charles John Thomas, Bugler.

First platoon: Willis Coplan, second lieutenant, George Gould, sergeant. Privates: Jesse W. Crosby, Jr., James Cragum, John Houston, David Cammeron, Mahonri Snow, William Meeks, William Edwards Cowley, Henry McFate, Archibald Sullivan, John Lay.

Second Platoon: Woodruff John Freeman, second lieutenant; Thales Hastings Haskell, sergeant. Privates: Alfred Ford, Hiram Pollock, Thomas Jefferson Clark, Samuel Newton Adair, Frederick Dickerson Riggs, Lehi Smithson, William Gardner, William Slade, Bennett Bracken, Benjamin Knell.

Third Platoon: Thomas Dennet, second lieutenant; George Petty, sergeant. Privates: George Williams, Albert Beebe, George Isom, Charles Pinney, James A. Stratton, Robert H. Brown, Elijah Everett, Jr. killed, Gardner Potter, Walter Winsor, William Riggs.

Fourth Platoon: Albert Minerly, second lieutenant; Elijah H. Maxfield, sergeant. Privates; William A. Bringhurst, John S. Adams, Joseph S. McCleve, John Batty, George A. Wadsworth, Lemuel H. Redd, Francis Prince, Robert Richardson, Eli N. Pace, James Brigham Thompson.

Fifth platoon: Joseph Fish, second lieutenant, Privates: William C. McGregor, Enoch Wardle, George Richard, Thomas Robb, John White, Thomas Rowley, Richard Heber Benson, Edward Parry, Samuel Wood, Andrew Corry, Horatio Morrill.

8

AN EXTRACT FROM JAMES M. PETERSON'S DIARY.

The following is culled from the diary of James M. Peterson of Richfield which gives some additional data. Mr. Peterson who is the founder of the first bank in Sevier County: "April 15th, 1866. I am now sixteen years old and subject to military duty. My first service in the Black Hawk War was on the 26th of April when I was on guard.

May 3rd, together with Sheriff Nathaniel Hanchett and five others I started north with fifty head of cattle to buy arms and ammunition for the people of Sevier county; we went by way of Scipio for safety.

Tuesday, May 5th, we began to trade for guns at Payson and we also traded at Springville. We paid for revolvers thirty to forty dollars each; we finished trading in Salt Lake City on the 14th and returned home on the 21st under guard of twenty men. During our trip we bought eighteen rifles, eleven revolvers and one hundred and forty pounds of ammunition, which we had purchased at an enormous price; but these articles were indispensible. June 5th I was on picket all day and stood guard at night.

Sept. 8th a company of militia camping between Richfield and Glenwood took a man prisoner supposed to be a spy from the Indians.

DEATH OF BLACK HAWK.

Black Hawk, the Indian chief who figured so prominently in the Utah Indian War in 1865-1867, died at Spring Lake Villa, a small settlement situated between Payson and Santaquin, Utah County, Utah, in 1870.

The following letter gives interesting details:

A LETTER FROM WILLIAM PROBERT.

Dated at Provo, Utah, July 1st, 1915.

Mr. Peter Gottfredson, Springville, Utah.

Dear sir:—I am glad to comply with your request to give some items of history of some of the Indian troubles in and near Round Valley (Scipio) and in the following narrative I am sure some of the eroneous stories told in regard to the death of Black-Hawk, the great Indian Chief, and also Panacara, an inoffensive Indian who made his home in Round Valley, may be corrected and the truth of the matter given to the people in your proposed history of the Indian troubles of early Utah days.

There are probably a dozen men in Utah who claim the honor of killing Black Hawk, none of which is true.

It is true that Black Hawk was severely wounded in the fight at Gravelly Ford on the Sevier River, near what is now called Vermillion; but he lived three of four years after receiving the wound; and before his death Black Hawk obtained permission from the military authorities of the Territory to visit all the places where he and his tribe had caused trouble or raided. And accompanied by a few (seven or eight) warriors, Black Hawk visited every town and village from Cedar City on the South to Payson on the north and made peace with the people. On this mission of peace he was provided with an escort, usually from two to six citizens, from town to town. Ansel P. Harmon and myself acted as such escort from Holden to Scipio, Millard County.

Black Hawk told the people wherever he went that he was going home to die and before the end came he desired to be at peace with the pale faces. Black Hawk died at his wigwam near Spring Lake in 1869 or 1870; the exact date I am unable to give. He was buried in the foot hills immediately east and south of Spring Lake Villa, Utah County.

Because of the killing of the old man Ivie (James Ivie) in Round Valley (Scipio) a few years before by members of the Black Hawk tribe it was feared that the old warrior would be harshly treated by the Ivie family on the trip through the valley, unless provisions were made in advance for his protection from assault from that source.

The Ivies had previously sworn vengeance, and some time before Black Hawk's appearance on his mission of peace, the old Indian, Panacara, had been shot to death by James A. Ivie. In order to justify himself, Ivie charged that Panacara was a spy for the Ute Indians on the south, which was not true, as Panacara was a special friend of the white people in that vicinity and was hated by the Utes. On one occasion a band of Utes came to the valley for the sole purpose of killing him. Panacara was for a number of years before his death "medicine man" for the Pahvante tribe whose home was in Millard County, and this tribe of Indians was always friendly with the white settlers.

Panacara's death at the hands of Ivie was brought about in this way: The Old Indian came to the town of Scipio, and as was customary he carried a gun. This custom was objected to by the military authorities and a rule was adpoted that Indians should not carry arms when visiting the settlements. Accordingly the acting justice of the peace Benj. Johnson, prevailed upon the old Indian to give up his gun. The Indian willingly gave the gun to the justice and started out to cross the hills in the direction of Oak Creek, when Ivie followed him, and out on the flat, about two miles from town, he overtook the Indian and without warning shot him dead. He was buried where he was killed.

According to the Indian custom it was "a life for a life" and it did not matter to them who it was just so they got their revenge by killing a white. For the death of Panacara I came nearly losing my scalp at the hands of "Nun-ka-tots" (a particular friend of Panacara), who lived most of the time with him. I was on my way from Deseret to Scipio with a load of wheat and on reachng a point on the desert near Mud-Lake the reflection of a gun showed an Indian in hiding behind a mound near the road. I jumped off the wagon, ready with my rifle for action when the Indian rode away. For seven years this Indian avoided me and finally came to me and asked if I was "tobuck" now. I told him I was not "tobuck" and he said "me no tobuck now'; and from then on this Indian and myself were good friends.

(Signed) William Probert.
Manti, Utah, Feb. 12, 1914.
Box 109.

ATTACK ON THE J. P. LEE RANCH NEAR BEAVER, JOSEPH LILYWHITE WOUNDED.

Dear Brother Gottfredson:

When I began reading to mother the manuscript you inclosed, she began saying, "That is not quite

right, you must correct that;'' and by the time it was
finished she said, ''I wish you would just lay that
aside and write the whole story in your own way,
and I will help you with the facts. I think we can in
that way make it more clear than by correcting this.''
I have done so, and Mother says, this is the only
really true version of the story that has ever been
told. She is the only survivor of the three grown
persons present at the affair, and you are the only
person in all these years who has ever asked her for
the facts.

She hopes you will thus apply at headquarters
for all your other Chronicles, and get them as true
and straight as this one is.

With kind regards from Mother and myself .

L. L. Dalton, Lucinda Lee.

THE INDIAN ATTACK ON LEE'S RANCH IN BEAVER COUNTY.

In the fall of 1866, Mr. John Percival Lee, with
most of his family, was on his dairy farm (called
Hawhorne Dell, situated about eight miles southeast
of Beaver on a bright little stream called South
Creek,) busily pushing preparations to return to
town for the winter.

He usually spent the winters in town, employed
in teaching school, and the summers at Hawthorne
Dell, farming and dairying. Already he had turned
out some thirty milch cows with their calves along
with the dry stock, to forage on the good bunch grass
until spring. The grain was standing in stacks ready
for the thresher, and Mr. Lee and his young hired
man, Joseph Lillywhite, were gathering potatoes,

with the help of several children who assisted to pick up the tubers. The plan was to fill the double-bedded wagon full, and early next morning take that load to town and there make ready for storing the whole crop. This was the 22nd of October, and Mr. Lee intended to take his helper with him, and rather thought they could not return on the same day, having so much to do there.

It was sunset before the load was completed, and all the busy workers noticed that the wolves were very noisy, and seemed to answer each other from many directions. They took no hint, however, even when a neighbor from town, Mr. Elliott Willden, who had been out on the range, and who tarried to take supper with the Lees, remarked that Indians often used wolf howls to signal each other and to drive cattle together.

After the guest went on his way, Mr. Lee said to his helper: "Joe, it does seem foolhardy to live on a lonely place like this and pay so little attention to our firearms. Say, we clean them all up tonight and get our ammunition all ready. Then, if we do stay in town tomorrow night, Mrs. Lee will not be quite defenseless you know." Lightly spoken words and long remembered!

The firearms consisted of one large double-barrelled shotgun (Mr. Lee's favorite weapon), one new, excellent repeating rifle, and one good six-shot revolver. The stock of ammunition was found to be pitiably small and Mr. Lee resolved to buy some on the morrow while in town. The magazine of the rifle contained the whole of its stock of cartridges. The shotgun and revolver were both loaded up with re-

volver balls, with plenty of powder behind them.
Mrs. Lee assisted in the loading to be sure of understanding all about it, with this preparation the family retired to rest in blissful unconsciousness of the
danger that was even then hanging over them. All
night, however, the wolf howls continued and the
two dogs barked and fretted.

Before light next morning, the family was astir
and as soon as the back (west) door was opened,
the dogs barked so furiously toward a low ridge only
a few rods away on the north, that the two men took
their guns when they stepped out to reconnoiter.
There was still no daylight, but the sky line showed
faintly the ragged crest of the brush crowned bench.
"Mr. Lee," said Lillywhite, "I see something moving. Shall I fire?" Hail first, Joe," answered Mr.
Lee, "for if it should be Indians, and we fire first,
it will be said that we brought trouble on ourselves."

Accordingly the young man hailed; and for reply received a volley of bullets, one of which went
through his right shoulder. He reeled and the gun
fell from his helpless hand; but he staggered into
the house before he fell. Mr. Lee, with other bullets singing past him, watched the young man till he
gained cover; then fired one barrel of his shotgun
at the place where he saw the flashes, and sprang
into the house, forgetting to recover the rifle.

The doors and windows had not yet all been
opened. Such as were open were now hastily closed,
just barely in time to prevent the entrance of the Indians as they rushed yelling down the hill.

The front or east door had only a wooden button on a screw for a fastening, and the west one had
a broken gimlet stuck nail-fashion into a small hole;

so that it was necessary to reinforce these frail fastenings with furniture.

For the first few minutes the whoops and yells of the Indians, punctuated as they were with heavy blows on the doors and with shots through both doors and windows, were something terrific. The windows, fortunnately, had strong wooden shutters, secured with iron hooks on the inside. When these were all closed, the house would have been very dim had the sun been shining; but now, just at the break of day, it was quite dark, and a tallow candle had to be lighted to enable Mr. Lee to reload the empty barrel of his shotgun.

After raising such a hideous storm around the house for what seemed an age, the Indians grew quiet and one advanced to parley. During this lull in the strife, it may be well to introduce to the reader the remaining members of the household.

Besides Mr. and Mrs. Lee and Mr. Lillywhite, there was a young daughter not quiet sixteen years old, who lived to become Mrs. Mary C. Black, now (A. D. 1914) a skillful apiarist resident in Fruita, Cal. Another daughter, twelve years old, who afterward became the wife of Judge J. G. Sutherland, an eminent jurist in Salt Lake Ciy. Before her marriage, this lady had studied law, passed a successful examination and been admitted to practice before the bar. She was then Miss Emma Lee.

Next was a son, Chas. A. Lee, an enterprising lad of nearly ten years, who is now an apiarist and orchadist in Fresno County, Cal.

Next was a little daughter between seven and eight years old, now Mrs. Ellen L. Sanders, living in Nacozari, Sonora, Mexico. This lady is consid-

ered to be one of Utah's foremost literary women.
Last was Baby Rosamond, only fifteen months
old, who is now Mrs. Geo. Sutherland, wife of the
U. S. Senator from Utah. Besides these five children of their own, there was a little English girl
named Jane Hall, whose father had left her temporarily with the Lees while he went in search of a
home and employment. She was about thirteen
years old. These six children would have made a
costly sacrifice to be offered up on the alter of
redhanded violence.

The Indian spokesman who hailed Mr. Lee by
name, said that he was Too-witch-ee-Tick-a-boo,
a very good friend, who was hungry. Would his
friend John open the door and give him break-
milk-matches, etc., Mr. Lee, after some talk, said
to his wife, "We have always been such good friends
with the Indians, can it be possible that all this is
a mistake?" "Not possible!" she replied "that all
this shooting is any mistake." The Indian continued to plead and protest until Mr. Lee said again
to his wife, "I have so little ammunition that I can
not fight long; and when it is all gone, we should be
at their mercy, and they would be still more angry than they are now. What do you think?"

"I think just this: They are not angry at all—
have no occasion to be so. They have simply made
up their minds to kill us. We will fight as long as
there is one shot left, and trust in God. Let me
answer once." "No," she called to the Indian,
"you are not Tick-a-boo! We will not open the
door! If you come in here, we will shoot you!"

The Indian laughed, and said, "Oh! Squaw
shoot! Now me scared! Yes, now me scared!"

Mr. Lee hastened to speak again lest the enemy suppose that the woman had spoken because he was disabled.

Now the defenders learned the real reason for the stay of proceedings and the parley; for little puffs and lines of smoke began to come in between the roof and the walls of the unceiled rooms. The Indians had brought sagebrush and pushed bundles of it with poles up under the eaves, and fired them.

Providentially, there had been snow sometime lately, and although the most of it was gone from sight, the roof of boards and slabs was so damp it would not blaze. The underside, with the burning brush against it, took fire but only smoudered, and poured into the rooms clouds of bitter smoke. It floated high for awhile, and then settled down like doom upon the defenseless inmates. It grew so dense that strangulation threatened; and baby Rose gasped and struggled so that she seemed about to die. At one time some one discovered that under the best bed was better air, and Mary was appointed to take the child there and tend her. The other children stuck their heads into cupboards and even the dutch oven, and wherever they could find a little air. There was still a little water in the house, which was hoarded carefully. The wounded man continously moaned for water, the baby drank eagerly, the others must have a few sips, and there was very little to spare for the fire, but that little was cautiously applied so as not to waste one precious drop.

Emma had used some to make a cup of coffee for her father who dared not be off his guard for a single minute; and she had also given the children drinks of milk and bits of bread; but the parents had no time for eating.

The smoke thickened till the wounded man groaned in distress; and Charles, Emma and Janey Hall took turns in fanning him while they breathed through damp handkerchiefs, and coughed in a way that must have been music to the ears of their would-be murderers. Charles could even lift the head of the fallen youth to give him water, and did so until he was nearly as bloody as the patient. As the din increased, and more shots flew through the stifling smoke, Charles and Janey went together to the mother to ask what they could do to help.

"You poor children," she answered, "there is nothing more you can do with your hands; but you might pray with all your might for God in heaven to help us—He only can;" and those two children knelt down amidst all that blood and smoke and uproar, and prayed with all the unstudied earnestness of trusting childhood; and who shall say they were not heard?

About this time some Indian inserted the tines of a pitchfork into the closing of the east door, and burst off the frail wooden button, but the cupboard barricade did not allow the door to open more than an inch or two. Here the darkness within gave Mr. Lee his first real advantage over his assailants. He saw, without pressing near enough to be seen, an Indian raising his gun to fire through the crevice; and he turned loose with the old shotgun at point blank range.

A wild yell, followed by dreadful shrieks, groans and howls, was the result of this, the second shot from the gun, which fairly tore away the right shoulder of the Indian. Almost immediately, Mr.

Lee saw another Indian at a few rods distance ramming a load into his gun. He sent the load fromt he other barrel after this besieger, and handed the gun to his wife to be reloaded; while with his revolver in hand, he continued his watch through that dangerous but convenient opening.

The Indian who received that last shot, had seemed to think he was out of range; for when the charge struck him, he dropped his gun and sprang straight upward with a suppressed, guttural cry that seemed to express as much surprise as pain. By this time the Indians decided that they had no use for that narrow opening in the door, for the pitchfork was cautiously removed; and the besieged hastened to drive in a stout nail.

During this part of the action, Emma had found an ax in the kitchen and stationed herself by the west door, saying grimly that she would do her best to chop off a leg from the first Indian who came in there. Had the occasion and the moment been less tragic and desperate, this might have been amusing; for she was a delicate girl and small for her age; but she meant it.

Her mother smiled drearily at such training for a dainty girl, but her keenest anxiety in this terrible situation was for her daughter Mary. She found and gave to Mary a small dagger in a sheath attached to a narrow leather belt; and while directing her to buckle it around her waist, said solemnly: "My daughter, our case is desperate; and if the worst comes, if the Indians do break in on us, your father, I and most likely all the rest of us except yourself will be killed at once; but I fear they would take you alive and put you to tortures worse than death, as

is their way with women prisoners. Let me beg you
to wear this dagger and do not let them take you
alive.''

Mary who had been so brave until now, almost
fainted on hearing this; and, pale to the lips, she
sighed "Oh, I couldn't—hurt a fly.'' Her mother
urged her to be brave, and added, "I wore that dagger through a time of danger—'' and Mary, with a
great effort, put by her weakness and returned to her
duties.

The uproar on the outside gradually subsided;
and the smoke on the inside thinned a little, probably
being drawn up through the two chimneys.

The besieged waited with straining ears to learn
what new deviltry was to be practiced on them, while
the slow minutes dragged along. The baby, pale
and gasping, grew so weak and faint, that the mother
in desperation took her to a west window which she
opened enough to give the child a few breaths of
outside air. The father ran in alarm to see what
had happened; and on seeing the condition of the
child, took up his guard there as long as they both
dared. Then he said, "I will rush out and get
water to drink and to throw on the fire.''

The wife protested earnestly, against this, so
did the children. Mrs. Lee believed that the treacherous foe had only pretended to go away, hoping to
entice him, the only fighting man, to go on this very
errand, so they might pick him off easily. "If he
were killed,'' she urged, "the others very soon
would be.''

He yielded to their entreaties; and Mrs. Lee,
who was never known to flinch in the face of duty,
and Mary, who had already concluded that an In-

dian bullet would be far better than a dagger in
her own hand, took buckets, and when the barricade
had been removed from the back door, while the
husband and father stood at guard for them, they
ran to the stream, only a rod or two from the south
end of the house, and secured water.

The opening of the door (which was hastily barricade again) released a volume of smoke, the
water relieved their aching throats and smarting
eyes, and with it they finally extinguished the fire.
There had been no demonstration whatever from the
enemy for nearly an hour; and hoping that the Indians were really gone began to struggle with the
fear of an ambuscade, when Charles came to his
parents with a grave proposal that they allow him
to run to town and ask for help.

They were horrified at the bare thought of
sending out so young a child to go eight miles on
foot, more probably, to be shot down before their
eyes by their lurking foes. But the boy had the look
of one inspired while he urged, "I know I can go
and not be shot;" and said he would not follow the
wagon road, which wound among the ridges, but
would take a straight shoot across the country,
which would shorten the way two miles or more.

The parents then looked into each other's eyes
and agreed without words. "God is with the child,"
said the father, and laying his hands on the head of
his grave little son, he solemnly blessed him. The
mother kissed him just as solemnly, with all the dust
and blood upon him. Then they opened the west
window looking toward town and the boy sprang
through and ran like a deer until lost to sight among
the stunted cedars and sagebrush on the hillside.

His father remained by the open window watching for sign of an enemy until the flying figure disappeared. Then he closed the window and with his tired wife and weary children, prepared to face another interval of inaction and suspense. But just here, Janey raised a diversion by requesting Mr. and Mrs. Lee to let her also run away to Beaver. This they assured her they would never do. She was a girl—nearly thirteen years old—not even their own —oh! no! that was not to be thought of—not for one moment!

But the more they explained these things to Janey, the more persistent she grew, and the more fiercely she accused them of allowing one of their own to escape and save his life, while they kept her to be killed. After fifteen minutes to half an hour of screams and tears, and alternate entreaties and upbraidings from Janey, Mr. and Mrs. Lee decided that only God in heaven knew whether it were less dangerous to go or to stay; and they let her go.

Mr. Lee stood at the window as before to keep his futile watch over the child until she went out of his sight around the bend in the road.

The sequel proved that at this very time the Indians were really gone to join their companions who were passing with droves of cattle; and happy would the Lees have been could they have known it.

When Charles set out, he felt, as he said afterwards, as though he could fly. He fixed his eyes on a landmark and never went a round a rock or a bush, but leaped over them. He had no sense of fatigue until he reached the little suburb of Beaver which had been named Pleasant Point, but nicknamed Jackson County. There he saw Mr. Anderson just about to mount a horse to ride over to Beaver, about a mile distant.

Seeing the boy all bloody and wild, he paused to make inquiry; and the boy panted out, "The Indians —fighting—Hawthorne Dell."

"Poor boy," said Mr. Anderson, "Sit down here and rest and I'll stir up Beaver in a hurry."

He mounted and galloped away, and the boy sat down on some timbers and felt like he never could move again. He had lost hat and shoes, scratched his flesh and torn his clothing to rags; but he had accomplished his errand in a marvelously short time.

So did Mr. Anderson; for the boy was still sitting in the same place when a band of mounted men whom he had "scared up," passed on their way to Hawthorne Dell. They shouted "Hello Bub," but never drew rein. Near Birch Creek, about half the distance to the ranch, they met Janey Hall, who, to their surprise, did not seem frightened nor excited, but was walking leisurely along the road, and chewing gum that she had picked by the way. They greeted her and passed on, and she finished her long walk alone but safely.

When the horsemen reached the ranch, sometime before noon, they found no Indians, but scouted about and found plenty of signs. Patches of frothy blood on the top of the ridge whence came the shot that brought down young Lilywhite before he had a chance to fire once; other blood on the ground east of the house, and indoors, too. The dropped rifle was found and utterly ruined, and with its magazine quite empty. Harness, saddles, tools and many other things were destroyed, all the horse and cattle inclosures were left empty, and untold damage done; but of the nine persons beseiged only one had been hurt, and the grain stacks were safely standing. For these mercies Mr. Lee was a thankful man.

A few of the men remained to assist the family while the others pushed on after the Indians.

It did not take those on the trail very long to understand the situation. The range was silent and empty, and the fat young cattle found shot along the trail, told them the whole story. They knew that the relations between this family and their Indian neighbors had always been friendly, therefore it was highly improbable that this attack had any personal ill will behind it; but was made solely because the little ranch lay in the track the Indians wanted to use in a great cattle raid. Although they must have known that the family was hurrying to get away for the winter, they could not postpone the raid because they also knew the white men were preparing for an extensive roundup, and they, the Indians wished to be beforehand.

These men followed the Indians and cattle sixty or more miles without overtaking them, swift as they had been to follow. There they were forced to turn back because their hasty preparations were so inadequate to a long march or for a hard fight.

At the farm the great concern was to get the wounded man and the family away before night. The team was gone, the harness demolished, the wagon heaped up with potatoes; and the only vehicle that had come from town was a very light buggy belonging to Bishop R. Murdock. This could not even convey the wounded man, who was too weak from loss of blood to sit erect. Just here the memory of

Mrs. Lee (now 84 years old) under whose sanction and prompting this chronicle is made, fails her; and the pen woman, who was not an eyewitness, supplies from impressions received at the time this one statement, believed but not guaranteed to be true.

A good brother named Alonzo Colton, from Minersvile, was on his way to a sawmill farther up in the mountains to get a load of lumber. He arrived at Hawthorne Dell when it began to look as if there was nothing to do but to send to Beaver for conveyance and await its coming, a most dread alternative. On hearing of the dilemma, Mr. Colton promptly unhitched his team, and leaving his "running gear" standing, hitched on to Mr. Lee's wagon, from which the potatoes were hastily "dumped." The sick man in his bed and the wife and children were then loaded in, and Mr. Colton himself drove them down the mountain road to their home, where they arrived at about five o'clock, p. m.

Now if this statement be not correct, Mr. Colton or any surviving member of his family is at liberty to deny it; and she who wrongfully accuses him stands ready to apologize amply. One thing, however, that she knows to be a fact, is that when, some days later, threshing was done, this same Mr. Colton with his own wagon and team brought down one or more loads of the crop, and never would accept one cent of pay. For this kindness to fellow-creatures in distress, he is gratefully remembered to this day; also others who freely rendered assistance at a time of need.

This murderous and unprovoked attack took place on the 23rd of October, A. D. 1866. Mr. Lee,

who is not now living, always considered it a divine
intervention that prompted him to put his fire-arms
into good condition just on the eve of such dire
need. He fired only three shot, (having no ammunition to waste), but every one reached its mark. The
Indians at the time made themselves scarce, and
knew absolutely nothing; but in after years they
said Mr. Lee was a Big Chief—a Brave—and that
he had killed three bad Indians who had tried to kill
him. These were the Piutes, whose home was in Beaver County, and who knew every member of Mr.
Lee's family well, and often visited them at the farm.
It is even probable that the very matches used to fire
the dwelling had been begged from the intended
victims. One queer thing not yet mentioned is that
when the east door of the house was finally opened,
it was found piled high with sagebrush that had not
been fired; and after much wonder why this dry
door was left unburned while the wet roof had so
much effort spent on it in vain, the conclusion was
finally reached that after the brush was heaped
against the door, the Indians found they had used
all their matches. If so, it was certainly an error of
judgment on their part, because the door would have
burned readily.

Joseph Lillywhite recovered from his wound;
but it is said that he never became the strong man
that his robust youth promised, and did not live to
reach middle age.

Such were many of the experiences of the early
settlers of Utah.

ACCOUNT OF THE WAR IN WASATCH COUNTY AND VICINITY.

Wasatch County, Utah, which was somewhat adjacent to the Indian rendezvous in the DuChesne country had its share of Indian troubles during the Black Hawk war in 1866. The following from the writing of John Crook of Heber City:

In the early spring of 1866, instructions came from military headquarters, Salt Lake City to prepare for Indian troubles, and to guard our stock and vicinity, and we were informed that officials would arrive to organize us and place us on a war footing.

In the month of April, 1866, we began to build corrals for our dry-stock in Ross Hollow, eight miles north, and also a large corral in Heber City for the cow-herd.

On the 25th of May, 1866, Col. Robert T. Burton and Drill Sergeant D. G. Ross arrived, and organized the militia in the valley, with John W. Witt as Major and Charles H. Wilkins as adjutant of company (A) "cavalry." Company (D) was composed of Silver Grays, and these two companies formed the first Battalion.

Companies B and C formed the second battalios, and was commasded by John Hamilton as major and John Crook as adjutant.

All on the west side of the Provo River principally Midway formed a separate command, a battalion, with Sidney H. Epperson as major and David Van Wagonen as adjutant, this company consisted of both cavalry and infantry.

All the settlers on the east side of the Provo River moved to Heber City. On the 25th and 26th of May a two days drill was ordered, and a sham battle was participated in on which occasion Col. Robert T. Burton called the troops into a hollow square. This being done Col. Burton said, "Now you are organized on a war footing, go to work and put out your guards and scouts, and protect yourselves."

The previous winter had been a very severe one, and with deep snow in the mountains we did not expect that the Indians would come over so soon.

FIRST INDIAN RAID.

About the middle of May, 1866, a band of Indians came over the mountains, no doubt in the night, the snow being crusted. They gathered up some forty or fifty head of stock on the east range, and drove them over no doubt while the snow was yet crusted. Wm. McDonald while hunting cattle came across the trail. Adjutant Wilkins and Lieutenant McDonald started with a posse of men in pursuit and reached the trail in the middle of the day. The snow being soft the horses plunged to their bellies and the expedition had to give up the chase and return home. Wm. Bradley Sessions who had a big family lost seven cows in this raid, the Indians taking all he had. This raid was made before the county militia was organized.

For information I will describe the lay of the country. Three canyons leads from Provo Valley to the dividing ridge between said valley and the Indian Reservation. The center one is Lake Creek

running due east, through this canyon an Indian
trail leads over into the west fork of the Duchesne
River, and it was only forty miles from Heber to
the Indian colony on said river by way of this trail.

After re-organization of the militia we placed
guards, "The Silver Grays," on the north
and south of Main Street in Heber City and a
guard at the grit mill, one mile east, also three
sets of scouts for the three canyons, patrolling the
ridge between the Reservation and Provo Valley.
They were on duty both day and night, and were
changed every four days.

On the 27th of May an expedition started to the
Uintah Indian Reservation. Col. Head, the Indian
agent, was along with Col. Robert T. Burton and
Sergeant Ross, with supplies for the Indiass; there
were also three men with one hundred head of beef
cattle for the Indians, a present from Brigham
Young (church donation) Col. Head asking for an
escort of the militia, the following were chosen to
compose the escort.

Captain Wm. M. Wall, Lieut. Joseph McDonald,
Serg't John McDonald; Privates: John J. Cummings, Wm. B. Sessions, Hyrum Oakes, Joseph Mc-
Carrol, George Boner, Nymphus C. Murdock, William Forman, Stanley Davis, Steven Taylor of Salt
Lake City, Alma Huntington, George Carlile. The
expedition was gone twelve days.

The personnel of a Second Platoon composing
the escort is the following:

Lieut. Patrick Caroll, Serg't Edward Brunson
Privates: Wm. Giles, Jr., Eph. Van Wagenon, Jerry
Robey, Zeke Bates, Emanuel Richman, James Carlile,
John Acomb, Stephen Moore. Teams and teamsters:

N. C. Murdock's team, Ben. A. Norris, driver, John W. Witts team, Willard Carroll driver, Hyrum Oakes, team, Isaac O. Wall, driver.

This Platoon and outfit was gone ten days. They were corralled four day in a log cabin surrounded by three hundred "to-buck" (angry) Indians, who didn't want the cattle but wanted Mormon scalps. The agent prevailed on the Indians to let them go.

On July 8th, 1866, a second expedition was sent to the reservation with Indian supplies.

Following are the names of the parties, constituting this expedition:

Major John Hamilton, Lieut. Joseph McCarroll (infantry), Adjutant Charles Wilkin, Capt. Wm. M. Wall, Lieut. Wm. McDonald, and Privates Nymphus C. Murdock, George Giles (blacksmith) William Gallagher, Joseph Thomas, George F. Giles, Henry Luke (interpreter) Albert McMullen, John Harvey, Jr., James Allred, Richard Jones, Wm. M. Giles, Moroni Duke, James Shanks, commissary for the expedition and Privates Ira N. Jacobs, George Boner, James B. Hamilton, A. Thompson and Emanuel Richman (teamster.)

This expedition numbering 23 men was gone eight days, from the 8th to the 16th of July.

While this party was over at the Reservation a raid was made on Thomas Handley's corral, in Heber City, where Indians took two oxen and a heifer.

This raid will be explained as the raid in which Jas. A. Ross and others figured.

SECOND RAID ON STOCK.

After the second expedition had started for the Reservation and while the expedition was still there between the 8th and 16th of July, 1866, some Indians came into the eastern part of Heber and took two oxen and a heifer from Tom. Handley's corral; they left a bell-cow. William Foreman, who was on guard at the lake, found the tracks at daylight. A shower having fallen during the night he rushed to Heber and reported. Handley's stock being found missing, James A. Ross, Joseph S. Parker, Sid Carter and Isaac Cummings started in a hurry on the trail and when down about eight miles on the west Duchesne they saw smoke in the timber. Leaving their horses and crawling up close to the timber, they saw the Indians roasting meat, they having killed the heifer. One Indian was sitting on the paunch while the others were lying down. By signs each of the men in pursuit took aim at an object and fired. The Indian on the paunch fell over and the others crawled into the brush. The boys got the oxen and also the Indians' horses and effects and some of the meat, which they brought home, and they did not look to see how many Indians were killed.

This occurred when the militia was at the Reservation. Lieutenant McDonald was conversing with some Indians when another Indian rode up very excited pointing to the hills and motioned for another horse. It was rumored that a wounded Indian was brougt in before the company left. Putting these items together, they tally with circumstances connected with the raid on Mr. Handley's cattle at that time.

By request of Commander James D. Shanks. Adjutant Lindsey sends an account of an incident which happened in conection with the second expedition from Provo Valley. After delivering the supplies to the Indians, part of the company decided to come back to Heber by way of the short cut, or Indian trail. Captain Wm. M. Wall, Charles H. Wilcken, Nymphus C. Murdock, George Bonner, Jos. McCarrel, Ira Jacobs and Wm. Gallagher and two or three others were in this company. This route led them down Lake Creek Canyon which is east of Heber and runs to the ridge between this Valley and the old Reservation, scouts were kept on this ridge all through the summer. The day before these men came over the ridge the scouts came to Heber and reported that they had seen Indians encamped in a grove near the head of Lake Creek.

Twelve men on foot were sent out that night with orders to get well up into the canyon before day light to surround the Indians. They reached the appointed place by nine or ten o'clock a. m. and examined the grove. They saw no Indians, but found a fresh trail leading down towards Heber.

This company consisted of W. B. Sessions, Isaac Baum, John and Geo. Muir, Jesse Bond, Lewis Mecham, Thos. Handley, G. A. Wilson, Dickson Green and three others. After following the trail three miles, they came onto what they supposed were Indians, lying in a sort of grassy and shady place, and without waiting for orders two of the men fired. The result was that N. C. Murdock was grazed by a bullet on his left wrist and shot in the right leg.

The bullet shattering the shin bone. George Bonner was shot through the thigh, the bullet coming so near through that it was cut out with a pocket knife.

Wm. M. Wall had a marvelous escape, a bullet passed around the rim of his belly, making nine holes in his vest and shirt, but never breaking his skin. It has always been considered a miracle that Captain Wall was not killed. It was also through the alertness of our scouts just a few days before, that J. A. Ross and three companions were able to overtake those three Indians who took Thomas Handley's oxen and heifer out of his corral, right in Heber, and they brought back the oxen and the Indians' horses, also a white mule that had been stolen by the Indians down on the Sevier River.

One Indian was known to have been killed at the time, and another wounded; one got away.

Written by Wm. Lindsey, and corroborated by James D. Shank, commander Wasatch Department, Indian War Veterans,—who was Commissary at the time.

THIRD RAID.

About August, Indians took John Muir's mules and John Turner's horses out of a pasture adjoining Heber City east. Through friendly Indians Mr. Turner got back his horses, but Mr. Muir's mules, two fine ones, failed to return.

FOURTH RAID.

About the 20th of August Indians took John Lee's horses from his pasture, one mile east of Heber City. Mr. Lee had moved from his farm to the east line of the city, and had just taken the animals to the pasture, when on looking east, he saw the Indians driving the horses out of the pasture. He gave the alarm. The Indians drove the horses along the foot hills, east and north aiming to strike the Park City road north of Heber. A company of men started to head them off. William McDonald who lived on his farm on said road and owned a good horse, mounted this horse bare back and started in pursuit, but the Indians struck the road before Mr. McDonald. A race ensued, but before Mr McDonald could reach the river bridge six miles north, the Indians ran the horses across the Provo River and into some brush where they left them, and then hurried away.

The boys brought the horses back. About ten days later the Indians stole the same horses again, out of the same pasture. On this occasion Mr. Lee got one horse back by paying an Indian for getting it.

FIFTH RAID.

In September, 1866, the Indians broke into Wm. Bell's stable south of Heber and stole a fine pair of mares "called Island stock". These animals were young and full of life, and had not been handled much. It appeared that the Indians had had a struggle with them in the sage brush. The next morning they were found shot. About this time, or perhaps a little later, Charles H. Wilkin went to his saw-mill in Center Creek canyon with two yoke of oxen, which he turned out in the evening. The next morning they were gone. Major Witt and Adj't. Wilkin went to the Reservation and got three of them back; one had been killed and eaten. It was

quite a risk for these two men to go on such an
expedition alone.

From a report filed Oct. 8th, 1866, by Major
John Hamilton, who was in command, we learn that
Indians had stolen some horses from stables in the
south part of Heber City, and had driven them
south, following a ridge to the river. Thence up a
canyon over the ridge, thence into American Fork
Canyon, and thence down to the north end of Utah
Lake, across Jordan Bridge and thence into Cedar
Valley, going west.

A company of sixteen started in pursuit and
when they reached the Jordan Bridge they learned
that the Indians had crossed there before day-light.
The boys followed the thieves into Cedar Valley and
met some teams hauling wood. The wood-haulers
said that they had seen some Indians and horses
two hours previous on the run. As the pursuers
realized that they were at least two hours behind
the Indians they concluded that following further
would be a fruitless chase, as the Indians before
they could be overtaken would be on their own
grounds and the horses hidden away. It was therefore decided to give up the chase, and the boys consequently returned to their homes.

Following are the names of those who participated in this expedition:

Major John Hamilton, Capt. Wm. M. Wall,
Lieutenants James A. Ross and Patrick Carroll,
Sergeants Philip L. Smith and Geo. A. Wilson and
Privates John Acomb, Joseph Parker, A. McMullen,
Sol. Sessions, Geo. F. Giles, Wm. Gallagher, Wm.
M. Giles, Orson Hicken, Robt. Broadhead and Frank
Fraughton.

ACCOUNT OF THE WAR IN WASATCH COUNTY CONTINUED.

The spring of 1867 was late and the snow deep in the hills. We put out our guards, but no Indians troubled us until about the middle of July. We had a special scout independent of the usual scouts, namely John Cummings, who on a certain occasion found in a side Canyon an Indian who had skinned an ox and was in the act of cutting up the meat. Mr. Cummings covered the Indian with his rifle and drove him ahead of him to Heber City where he was kept under guard three days. A court marshal decided to write a note to Chief Tabby, advising him to keep his Indian at home, and also asking Tabby to come over and make peace with us. We gave the note to the Indian and told him to go immediately to the Reservation, give the note to Chief Tabby like a good Indian. Two guards went with him to see him over the ridge.

About a month later. or about the 15th or 20th of August, Chief Tabby with his whole tribe, squaws, pappoosses and peaceable Indians that he could control came here. The Chief said that he could not control those of his Indians who were with Black Hawk. We had a bowery in which we held summer meetings, and in this we set large tables, and the ladies furnished a good picnic for the Indians. An ox was killed and roasted, (a fine barbeque) and the Indians filled up good; the pipe of peace was passed around, and the Indians after stopping a few days returned home with a few good presents. On leaving our valley these Indians stole thirty of our horses.

This occurrence ended the raids in our valley, and we still kept up our guards and scouts in the hills.

Concerning further Indian troubles in Wasatch County in 1867 John Crook wrote the following:

The expeditions reported in the foregoing details are from the original records in charge of John Crook who was adjutant to Major John Hamilton at the time. Other information is from parties who took part in the different expeditions and from personal knowledge and memory. The guards and scouts were mostly from the infantry and the Silver Grays. The cavalry was kept as minute men to be ready to go at a minute's notice. There were about 260 men enrolled in the militia in Provo Valley. At this time (1914) the survivors are reduced to about thirty-five.

I have written this by an order and sanction of the Veterans and they pronounce it O. K. this 7th day of November, 1914. *John Crook.*

COL. PIERCE AND ANDREWS ENGAGE
INDIANS NEAR ST. GEORGE.

Early in January 1867 the Navajoes made a raid on the horse herd in Washington County. This being just after New Year, it was an intimation of what might be expected in other places; in this instance however, the success of the savages was of short duration. Captain James Andrus led a party of Saint George cavalry in pursuit, overtook the thieves, killed eleven of them and recovered the horses.

RAID ON PINE VALLEY, INDIANS OVERTAKEN, ELEVEN KILLED.

From David Chidester the following additional particulars are obtained. On the night of Jan. 18th, 1867, the Navajo and some Shevete Indians gathered stock from Shoal Creek down along Black Ridge. When Col. J. D. L. Pierce and his company found the tracks, they followed them to the end of the ridge, some ten or fifteen miles. The militia kept in a wash as much as possible, and saw in the distance what appeared to be a small whirl-wind, but which proved to be smoke from the Indians camp-fire. The cavalry came upon the Indians unawares, and killed twelve of them and put the rest to flight; they recovered nearly all the stock, about two hundred head. but some of the Indians had separated were seen, but not found. While the fight was in from the rest, as the tracks of two large mules progress the stock started back the way they came, and were not overtaken till they had proceded about six miles.

As spring advanced Black-Hawk and his band from the Elk Mountains region made, their way northward. In March, 1867, General Snow was in Glenwood confined to his bed with sickness, and the people were not looking for trouble with the Indians so early in the season. However, they were preparing for future trouble by building a rock fort about two miles west of Glenwood, which was considered a safer place than Glenwood, being farther away from the mountains, or out in the open valley, but the location was not good, as it was low land and without

PETER GOTTFREDSON AND FAMILY 1882

I married Amelia Gledhill in April, 1872, and contracted with her sister's husband, Bernard Snow, to bring logs to his saw-mill to be sawed into lumber, each to have half. I took my young wife to the mill to cook, and engaged her brother, Thomas Gledhill, to help me get logs to the mill, with three yoke of large oxen. We worked there till the 26th of September, when Indians from ambush killed one of our number and wounded another.

In 1882, at the age of 36, when this picture was taken. I was requested by the editor of our local paper, the Richfield Advocate, to write up the circumstances for publication, which I did, with the assistance of my wife, her brother Thomas, and my brother-in-law. Colonel John L. Ivie, which was the beginning of the compilation of this history.

ORSON P. LEE
Commander Sevier County Department
UTAH INDIAN WAR VETERANS

OLE P. BORG
Who did harness and saddle work during the Black Hawk War for the Cavalry. He was also miller.

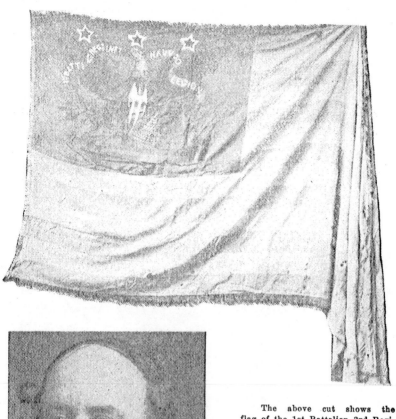

MARK LINDSEY

The above cut shows the flag of the 1st Battalion 3rd Regiment of Infantry Nauvoo Legion. This flag was carried by Mark Lindsey, of Captain James C. Livingston's Company under the command of Major Andrew Burt, which company was mustered into service July 25, 1866. Mark Lindsey was chosen to carry this flag on account of his height, which was 6 feet and 3 inches. Mr. Lindsey was born in Trowbridge, Wiltshire, England, January 22, 1832, and came to Utah with the Utah Handcart Pioneers in 1859. He was the Pioneer Pleasure Garden man of Utah and owned what was known in pioneers days as "Linsey's Gardens", which occupied a quarter section in the North-east part of Salt Lake City. He died in Ogden, Utah, February 12, 1900.

PRESIDENT WM. H. SEGMILLER AND WIFE

of Sevier Stake, closely connected with the colonization of Indians in Grass Valley.

drainage, and surrounded by springs and swamps. Yet the town being so near the hills was too much exposed for safety; hence, the move. The Fort, however, was never finished.

J. P. PETERSEN, WIFE AND MARY SMITH KILLED NEAR GLENWOOD. A SKIRMISH AT GLENWOOD, STOCK RECOVERED.

Early in the morning of March 21, 1867, Jens Peter Petersen and wife, and Mary Smith, a neighbor girl, aged fourteen years, left Richfield, Sevier County to go to Glenwood about five miles distant (east) with an ox-team to do some trading. Stores being few in those days. Warren S. Snow had brought a load of merchandise to Glenwood to trade for stock and produce, and in order to get some needed articles, these people ventured out, thinking that by starting so early in the day there would be no danger, but as the roads were muddy, they could not travel as fast they had expected. It may here be added that it was contrary to council at this time for anyone to travel between the settlements without armed escort. The Petersens left their baby girl, eighteen months old, at Jorgen Smith's at Richfield; she is now Mrs. Christine Christensen of Koosharem, and mother-in-law of Louis Hatch (the Indian Missionary). When they got to the so-called Black Ridge east of the Sevier River, Indians were gathering the stock along the river bottoms; and the Indians seeing the people on the road, immediately attacked them and killed all of them, mutilating their bodies in a most horrible

9

manner, especially the women; they also killed one
of their oxen. Just at that time two boys from
Glenwood, Joseph Hendricksen and Joseph Frankum
happened to be down in the field near by after some
cows. They had some difficulty in starting the
animals and looking back they saw two persons coming down the dugway. One of the boys said to the
other: ''There comes some boys, we will ask them
to help us to start the cows.'' But they soon discovered they were Indians and then ran for town.
The Indians squatted down and took a shot at them,
but missed their mark. Hendricksen reached town
first and reported. The murderers drove the stock
which they had gathered north to the crossing of
Cove River, near the so-called Herrings Hole. The
stream being difficult to cross, they were delayed
somewhat in getting the stock over. Some of the
men in town requested that no one should leave the
settlement lest the Indians should come and over-
power the people. But when Dr. Elias Pearson,
called for men to follow him, ten or more responded
among whom were the following: Dr. Pearson, Artemus Millett, James Killion, J. K. Petersen, Joseph
Snow (son of General Snow), Archibald T. Oldroyd,
Joseph Herring, George Pectol, J. K. P. Sampson,
and Hans J. Gottfredson (a boy who was on his
way to work on the fort) Some of these men got
between the stock and the hills, and exchanged several shots with the savages; and the Indians who
would not fight in the open, made for the hills and
rocks. One redskin endeavored to stampede the
stock by shouting and shaking his blanket, and
two or three others were hiding among the cattle,
but the stock did not seem to scare much on this oc-

casion. The Indian with the blanket was wounded and ran to the hills, and the savages reached a creek later called Indian creek, where they made a stand and fought for some time. It was amusing to see J. K. Peterson maneuver, he would dodge around here and there and when he saw an opportunity he would squat down and fire, throw himself down on his back, while reloading, and get up again to repeat the performances. Some of the men kept the Indians back, while the younger boys drove the stock to town. About a dozen men came out from town to meet those who had been out and helped to drive the stock in. Some Indians rode out onto the point of the hill, and the white horse Chief "Shena-vegan." rode around encouraging his braves The boys picked him out for a target and ran him to cover. John Frankum, whose gun was out of commission, obtained another gun from a boy (Tom Goff) and together with some others went up towards the Indians on the hill. Here Frankum was shot through one shoulder which disabled him, but Hans. J. Gottfredson assisted him to reach town. The Indians finally pulled off into the hills, but got away with a few horses and a mule or two. One of the mules belonging to Peter Oldroyd. It was recovered at the Spring City fight the next fall.

After the skirmish and recovery of the stock, George Crowther of Monroe, who had been working on the Glenwood Fort for Peter Oldroyd, started for home. Archibald T. Oldroyd and some of the other boys who had been in the fight started with him to escort him part way, and when they reached the dugway on the hill near Glenwood they found the wagon, and the murdered people. It appeared that when the

Indians had shot the ox, the people jumped from the wagon and started to run. Petersen had gone but a short distance from the wagon when he was shot down. After being shot he had been horribly beaten about the head and face; his nose was mashed onto the side of his face, and he was scalped. Mrs. Petersen who was in a delicate condition had run a short distance up the road. Miss Mary Smith being young, had nearly reached the top of the hill before she was overtaken. Both women were stripped and horribly mutilated. Before George Crowther and his escort left the scene of the tragedy, they were joined by a company of men from Richfield. One of the party was sent back to Richfield after a conveyance to take the dead people home.

At the time of the killing of the people on Black Ridge, Ole P. Bork, a Richfield harness maker, then a boy, was going down into the meadows to look for stock. Just at sunrise he heard shooting; the air was a little hazy, but he could see that the shooting was done by Indians, and knowing also that Petersen had gone to Glenwood, he thought the Indians were after them. He therefore ran for town, but when about half way to the settlement a man on horse-back (who had been down at the river) passed him and gave the alarm. The drum beat, and when Borg got to the fort at Richfield a number of men had already started for the scene, but arrived there too late to render much assstance. The Smith family claimed the little girl who had been left with them, as their daugther had been killed, but Major Claus P. Anderson who was a relative claimed her, and raised her to womanhood.

Ten of the Richfield boys participated in the

expedition named. They were ordered to go to the upper, or south end, of the Black Ridge and follow down the same. When they came to the place where the people were killed they met the Glenwood boys. Some of both parties (Joe Snow with them) went after the Indians; they traveled up Indian Creek, the way the Indians had gone, and followed the trial to the head of Lost Creek, where they abandoned the chase and returned.

SEVIER, PIUTE AND PARTS OF OTHER COUNTIES VACATED.

Richfield as well as Monroe and Glenwood were vacated April 20, 1867, by their inhabitants because of the Indian troubles. About the same time many other places were temporarily deserted. Thus Piute County was entirely vacated as well as the settlements of Berryville, Windsor, upper and lower Kanab, Shunesburg and Northup and many ranches in Kane County; and so also were the settlements of Panguitch and Fort Sanford in Iron County.

These timely movements undoubtedly saved many lives, for the hostility and strength of the savages left no doubt as to their determination on aggressive measures. Troops were accordingly mustered into service in the counties of Sanpete, Juab, and Utah.

GEN. R. T. BURTON AND COMMAND ORDERED TO SANPETE.

April 15th, 1867, General Daniel H. Wells called upon Major-General Robert T. Burton of Salt Lake County to raise three platoons of cavalry to march on the 22nd for Sanpete; this detachment numbering seventy-two men, under command of Captain Orson P. Miles reported to General Pace at Provo who had been appointed to succeed General Snow in command of the Sanpete district.

CAPT. WM. L. BINDER'S INFANTRY LEFT
S. L. CITY FOR SANPETE.
ADAM PAUL OF CAPT. MILES CAVALRY
COMPANY WOUNDED.

On the 22nd of April 1867, Captain William L. Binder left Salt Lake City with a small company of infantry and reported for duty to General Pace, whose headquarters had been established at Gunnison; General Pace's own district. Utah County had also sent a company of cavalry under Captain F. P. Whitmore and one of infantry to the front. With these reinforcements and the energetic preparations made by local troops it was hoped that the savages might be deterred from further depredations.

An engagement occurred in May 11, 1867 in which Adam Paul of Mile's Salt Lake cavalry was wounded.

ATTACK ON FOUNTAIN GREEN COWHERD
LOUIS LUND KILLED.

At Fountain Green, Sanpete County, it was customary for a guard of ten men to be with the cowherd, but in the morning of June 1st, 1867, only five were with it, and Mathew Caldwell, the man in charge of the guard, was detained in the settlement and getting his horse shod. Feed being plentiful, the herd only went a short distance from town to graze. Two of the herders were stationed a short distance east of the herd on a knoll where their horses were feeding just below. The other three herders were on the north. Wm. Adams, Jr., who happened to be in the edge of town saw ten persons riding fast from the east hills towards the herd. Thinking they were the ten herds-men he took no more notice of it until he heard shooting in the direction of the herd; then he was convinced that the men he had seen were Indians. Before the Indians reached the herd, they separated, six going east and the other four west of the herd. Jasper Robertson, Swen Anderson and Louis Lund who were north of the herd, had killed some rabbits and were cleaning them in a hollow by the water hollow ditch, and did not know anything about the presence of Indians until the savages rode to the brink of the hollow and shot Lund through the region of the heart. He immediately fell forward into the water, and the other two jumped up and ran. Jasper Robertson was shot through the thigh, while Anderson escaped unhurt. Albert Collard and Charles Jones, who were on the east of the herd, heard the shooting and ran toward the place where their horses were. The Indians tried to head them off, but the boys had the start and were not overtaken. W. H. Adams and Thomas Caldwell, hearing the shooting, thought it was the boys and Indians fighting, and they mounted their horses and went to the scene of action as speedily as they could. When they got about two miles from town they saw cattle which had been shot along the trail on which the Indians were driving the herd. They followed the herd to the pass that leads over into Water Hollow, and thinking it unsafe to follow farther they returned. William G. Caldwell, a boy was taking an old mare to the herd, seeing the Indians, turned and rode for town. Some of the Indians tried to head him off and shot at him several times, but he escaped unhurt and gave the report in town. As Adams and Caldwell were returning, after following the Indians, they saw two men, Noah T. Guyman and Charles Johnson, and on reaching them they were informed that Louis Lund had been killed somewhere on the Water Hollow Ditch, but they could not find him. But as Adams knew where the first shooting had been done, they soon located him and found him lying with his head in the ditch with the water running through his hair. He had also been shot in the center of the forehead at short range, his face being powder-burned. Adams and Caldwell carried the body out of the hollow and by this time others had arrived. Most horses are frightened at the smell of blood, and as Adams had a gentle horse and Parley Allred had a saddle on his horse, they took the saddle off and put it on Adams' gentle horse, placed the corpse in it in an upright position, and with Swen Anderson walking on one side and Adams on the other they held in it the saddle until they reached the edge of town, where they met Thomas Crowder with a wagon. They then placed the body in the wagon and took it to the fort, only about two hundred yards distant. Bro. Lund's body was taken to his mother's room; he was her only child.

As soon as possible a company of men followed the Indians who were driving away two hundred head of stock and horses belonging to the settlers. On reaching Thistle Valley they met Colonel John L. Ivie and his company of cavalry from Mount Pleasant and together they now followed the Indians and soon captured the cattle, but the Indians who had changed horses and were riding fresh horses belonging to the settlers hurried away, knowing that they were pursued. They rushed the horses into Spanish Fork Canyon and got away with forty head.

Col. Reddick N. Allred gives the following particulars of the Fountain Green tragedy.

Springtown, June 12th, 1867.

Editor Deseret News:—

In regard to the Indian raid at Fountain Green, some people may wonder why forty-five men, coming up with twenty-one Indians could not kill or capture them and recover the stock,--we were led to believe, from the report of the express riders and telegram from Moroni, that twelve Indians had gone with the stock, and that a war party was left behind fighting for two hours. On learning this, and that Major Bradley had sent assistance, I raised fourteen men from Springtown and followed Col. Ivie as fast as I could to Thistle Valley, to intercept the Indians. He (Col. Ivie) arrived in Thistle valley with twenty-three men from Mount Pleasant and Fairview, and saw the Indians about three miles distant, and near the canyon. Finding themselves hard pressed they killed and wounded some of the cattle, mounted fresh animals, driving only horses before them and reached the canyon before Col. Ivie came up. He took the precaution to flank the canyon, not knowing but that a heavy reserve was lying in wait. In a few moments he became satisfied that twelve Indians were about the whole number in the canyon, but supposed that the war party was still behind, and kept a rear guard to watch for them. That guard twice reported Indians in the rear, but they proved to be our re-inforcements. Col. Ivie pursued the Indians about three miles, into the mountains, but finding that their jaded horses were unable to compete with the fresh horses that the Indians had just mounted, they gave up the chase. I formed a junction with Maj. Guyman and twenty-three men from Fountain Green and Moroni, in the south end of Thistle Valley, and met Col. Ivie at the mouth of the canyon. After hearing his report I decided to return. The distance our men had to travel was from fifteen to thirty miles, which was done on the run, I believe that the officers and men generally did their best in trying to capture the raiders, but the want of vigilance on the part of the guards gave them the advantage; and the want of telegraph office in each settlement was all that prevented us from cutting them off. The distance rode from the point of attack till I met Col. Ivie was at least fifty miles.

Yours,

R. N. Allred.

MAJOR VANCE AND SGT. HOUTZ KILLED AT TWELVE MILE CREEK.

On the 2nd of June, 1867, Major John W. Vance (of Alpine, Utah County) Brigade Adjutant on General William B. Pace's staff, was returning with Captain Orson P. Miles, Sergeant Heber Houtz, and Nathan Tanner, Jr., of the Hiles Company from a military drill at Manti to headquarters at Gunnison, at dusk, while halting at Twelve Mile Creek to let their horses drink, they were fired on by ambushed Indians at close range; at the first shot Major Vance and his horse fell dead, and Sergeant Houtz with a groan also fell from his steed as the animal wheeled suddenly out of the creek. Believing their companions both dead, Captain Miles and young Tanner rode rapidly back to Manti, where a detachment under Lieutenant M. H. Davis of Salt Lake County was ordered to recover the bodies of the dead men.

Vance was found pierced with two bullets and lying where he fell within a few feet of the creek; Houtz had evidently recovered himself a moment after the first fire, for his body shot with two bullets and several arrows lay about five hundred yards from the scene of the ambush. The remains of the deceased were reverently conveyed to their respective homes, where obsequies were conducted over Major Vance on the 5th and Sergeant Houtz on the 6th of June, 1867. The services closed with military honors.

THE PARAGOONAH RANGE SWEPT BY INDIANS.

Indians raided Beaver and captured a herd of stock, June 14, 1867. The Paragoonah range was swept by Indians June 22, 1867. Major Silas S. Smith gave chase and succeeded in cutting the Indians off from the mountain passes; a maneuver which caused the thieves to leave their booty. At this raid an Indian named Albert Hanks, who had been raised by a brother Hanks at Parowan captured a Spaniard who had been captured by the Navajoes and kept as a prisoner for several years. He was trying to get away from the Indians when captured. He afterwards made a speech at Paragoonah, giving a detailed account of how he had been captured by the Indians. Among other things he said that they burned the bottom of his feet in order to cripple him, so he could not get away; he was kept as a servant or slave by the Navajoes, and he said that this was the first opportunity offered him to escape.

RAID ON THE STOCK AT LITTLE CREEK, BEAVER COUNTY.

At dusk on July 21, 1867, a descent was made upon the stock at Little Creek near Parowan, Iron County. The guards gave the alarm, the local cavalry was quickly in motion and headed off the Indians at the mouth of the canyon, charging them and turning back the stock. The savages re-formed and charged twice, but were finally repulsed. The fighting lasted nearly all night.

WM. J. ALLRED RECOVERS HIS HORSES, KILLS TWO INDIANS.

William Jackson Allred was the first Bishop of Circleville. When that town was vacated on the 28th of June 1866. He went to Parowan, Iron County, and later in the fall moved his family to Beaver. The next summer he worked a farm on shares at the Buckhorn Springs, south of Beaver, leaving his family at Beaver.

One morning (Nov. 10th, 1868) when he got up, he sent his little boy to look for his horses and as the boy was gone longer than he thought he should, he went to look for him. The boy who had found the tracks of the horses, could see that they had been taken by Indians, and showed his father the tracks. Allred then took with him his five-shot revolver and followed the trail of the thieves all day, going northeast through Cottenwood canyon. Having crossed Buckskin Valley into Hawkins Canyon, he discovered a smoke about a mile distant. He crawled carefully to the place where he saw the smoke and here the three thieves were located in a deep wash sitting by the fire. He stopped to reflect as to what was best to do and seeing one of the Indians with a gun laying by him Allred fired at him, and he fell over; the other two jumped up and ran. He fired at one of them killing him, the other got away. When Brother Allred went down in the hollow where he shot the first Indian he found that the Indian was not dead as he raised up and shot an arrow at him; it grazed his face and went up through his hat. Allred then shot the Indian in the head. He recovered his horses, and before leaving the place he dragged the dead Indians together, covered them with brush which he set on fire, and got back in the night.

SPRING CITY FIGHT, J. MEEKS AND A. JOHNSON KILLED.

An account given by Marinus Lund of Spring City, Utah. During the month of April a company of "Minute Men" was organized at Spring City, Sanpete County, Utah, for guarding, scouting and general service in protecting the settlers from the Indians; the company was composed of ten picked men, who were on duty all the time during the spring and summer of 1867. Everybody moved along quietly until the morning of August 13th, 1867, when about twenty men with teams left Spring City for the hayfield which was about six miles south-west of the town. Contrary to the usual custom, the scouting ahead of the cowherd was not done that morning. A company of Indians, who evidently had spent the previous night in the stone-quarry hills, about a half mile south of the hay road, saw the cow-herd coming over the hills north of the road. In their effort to reach the herd the Indians encountered the hay teams; the minute men were guarding the cow herd and were attracted by the reports of the guns fired by the Indians in their attack on the hay teams. William Scott, Sanford Allred and myself rode to the place where the firing was heard. On our way we saw Andrew Johnson, a driver of one of the hay teams, going north with an arrow in his back. He had been shot by an Indian while on his wagon. Sanford Allred, who was armed with a cap and ball pistol, went to Spring City, to report. William Scott left me and rode down west. I yelled and asked him to wait for me. I had nearly reached him when Mr. Scott said "Look behind you." I then discovered that several Indians were riding close behind me. I turned in my saddle and fired at them, when they rode away.

When I reached Scott, I asked him where he was going? He said that he was afraid his father-in-law, James Meeks had been killed. I then left Scott and rode north to the cow herd. On the way I met William Blain who had been shot through the ear by the Indians. Mr. Blain told me not to get scared. I showed him the nearest way to town and told him to go there as fast as he could. The Indians were then all south of us.

I then met Jack Allred and asked him where he was going. He said that he was going down to get his horse out of the band which the Indians had stolen. As he was crippled I told him that I would go with him and help him catch his horse. I suggested that the Indians might kill him; to which he replied that he did not care. We went east to a place where other minute men were stationed on top of a hill. At the foot of this hill two Indians rode by without seeing us; neither did we see them until they had passed. When we arrived at the top of the hill, I dismounted and tied my horse to a cedar tree; as I dismounted three Indians rode by. I shot at them three times. Captain John Hitchcock asked me if I was shot. I told him "no." He then said

that my horse was shot, if I wasn't, but my horse
was not hurt. Jack Allred said "You hit an Indian."
"I am not certain whether I did or not," was my
reply. Later we caught a mule which one of the
Indians that I shot at had been riding. This mule
had been stolen from Peter Oldroyd at Glenwood at
the fight in March, 1867. I then rode towards Spring
town and met members of the militia who were
coming to the rescue of the herd and hay teams. The
Indians had stolen twenty-eight head of horses and
started to the mountains with them. We followed
the Indians up the trail south of Bill Allred's canyon and the militia had a small engagement with
them on the mountain-side. The Indians were followed to the top of Horseshoe Mountain, and on
the way up my horse gave out. Thomas Coates,
and a tame Indian from Moroni, and I followed to
the top of the Horseshoe. When we arrived there
we discovered that all the militia-men had returned to Springtown and we did not see any Indians
there. Then we returned to Springtown where we arrived about nine o'clock at night. Here we learned
that William Scott's father-in-law, James Meeks
had been killed. and also that Andrew Johansen who
had been wounded, died that night.

RAID ON SPRING CITY
By H. S. Ivie

"About nine o'clock as reported on the morning of the Spring City fight I was riding down to
the hayfield with Sidney H. and James R. Allred,
when about half way between the stone-quarry and
the meadows we heard some shooting. Christian

J. Larsen, who had a pair of gray horses (pretty good runners) was not far behind us. About eight Indians on horses came from towards Pigeon Hollow towards him. Larsen who had a small boy with him, whirled his team around and went back as fast as he could go, while the Indans rode along beside the wagon, shooting at him and the boy. They shot several holes through his clothes, and also shot his gunstock in two, but he was not hurt. The main lot of Indians had been hidden in the cedars above the stone-quarry, south of the road. When we saw what was up, we turned and drove back till our horses got out of wind. The Allreds unhitched the horses and went to where the figh hitched the horses and went to where the fighting was going on. Two men from Ephraim came along and one of them took me on his horse over the hill and let me down, when Con Rowe, who was coming out, took me into town on his horse. When we got to the foot of the stone-quarry hill, we saw James Meeks lying by the road dead; he had been shot through the right breast and under one eye; his pants and hat had been taken; his pipe lay by his side and his ox team was out in the brush a short distance from the road.''

Colonel Reddick N. Allred in his journal, says: ''I went to Ephraim to meet General Pace and General Robert T. Burton and to hold inspection only taking J. T. S. Allred. Sr. and daughter with me. I knew not that a band of Indians were lying in wait in the cedars to take the herd as soon as it was driven out. They made a break on the herd, killed James Meeks wounded Andrew Johansen and wounded Wm. Blain slightly. When we arrived at Ephraim we received a telegram from Mount Pleasant giving the news of the raid, and we joined Captain Louis Larsen's Minute men who later joined men from Springtown and Mount Pleasant under Colonel Ivie. But the Indians had made good their escape into the mountains, taking only the horses from the herd. We pursued them to the top of the Horse shoe Mountain after exchanging a few shots with them.

The "Deseret News" of August 28, 1867, published an account of an interview which Superintendent Head of Indian affairs, who had just returned from the Uintah Reservation where he had met and had a talk with the notorious chief, Black Hawk, who came there with his family, unattended by his braves. Black Hawk said he had 28 lodges under his sole control, and that he was assisted by three Elk Mountain chiefs who each had ten or twelve lodges with him. These Indians were scattered all along the valleys from the north of Sanpete county to the southern settlements, watching opportunities to make raids. Nevertheless he expressed a personal desire for peace and said that inasmuch as the others looked to him as head chief, he thought he could influence them to bury the hatchet and perhaps consent to a conference with Superintendent Head in the near future. He declared he had made a covenant when he commenced to fight that he would not have his hair cut, and that he had found much fault with Tabby and Kanosh, who had had theirs cut like the white men. Now that he was willing to make peace, however, he expresses a desire that the Superintendent shear his locks for him, which Colonel Head very kindly did.

Brief obituary notices were published in this week's issue of James Meeks and Andrew Johansen, who had been killed, as reported in this department last week, by Indians at the Springtown herd grounds. Mr. Meeks was 69 years of age, a native of England, and came from that country to Utah in 1853; he was one of the earliest settlers in Springtown. Mr. Johansen was 30 years of age, a native of Sweden, and had only arrived in Utah the previous year.

JOHN HAY KILLED NEAR WARM CREEK WHILE ON GUARD.

Communication from General Wm. B. Pace to Deseret News Sept. 5th, 1867.—Last evening about 11 o'clock private John Hay of Captain Binders company was shot dead by Indians, while tending the fire at the lime kiln near Warm Creek. The Indians crawled up within twenty feet and fired one gun only, then fled. It appears the guard had changed their position for some reason, leaving this avenue open. Detachments from Manti and this place were immediately placed upon the trials to interecept them without success. A reconnoitering party since daylight report signs of only three Indians on foot, who, from the course and length of steps must have made twelve mile canyon in less than an hour from the time of committing the murder, Reconnoisances are out in search of their rendezvous.

Yours, Wm. B. Pace.

On Sept. 4th near Warm Creek (Fayette) Sanpete County, where three of Captain Binder's Salt
Lake infantry were on picket duty, Indians stole
up in the darkness, and by the light of the camp-
fire were able to single out John Hay, upon whom
they fired with fatal effect. His comrades gave the
alarm to eight other men stationed near by, and
taking the dead man with them, the detachment made
good their retreat to the settlement. Soon afterwards the Indians withdrew for the winter, and the
militia were able to devote the few remaining weeks
of autumn to the pursuit of peace. During this summer and autumn a stone fort was projected and
partly built at Gunnison for protection against the
savages. The remains of this fort, which was never
completed still remain as a reminder of times past.

From Whitney's History of Utah, Vol. 2, page
208-9-10.

GEN. WELLS ISSUED ORDERS FOR A
GENERAL MUSTER.

Sept. 17, 1867. Lieutenant-General Wells issued
orders for a general muster of forces in the various
military districts of the Territory, which orders
were generally observed. At this time Adjutant-
General Clawson was absent in the east, and the
duties of his office were performed by Assistant
Adjutant General Thomas W. Ellerbeck; Colonel
John R. Winder, who had acted as General Well's
Adjutant in Sanpete in 1866, assisted in drawing up
a report of operations of the militia, during the
three years campaign just described, which was presented by General Clawson to the Governor, and by

him to the legislature in January 1868. It is dated December 31st, 1867. **From this document** it appears that the militia of the Territory consisted of one Lieutenant-General, with a staff of eighteen officers; thirteen topographical engineers, six officers of the ordnance department, two Major-Generals, with a staff of fourteen officers. Nine Brigadier-Generals, with fifty officers in the staff, twenty-five lieutenant-colonels with eighty five officers in the regimental staff, 112 majors with 113 of battalion staff, 236 captains, 228 first lieutenants. 906 second lieutenants, 896 sergeants, 322 musicians, and 82 teamsters, making a total of 12,024. The cavalry consisted of 2,525. The artillery 179, and the infantry of 9,207, the remainder being the general officers and staff, and a topographical and ordnance department. The arms and equipment of this body were reported as several pieces of artillery, 2,838 horses, 2,476 saddles, 4,926 revolvers, 252 swords, 6,960 rifles, 1,719 muskets and shotguns 25 bayonets, 431,375 rounds of ammunition, 77 trumpets, 96 fifes and 107 drums.

General Clawson in his report dated February 9th, 1869, to the Department at Washington, tersely tells the story of these military operations and supplies vouchers, showing the expense of the Indian War during the three years to be $1,121,037.38, not including charges for vast amount of service in the home guard, which would have materially increased the total. The report bears Governor Durkee's official endorsements and quotes from the reports and communications of Colonels Irish and Heath to the Commissioner of Indian Affairs.

Accompanying it also was a memorial to Congress adopted by the Legislature in February 1868 and approved by the Governor, asking for the payment of the expenses. The document pointed out that Colonel Irish had applied to General Connor for military aid in putting down the renegades, and that Colonel Head, had addressed himself to the same effect to Colonel Potter and that in each case the request had been refused whereupon it became necessary to call upon the militia: that notwithstanding their ready response and their energy and courage, six flourishing settlements in Sevier and Piute Countes, four settlements in Sanpete, fifteen settlements in Iron, Kane and Washington Counties and two or three in Wasatch County had been abandoned, with an almost total loss of stock and improvements; that about seventy-five lives were lost, and that in furnishing its own soldiers, arms, transportation, horses and saddles the Territory had borne a heavy burden, wherefore an appropriation of $1,500.000 or so much thereof as might be necessary to cover the expenses was respectfully asked. The petition was never granted and the just debt of the General Government to the then struggling Territory remains unpaid to this day.

RAID ON BEAVER, 200 HEAD OF STOCK STOLEN.

September 18th Indians raided Beaver and stole two hundred head of stock.

CHAPTER III.

GIRL STOLEN AT WELLSVILLE, NEVER RECOVERED.

On April 1st, 1868, a beautiful little daughter of a Mr. Thurston who lived about three miles from Wellsville, Cache County, was captured by some of Pocatello's band of Indians, and in spite of every exertion she was never recovered. She was about three years of age, idolized by her parents, and her loss was to them a dreadful blow; far worse indeed than her death would have been, she was never heard from with certainty again, except that she was dead.

For detailed account of a sad story of this story of this stolen child the reader is referred to the "Contributor" Vol. 12; Page 75. 1868 Files Deseret News, April 22nd, Vol. 17.

BATTLE AT ROCKY FORD, JUSTESEN AND WILSON KILLED.

In the spring of 1868 it was believed that Indian hostilities were over and that it was safe for the people to return to the deserted homes on the Sevier.

A company was formed under the leadership of Frederick Olsen of Spring City, Sanpete County. Their intention was to resettle Monroe. There were twenty-three persons in the company with twelve

teams, namely, Frederick Olsen and son Ole, Richard
Davis, Benjamin Davis, David Davis (a boy), Axel
Einersen, John Knighton, C. C. Brown, John Fern
and his brother (a small boy), Walter Jones, Lars
Alexander Justesen and his step son (Simon T.
Beck), Adolph Tomson, Ira Sutton, J. W. Bohman,
Andrew Rasmussen, Rasmus Sorensen, and Louis
Barney. When at Cedar Ridge, (now within the
limits of the present Vermillion), near the Rocky
Ford, April 5, 1868, some thirty Indians, who had
just previously attacked George and Charles Wilson from Scipio, Millard County, a short distance
north of the Rocky Ford. These men were on their
way to Monroe after some mill irons. Charles Wilson was killed by. the Indians who cut the tugs
of the harness, taking the horses and supplies.

George Wilson escaped by running to the
river and hiding in a hole in the bank till night,
when he made his escape back to Scipio.

Some of Olsen's company had ox teams and
traveled slow. As they came along the upper road
the Indians came in behind them and when those
with horse teams saw the Indians, they stopped to
let the ox teams catch up. The savages circled out
around into the cedars on the west of the company
and got a little way ahead. The people seeing that
the savages meant mischief, corralled their wagons
as speedily as possible placing the back ends of
the wagons in such a position that each wagon would
shield the team on the next wagon to it from the
fire of the Indians.

As soon as the Indians were prepared, some
behind cedars and rocks and others in a ravine,

they opened fire on the company. A bullet from an Indian's gun struck a wagon tire; it glanced and struck Alexander Justesen, killing him instantly. Andrew Rasmussen turned his oxen loose with the yoke on; they wandered away and were never recovered. While some of the best marksmen did the shooting, others were loading guns, and still others were digging rifle pits, (holes in the ground), about three feet deep, and from six to twelve feet across. Th fight was kept up for an hour or more. In the meantime volunteers were asked for to go back to Gunnison for help; Axel Einersen and Adolph Tomson offered their services which were accepted.

The Indians had pulled off and gone towards the ford, and were seen holding a council. · When the expressmen started they were seen by the Indians who tried to head them off. Einersen rode a pretty good horse, and when he saw the Indians coming, he headed away from them towards the hills. The Indians, seeing that they could not overtake him, went after Tomson who was following the road. They gained on him and fired several shots; a bullet passed through his thigh, cuttting an artery and lodged in the saddle. He was also hit in the back with an arrow. Seeing that he could not get away from them, the impression came to him that if he would turn back and rush at the Indians, it would save his life. Consequently he turned, and with gun in hand rushed on them. The Indians opened ranks, seemingly surprised and let him pass, but then they gave chase. The men is camp seeing what was going on ran out, firing at the Indians, and one of them fell off his horse. The Indians then turned and went away, followed by the riderless horse; they returned in the night and carried away the fallen Indian. On his arrival in camp Tomson was nearly exhausted from the loss of blood; but the men removed the arrow and dressed the wounds as best they could; he was badly hurt, and it took a long time for him to recover. During the fight the White Horse Chief was constantly riding around, directing the movements of the warriors. Walter Barney was hit on the shin, the bullet going through his pants and boot, but did not cut his under garments. The men kept up a guard all night. The four boys in the company dug a trench about three feet wide three feet deep and covered it with a door which they took out of one of the wagons and placed some rocks on it, and laid there two deep on top of each other.

The next morning Einersen came with a posse of men to help the company back to Gunnison. In the meantime the Indians had left. All went back with the relief sent with Einersen. No further attempt was made to resettle the Sevier country until 1871.

The following additional information was written by Joshua W. Sylvester:

In the spring of 1868 I accompanied some Gunnison boys to Marysvale to do some prospecting, gold having been discovered there. There were six of us altogether, and as we were returning home we camped one night in the abandoned town of Monroe. Next morning we resumed our journey, and when we got to the Rocky Ford, about twenty miles distant from Monroe, we saw a lone horse on the opposite side of the river. We also discovered

fresh pony and cattle tracks, and upon crossing the
river we saw a wagon, and decided to stop there
for dinner. But when we reached the wagon we found
that the tugs had been cut off the single-trees, and
there were moccasin tracks around the wagon. Con-
cluding in a hurry that we did not want dinner, we
drove on, wondering what had happened. Upon reach
ing the road that led to Scipio we found a board laid
across the road upon which was written "we have
taken the dead man from Scipio to Gunnison." As we
drove along the west side of the river, the Gunnison
people could see our dust for quite a long distance,
and they imagined that they could see Indians following us; and as a squad of men had just arrived
from Manti, and were already mounted, they pushed
on to meet us, though the sun had gone down and
it was getting dusk . As they were coming up one
side of a slope we came up on the other, and when
we reached the top and saw their dust, we thought
of nothing but Indians, consequently we all reached
for our guns and pistols, but right then I took command, telling the boys not to fire a shot till I told
them to, and if the Indians made a move to surround
us we would let them have a shot and I would run
the team to the river bank where we could get breast-
works. The boys kept eyeing the squad and finally
I said that it might not be Indians, and then they
could see at a glance that it was not. There was a
big excitement at Gunnison, for they knew we were
coming. When we reached home we learned that
a company of men who were on their way to Monroe to put in crops had been attacked by Indians;
they had corralled their wagons, had entrenched

themselves and had stood off the Indians until Axel Einersen mounted on a smarter horse than the Indians had, broke through the lines to take the news to Gunnison. One man was killed in the affair.

RAID ON SCIPIO, FIFTEEN HEAD OF HORSES STOLEN.

Of other Indian raids which took place in 1868, we may mention that on May 7th, four Indians made a raid on Scipio, Millard County, and drove off fifteen head of horses.

On July 5th, Seth Childs was accidently shot and wounded near Gunnison, Sanpete County, by an Indian who proved to be friendly.

INDIANS STOP COL. IVIE IN SALT CREEK CANYON.
Copied from Deseret News, July 10th.

We met Brother Henry N. Larter of Moroni, Sanpete County, today, who arrived in town yesterday, in company with Col. John L. Ivie and the latter's family. He reports that when they were about four miles below the divide above Salt Creek Canyon, six Utes, among whom was Tabiona, rode up to them and demanded to know of Col. Ivie whether he was "Jim Ivie," the colonel's brother. On being answered in the negative they passed on. In a short time, however, they returned, rode in front of the wagon, stopped it, and reiterated the question. One of the Indians then said that it was not "Jim Ivie," but his brother. At this time, Tabiona had his hand on his arrows, and another Indian had his

rifle ready for use. The Indians, however, passed
along and after going a short distance they stopped
and held a council. The team was made to travel
at a lively pace. When the Indians saw this two
of them started after it, coming towards the wagon
about three hundred yards, but seeing their companions did not follow they stopped and went back.
One Indian was so drunk he could scarcely sit on
his horse, and the others had been drinking, but they
knew what they were doing. James Oscar Ivie, son
of Colonel Ivie, one of the children in the wagon
said, Lyman R. Peters was the driver. Mrs. Ivie
and her children were very much frightesed; the
mother covered the smaller children with the bedding
in the wagon. Colonel Ivie said afterwards that if
the Indians had overtaken them the second time, he
intended to jump out of the wagon and let it go
on and take his chances with them. He was well
armed.

INDIAN GRATITUDE.

*The following is an incident as related by Col.
John L. Ivie, to his son James O. Ivie:*

During the Indian troubles in the 60's—the
Indians had stolen some cattle, and driven them up
North Creek Canyon, between Fairview and Mount
Pleasant. Father John L. Ivie and his company of
minute men were in pursuit, and going up the mountain they gathered up several head of cattle which
had been left along the trail, on account of not
keeping up with the herd. And up among the timber was discovered a lone Indian covered up with
leaves; he was sick, and not able to travel with

the rest. Some of the boys wanted to kill him, but father said "no, we will not shed blood, unless it is necessary," so they left him and went in pursuit of the Indians and stock till nearly night, when it was decided to give up the chase and return home, taking back what stock they had.

On their return they came across the sick Indian sitting up against a tree smoking a pipe. The men still wanted to kill him, but father wouldn't let them. Some time after that, Father and two other men were standing guard over some stock in the north fort of Mount Pleasant; they would frequently meet and report to each other during the night, and had got together at the north side of the fort, when they heard and saw the cattle getting up from their bed-ground and moving away from what they thought might be Indians crawling among them. The cattle kept getting up nearer and nearer to where the three men stood, when father spoke to the others and said, "that they must be close by." After that they saw the cattle moving as if something among them was going away from them. When morning came nothing had been molested.

In the beginning of the 70's—after peace had been restored, an Indian and his family came to our house and spent a day or two. He told father of the occurrence at the fort, explaining that he and four other Indians were there on that occasion and had their guns lying across a cow ready to shoot the three men, when they heard father speak and say, "They must be close by." He said he knew father's voice and would not let the others shoot as father

had saved his life on the mountain when he was
sick. In appreciation he had now saved father's
life.

James O. Ivie.

SKIRMISH AT EPHRAIM, BATTLE AT ROCK LAKE.

July 11th, the Ephraim horse-herd was driven
to feed about two miles southeast of town, on the
south side of Willow Creek Wash; they were in
care of James P. Christensen, Sr., John Tompson
and Sam Beal, an Indian who lived with the settlers. N. O. Anderson and Andrew Overdale passed
the horse-herd and went to the mouth of Willow
Creek Canyon after wood; they heard some shouting
as if someone was driving cattle. They thought
it might be men with ox-teams after wood, but it
proved to be Indians driving animals which they
had gathered up in the morning before the horse-
herd came out. Anderson and Overdale began getting their loads of wood, when they heard some
talking and thought it was a scouting party, but it
proved to be Indians who came out into a clearing
and approched to within thirty yards of them. The
men being behind some trees were not seen by the
Indians who were making for the horse-herd. The
two men ran onto a hill south of the cedars, about a
half mile from the herd, and saw the Indians and
the three herds-men in battle for possession of the
horses. The fight lasted about fifteen minutes, when
the herders succeeded in getting most of the horses
started for town. The Indians, however, cut out
a few which they succeeded in getting into the hills

and drove off. Thompson and Beal drove the
horses, while L. P. Christensen rode in ahead and
gave the alarm. Soon two squads of men were on
the tracks of the Indians. One posse of about thirty
men went by way of Willow Creek Canyon, the
others went up Ephraim canyon which was a more
direct route to head off the Indians. This posse
consisted of Tory Thursten (Captain), P. C. Petersen, C. A. Larsen, Henry Oviett, Andrew O. Anderson, L. C. Larsen, Chris. Thompson (Balla), Chris.
Nielsen, George P. Jenson, John Thompson and
Sam. Beal, eleven in all. When they reached the
top of a high ridge between Willow Creek and
Manti Canyons, Indians came out and fired on them,
Thinking they could stop them or scare them back,
they did not check up, but continued on about two
miles farther to a small lake on the top of the mountain known as Rock Lake. Here they were fired
upon by the Indians from ambush at close range.
Three horses were wounded and one fell dead under its rider (P. C. Petersen.) The horse fell on
his leg and the dead horse served as breast-works
and a rest to shoot from. P. C. Peterson who
gives this information says that the battle lasted
about an hour. The Indians were at a disadvantage,
the brush that they were hidden in was thin and our
men could see them and disabled some of them, which
caused them to retreat and follow those who were
driving off some horses and cattle. Further pursuit was considered unwise owing to lack of horses
and being but eleven in number.

From Whitney's History of Utah.

PAH-VANT-SQUAW
and pappoose at Bear Dance 1914

CHICKENY' SHOOTEM'
or OLD TOM—more than 100 snows

CHIEF ANDREW HUN-COP, OF KANOSH
Successor to Chief Kanosh at steering wheel. Chief Walker Ammon of
Koosharem, Piute County, at his side, two squaws in back

EIGHTH ANNUAL ENCAMPMENT UTAH INDIAN WAR VETERANS
Provo Lake Resort, August 14, 1908

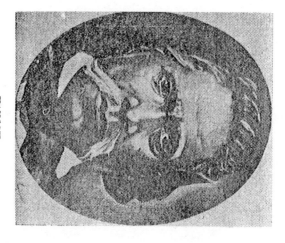

KANOSH
Chief of the Pauvante Indians in Millard County, with whom a treaty of peace ending the Walker War was made in May 1854.

WASHAKIE
Chief of the Shoshone Indians in Northern Utah, a peaceful Indian and a great friend of the pioneers.

A NATIVE SON OF UTAH

COL. HEATH'S TREATY WITH INDIANS
IN STRAWBERRY VALLEY.

On the 19th of August, 1868 the energetic Superintendent of Indian affairs, Colonel Head, succeeded
in negotiatng a treaty with the sub-chieftains of
Black Hawk's band and their still recalcitrant followers. Major Dimick B. Huntington was interpreter on the occasion, and Black Hawk himself who
had kept his pledge given a year before, lent
his personal influence. The young warriors were
loth to bury the tomahawk and boasted not a little
of their prowess and deeds of blood; one of them
especially, a handsome, feminine-looking stripling
named Aug-a-vor-un. After the war, Shenanagon
confessing his participation in killing Major Vance
and Sergeant Houtz and in other more daring and
less dishonorable engagements. Of the fellows
courage there could be no doubt. He had been wont
to ride a white horse, and as his reckless bravery
always led him to the front, where his example
served as a command to his associates, he was frequently the mark of military sharp-shooters, and
once when he fell wounded the cry went up that
Black Hawk himself had been killed. His defiant
eloquence was reinforced at this meeting by that of
other hot-heads, but it was patiently met and at
length entirely overcome by persuasion and threats
of the peace party. The treaty was signed and it
is believed was faithfully observed, although peace
was not completely restored until after the summer
of 1869.

10

NAVAJOES RAID HARRISBURG,
SOME STOCK STOLEN.

The earliest signs of trouble during the year came from the southwest where the turbulent Navajoes were the predominating tribe. A band of them invaded southern Utah in the latter part of February and drove off the herds from Washington and Harrisburg. A party of militia started in pursuit, recovered some of the stock and drove the thieves beyond the Colorado.

FRANKLIN BENJAMIN WOOLLEY
KILLED NEAR FORT MOHAVE.

March 21st, Franklin B. Woolley of St. George, son of Bishop Edwin D. Woolley was killed near the Mohave River, California; he had been on a business trip to San Bernadino, California, and was returning with goods for the St. George store and had been separated from the main body of his freight train and had gone to look for his horses that had strayed from the camp the night previous. They had gone back to the spring where the company nooned they day before, when it is supposed he was surrounded by a party of about fifteen Indians. He dismounted from his mule to parley with them, but finding that no compromise could turn them from their murderous purpose, he sought to make his escape. He fell pierced with arrows after running a few rods. His slayers stripped off his clothes and dragged his body to a place of concealment where it was not found until some days later by searching

parties. The remains were brought home for interment by the brother of the deceased, E. D. Woolley,
Jr., now president of Kanab Stake.

RAID ON KANE COUNTY, THREE FRIENDLY INDIANS KILLED.

May 1st. Raid on Kane County, three friendly
Indians were killed and the marauders drove off
eighteen head of horses.

RAID ON KANARRA, MANY HORSES STOLEN, SOME RECOVERED.

Joshua W. Sylvester.

I will now relate the next trip we made after
Indians:

We had moved from Gunnison to Kanarra; after
living there a couple of years, on October 31st,
1869, a very dark night, the Navajoes made a raid
on the place, and when I got up I found my fences
torn down and some horses gone. After breakfast
I rode to town, about a mile distant and found the
boys saddling the few horses they could get hold
of, for most of their stables were empty. A man
from Dixie had been stopping at the place and before going to bed he had gone out to see after his
mules in the corral. Finding the bars down he
put them up, thinking it would be best to hobble his
mules; he got the iron hobbles and put on them. Next
morning he found them shot with arrows; that with
the horses being gone gave the situation away; we
knew then that Indians had been on the ground.
We went after them, and owing to a light fall of
snow we could consequently track them easily. We

292 INDIAN DEPREDATIONS

pushed on until dark and discovered the Indians
making camp. They had just started a fire. We
crawled on, and just as we were ready to fire they
heard us, jumped up and ran, but we fired on them.
We recovered our horses, which they had taken, and
took their outfit. When we returned home we learned that a raid had been made that same night all
along the line for about forty miles. A man by the
name of Nebeker who was camping just outside of
Kanarra lost all his mules. Had we known they
were gone, we could have headed them off. We
afterwards learned that the Indians had been prowling around for a week or two gathering horses and
getting ready to make a general break in one night.
They had sat on the hill watching the men put
their horses in their stables, and where they could
find the door in the dark they took the horses.
They went to my stable and I suppose they could
not find the door. I had driven four cows and an
ox to a nice spot of grass near a spring on the
mountain. The Indians had camped there, killed the
animals and dried the meat. They drove stock from
all those points but the thefts were not discovered
until after they had gone. Had it not been that
they got angry and shot the mules because they
could not get the hobbles off, their success would
have been complete. That was the way it was all
the time. The Indians could sit on the mountain-
side and see where our stock were and what we were
doing and then making a dash, they would kill people who were at work in the fields, or traveling on
the roads, rush their stock into the mountains, leaving some to drive them, while others fell back and

waited in ambush on the trail for those who pursued. We hardly ever met them when they did not
have the advantage; therefore, whenever we were
out in the mountains, our wives, mothers and sisters
anxiously awaited to hear from us, and they were
actually the greatest sufferers. If they saw anyone riding fast into town, they all rushed to the
meeting house to hear the news. But while they
had women's fears they had soldiers' hearts; they
would get provisions ready for us out of their scanty
supplies,and often mould bullets for us, while we
were getting other things ready; but they never said
"Don't go."

NIELS HEIZELT KILLED AT
TWELVE MILE CREEK.

It has been stated that the Black Hawk Indian
trouble of 1866-67 ended all organized warfare on
the part of the aborigines in Utah. The spring of
1872, however, witnessed some desultory depredations by the savages, which threatened at one time
a general outbreak. The primal cause of disaffec-
tion among them was the treatment received at the
hands of some dishonest government agents and
acts of lawlessness committed by renegade white
men. These troubles did not originate in Utah, but
in the northern territories, whence they spread to
this region. During the previous autumn hostilities
in Southern Utah and Arizona had been barely
averted by the good offices of Jacob Hamblin, the
well known Indian interpreter, who at Fort Defiance,
on November 2nd, 1871, concluded a treaty of peace
on behalf of the people of this territory with the

principal chiefs of the Navajoes. When winter was
over the scenes of trouble was shifted farther north;
and while the majority of the savages were friendly
to the settlers, a portion of them seemed bent on
mischief. This was partly an effect of the warlike feeling exhibited at that time by hostile tribes
generally throughout the country.

Under these circumstances, Special Indian
Agent, G. W. Dodge, early in 1872, sought to redress
the grievances complained of by the Indians and
distributed large quantities of flour, beef, and other
supplies among them. The unruly ones, however, became more insolent with the efforts to pacify them,
and levied a burdensome tax upon the settlements
in central Utah by their persistent begging and
stealing. On the 16th of June in a raid by a band
of Shiberetch Indians upon Twelve Mile Creek, Sanpete County, Niels C. Heiselt, Jr., of Pleasant Grove
Utah County, was killed. The next two months witnessed a series of depredations in which several
white men were shot and a large number of stock
driven off. From friendly Indians it was learned
that the hostiles were mostly members of unorganiz-
ed bands such as the Capotas, Magoots and Elk
Mountain Utes.

During the period when the major portion of
these outrages were committed, several hundred Indians were paying friendly visits to the settlements in Sanpete, Sevier, Juab and Utah counties.
As some of them moved about in small companies,
there was difficulty in distinguishing which of the
roving bands were hostile. Colonel Dodge endeavored to simplify the situation by having all peace-

able red men return to the reservation, but these
could not be made to understand fully why they
should be restrained because of the actions of hostiles not of their tribes. Therefore, though they
consented to the measure at a council at Nephi on
July 5th and again at Fountain Green on the 14th,
and 16th of that month, they failed to fulfill their
agreement, thus complicating matters.

The aspect of affairs gradually became more
serious. Even Indians formerly disposed to be
friendly were implicated.

INDIAN OUTRAGES AT MANTI,
SANPETE COUNTY.

Under date of August 9th, 1872, James C.
Brown writes from Manti, Sanpete County, Utah,
to the "Deseret News":

The Indians are still around, and are meaner
than ever. They have been stealing horses every
night during the week from the range and also
from the brethern's stables. They took one of
mine a few weeks ago. I got him back, however,
by paying for him. They took the other this week.
They have tried for several nights past to steal from
the stable of Mayor Tuttle a fine span of bays, but,
as yet they have not been successful. They tried
it last night and on not getting them they crossed the
street to the stable of A. C. Van Buren and took
one of his. A party of them went down to the range
last evening and myself and three others who were
on our way home from hunting horses saw them just
about dark. We felt certain they wanted to steal
a band of horses that was close by, we went to work

and gathered the animals together and took them to town. I expect they were disappointed at losing the band, for they wantonly shot a mule with an arrow, mortally wounding it. They also went a little farther and shot down a steer and, with their knives cut it all to pieces. They manifest even a meaner spirit than they did before the last war. They went into a brothers the other day when there were no one at home but the latter's wife and because she did not give them bread, when they asked it, they struck her in the face. Several instances have occurred when they threatened women with violence for not complying with their demands. The people are fairly exasperated, but do not want to take any steps that would tend to start an Indian war, if it can be avoided. I am informed that a party of Indians went to a stable in Ephraim a few nights ago, and because they could not get the horses out of the stable, crawled in by a small opening and cut the animals in a horrible manner.

CHIEF TABBY SENDS WORD HE CAN NO LONGER CONTROL HIS INDIANS.

On the 12th of August General D. H. Wells received the following message from Colonel R. N. Allred of Spring City: "Tabby sends word to all the Bishops, that he can control his men no longer." He was in Spanish Fork Canyon yesterday. I with a detachment brought the herd from Thistle Valley yesterday, having started as soon as I got word of the raid at Fairview. The wounded boy Stewart is dead."

Next day R. L. Johnson of Fountain Green, telegraphed to Indian Agent Dodge for troops to defend the people against some of the bands of savages who had become incensed on account of obedience to Dodge's orders not to feed them as he would furnish them plenty on the reservations.

COL. IVIE SENDS DISPATCH TO GEN. WELLS.

Colonel John L. Ivie of Mount Pleasant sent the following dispatch:

Mount Pleasant, Aug. 17, 1872,

Gov. Geo. L. Woods, care of Daniel H. Wells—
Indian depredations here last night. Shall I call out the militia to defend the place for services generally in this county? The Indians attacked the telegraph operator about 11 o'clock last night in front of the office and, we fear, fatally wounded him.

John L. Ivie, Colonel of Militia

Also the following was sent:

ASSAULT UPON JEREMIAH D. PAGE AT MOUNT PLEASANT.

Mount Pleasant, Aug. 17th.—Gen. D. H. Wells—
As the telegraph operator, Jeremiah D. Page, was leaving the office last night about 11 o'clock, and when near the gate by the office, an Indian pounced upon his back and struck him three blows, with a tomahawk, upon the head, inflicting severe wounds, one penetrating through the skull. He was in a critical condition all night, but seems a little

better this morning. There were five Indians seen in town about the same time that the attack was made upon Mr. Page. Col. J. L. Ivie detailed a scouting party from the home guard this morning, and they were scouting the base of the east mountain. One scout reports no sign of Indians in that direction.

J. S. Wing.

INFORMATION ON ASSAULT, BY
BISHOP SEELY.

Under date of Aug. 20, 1872, Bishop Wm. Seely, of Mt. Pleasant writes to the Deseret News the following:

On Saturday evening suspicion rested on Richard Smyth as being the person who assailed our operator on the 16th. He was arrested, but on account of unavoidable circumstances, was held over until today at ten o'clock. An investigation took place, and when the prisoner was asked if he were guilty, or not guilty, he pleaded guilty of committing the horrible deed, after which he was committed to a higher court. The operator said that he was telegraphing a message to the operators of the county, and while so doing observed Smyth go into an adjoining room, and return and place himself behind him. He stood for about a half an hour, and as quick as the operator had finished the message and closed the key he was struck down and knew no more until he found himself lying on a lounge in the above named adjoining room with his head all mangled and his clothing all soaked in blood, and

Richard Smyth pacing to and fro with a hatchet in his hand. The latter continued to walk back and forth along side of the lounge, making remarks about the deed he had done. After making a pause for some duration, he said, Jeremiah, hold up your hands, I cannot spare your life any longer, your head is all chopped into pieces and your brains are running out. I have murdered you. The operator says he resolved in his mind, weak as he was, if a chance offered itself, to spring upon Smyth, take the hatchet and kill him, but there was no chance, so he thought again the best way was to direct his mind upon the best means of liberating himself and cover up the deed; so from that Smyth made him swear not to reveal what had happened for six months, and still kept him there for about five hours; without any assistance, soaked in his blood and perishing with cold. He was so weak and frightened that he dared not reveal anything after he got among his friends until Smyth had confessed he did the deed, when the operator made the above statement.

Signed W. S. Seely.

No justifiable reason for the assault on Page by Smyth can be ascertained, Smyth, it appears, was subject to fits of insanity, and was probably laboring partially under an attack of insanity, when he committed the assault.

The following is added by the historian Peter Gottfredson:

"The office in which Jeremiah Page was assailed by Richard Smyth was under the supervision of Anthon H. Lund. Besides the telegraph office Bro-

ther Lund also kept a daguerrotype picture gallery
in an adjoining room. It was quite customary for
young people to meet and visit there. Brother
Page was well thought of and a favorite with the
young people, but not so much with Smyth, and it
was the general supposition that Smyth was jealous
of Page and that this had much to do with the act.
I was a resident of Mount Pleasant at that time
and well acquainted with all parties concerned. Page
was learning telegraphy under Brother Lund and
was night operator.''

On the morning of August 17th, 1872, General
Morrow left Camp Douglas with a body of troops to
take the field against the hostiles by co-operation of
leading men in the settlements and friendly Indians,
the General secured a council with several chiefs,
and after a long pow-pow held in front of the residence of Interpreter L. S. Woods at Springville,
made a treaty which was signed by Chiefs Tabby,
Douglass, Joe, To-kawanah, Antero, Wandrodes,
Parrades and Tom. Colonel Dodge, A. O. Smoot,
Colonel L. John Nuttall, Bishop William Bringhurst,
General A. K. Thurber and General William B.
Pace and other citizens were present. The treaty
provided that the Indians should return at once
to the Reservations. General Morrow was to apply
to President Grant for permission for several chiefs
to visit and lay before him their grievances, or if
this was not agreeable, to ask that an investigation
commission be sent out by the government.

General Wells had an interview with Gen. Ord
and Governor Woods in relation to Indian affairs,
at which the former proffered all the men and sup-

plies necessary in any emergency. Gen. Ord and the Governor, thought, however, that there were sufficient troops available without making it necessary to call on citizens who were not in the immediate employ of the government. A body of troops left this morning for Sanpete and efforts were being made, which we presume were successful to obtain transportation for them from the Utah Southern track to the scene of their future operations. Generale Morrow will accompany the troops in person and will take an active part in endeavoring to bring about a pacific solution of the grave difficulty, and thus, if possible, avert, the dreaded calamity of an Indian war. We understand an invitation will be given to friendly Indians to use their influence with all the red men, and an offer will be made to them to the effect that if they feel so disposed a deputy of chiefs can be organized to go to Washington, with the view to visiting the chief authorities of the nation for the purpose of laying their grievances before the latter, if they have any, that they may have the same adjusted. Gen. Ord and the Governor informed General Wells yesterday that they desired to be understood by the people that themselves and their property would be amply protected. They also stated that should it be found necessay to call on the people to assist the regular militia, Gen. Wells would be notified to that effect.

INDIAN CONFERENCE

On Saturday evening Bishop Abraham O. Smoot and other leading citizens of Utah County

had a conference with the Indians at Springville
The co-operative herd having been removed from
Hobble Creek canyon recently, caused some uneasi-
ness among the red men,as they construed the re-
moval as a preparatory measure for war. Tabby
and Douglas, two chiefs did not attend the conference, but others of their tribe were there representing them. Tabby expressed his willingness to
return to the Uintah reservation on condition that
they are supplied with flour, but say some of their
people oppose him in this.

The Shiberetch, Capotah and Elk Mountain
bands with a number of Navajoes were still on the
war path. However, the troops were kept on
scouting expeditions against them.

TREATY CONCLUDED AT
MOUNT PLEASANT.

On September 17th, General Morrow, Apostle
Orson Hyde, Bishop William Seely, Bishop Amasa
Tucker, Bishop Frederick Olsen, Colonel Reddick
N. Allred and others met a number of chiefs who
had been present at the former council. Among
these were Tabiona, Angizebl, White Hare and some
who were known to have encouraged, if they had not
taken part in the depredatory incursions; all entered
into a treaty of peace, and it was believed that the
principal danger of a war was passed.

August 31st, some Indans made a raid on
Spanish Fork stealing some horses.

ATTACK ON FAIRVIEW COW HERD,

NATHAN STEWART KILLED.

August 13th, Henry Larter writes from Moroni. On Saturday afternoon Bishop George W. Bradley, of this place sent his two sons, James and Jephania into the cedars with a team, to get a load of brush. They went to a spring about three miles from here to get a drink, when a number of Indians with guns cocked, rushed on the wagon, and cut the harness to pieces and made off with the horses. The boys made their escape to town.

This same band of Indians crossed the hills to Fairview, where they were seen riding the Bishop's horses, and at which place they came upon the cow herd and commenced shooting at the herdsmen. They were Peter Larsen, Morten Petersen and Nathan Steward. Larsen was shot through the hand with a gun, and also shot with an arrow in the back of the neck, the arrow stuck in the bone, and one spike in his wrist was broken off, he rode home. Steward was wounded,but ran home; he died on the 12th. Petersen was pulled off his horse; one of the Indians struck him with his gun and told him to get. The savages took both of their horses. This happened on the 10th of August.

HORSES STOLEN FROM RICHFIELD.

During the late summer, (have not been able to get date), I glean the following account from Eskild C. Peterson and others:

During the night Indians came into Richfield and stole a pair of horses belonging to Andrew Killion. The animals were tied to his wagon in the southeast part of town. The Indians also took a band of horses belonging to Stanley Davis from the Prattville meadows. The trashing machine, horses and some others belonging to Archibald W. Buchanan at Glenwood were also taken. A company of fourteen men from Richfield under Captain Eskild C. Peterson started early next morning in pursuit; they went to Glenwood and awaited orders. In the meantime Brigham T. Young (son of Joseph A. Young) Stanley Davis, William H. Seegmiller, Cornelious Fairbanks and others were in consultation at Prattville and decided to send Brother Young to Manti to get a company from there to go out and head off the Indians; it is said he asked for two hundred men to go at once; but meeting with some rebuff, he telegraphed to Salt Lake City without results. Petersen's company having awaited in Glenwood till about three o'clock without receiving any instructions, decided that it was too late to follow the thieves; they went to Salina, where they remained during the night. There they learned of Brother Young going to Manti, which was the cause of the delay at Glenwood. Early next morning they rode up Salina Canyon by way of Soldier Fork; there they met Killion's horses which had got away from the Indians dragging a long lassoo. When they got to Gooseberry Creek they saw that the Indians had crossed it that morning, as the bank was still wet from them crossing. The company followed till they reached the summit where they could look down into Castle Valley. Not being prepared to camp out, they abandoned the chase and returned to Glenwood by way of Grass Valley, crossing into Kings Meadow Canyon at the head of the big willow patch through a very rought country and in a very dark night they got separated and came straggling into Glenwood after day-break hungry and exhausted.

HORSES STOLEN FROM FOUNTAIN GREEN.
(THE PURSUIT.)

About this time on a Sunday morning P. N. Guyman and Wm. G. Caldwell, two boys of Fountain Green, Sanpete County, went on the range after some saddle horses near where the wagon road passed through the hills toward Mount Pleasant, where the horses had ranged. Not finding them, they hunted further until they found tracks and followed them into the hills far enough to make sure that Indians had taken them. The moccasin tracks showed plainly where an Indian had been off his horse to cinch his saddle. They decided to return to town and report. When they reached town, Sunday meeting was in process and James Guyman, father of P. N. Guy man, was speaking. Young Guyman interrupted him by saying, "Let me say a word." He then related what they had found; the meeting was immediately discontinued and the minute men went in pursuit, but the Indians had too much the start and was not overtaken. A company of U. S. Soldiers who were in town, also went in pursuit, with Wm. A. Guyman as guide; they followed the Indians into Strawberry Valley where they found that the Indians separated and had gone in different

directions. Further pursuit would have been fruitless. They found some horses which the Indians had
ridden till they gave out; they were left along the
trail.

DAN MILLER KILLED AND SON
WOUNDED NEAR SPRING CITY.

The following sketch of the last killing of a
white man by Indians during the Black Hawk up-
rising, was originally prepared by Peter Gottfredson, of Richfield, for the local paper, about 1882.

The last man killed in the Indian Wars of Utah
was Daniel Miller of Nephi, Juab County. The tragedy took place on the morning of the 26 of September, 1872, at Snow and Douglas' saw mill, in Oak
Creek Canon, Sanpete County, three miles east of
Spring City. The mill had shut down about a month
before, it being considered unsafe to work there because of Indians, but William Higbee stayed there
as watchman.

I had a contract to get out a bill of lumber to
finish a new school house which was being built in
the Second District at Mount Pleasant, and Thomas
Gledhill, my brother-in-law, sixteen years old, was
helping me. I was working three yoke of oxen,
getting logs to the mill to be sawed on shares. Miller was building a house at Nephi, and he and his
son, (Dan M. Miller), thirteen years of age, was
working a pair of mules getting out logs for lumber to finish his house. All told, there were five
of us at the mill.

The 26th of September, 1872, was Saturday. We
were all going home except Higbee. The house in
which we camped was about two hundred yards be-

low the mill, between the road and creek, with the door toward the road east. About thirty yards east of the house at the side of the road lay a pile of poles. The Indians had placed two small poles, one on each end of the pile, and a large pole on top of them, making an opening to put their guns through There were marks in the dust where five Indians had lain, ready to fire, if we had all gone out together.

That morning we maneuvered differently from our usual custom. I arose at day-break and went up to the mill to saw out a few joints that I wanted, which were not in the mill yard, and to load my wagon. I called Gledhill to go after the oxen which were in the hills about a mile south of the mill. He left the house shortly after I did. Soon afterwards, Miller came up to the mill and loaded his wagon, and in a short time Miller's boy came up to the mill. Gledhill brought the oxen, yoked them, left them in the mill yard, and returned to the house. Soon after this I went down to breakfast and Miller and his boy started away. They passed the house with their load of lumber, drove about one hundred yards below the house around a patch of oak brush which hid them from view, and then stopped to tighten the binder. The Indians had run down behind a low ridge where their horses were tied to the oak brush, and from ambush fired five shot, most if not all, taking effect. Miller was shot through one arm and in the side under the arm, and one bullet passed through his bowels, breaking his back. The boy was shot through one thigh and through one wrist, the ball passing between the two bones.

We heard the shooting, but thought the Millers were shooting at a rabbit or wolf and took no more notice of it. We finished our breakfast and all three started up to the mill after my team. When about half way up, we heard the rattle of a wagon, and in looking back we saw a man standing up on the wagon driving as fast as he could make the horses go. Tom Gledhill said, "That fellow is driving pretty fast up hill." I remarked, "he must have had one drink too many this morning." Just then the man shouted, "There is a man shot all to pieces below the house.' We then knew what the shooting was we had heard and started back to the house as fast as we could run. We saw some horsemen south west of the house coming at full speed through the brush, and thought they were Indians trying to head us off from the house, where we had left our guns. When we reached the house we saw that the men were from Spring City.

The Miller boy, when shot, tried to run to the house, but the Indians headed him off. They had not yet reloaded. The boy turned and ran down the road toward Spring City and met these men going out to look for stock. They had received word that Indian signs had been seen the previous evening in the foot hills. Some of the men took the boy who was very weak from the loss of blood to Spring City and sent a telegram to Mt. Pleasant. Col John L. Ivie gathered up a small posse with which he pursued the Indians, but never overtook them. Later Colonel Allred took young Miller home and kept him until he recovered. Brother Allred's wife attended him like a mother without compensation.

We all went down to where Miller lay. When shot he had fallen off the wagon on the north side. The Indians, without mutilating his body, had dragged him about a rod from the wagon and laid his face on a large bed of cactus. They had taken his gun, pistol, food, bedding, and cooking utensils, and with the mules had made off in a northeasterly direction towards the mouth of Cedar Creek Canyon. It was then that R. N. Bennett, the man with the team drove up. He had seen the Indians leave, but thought they were white men. He saw the wagon, but did not notice that the tugs were cut. As he was passing the wagon he heard a man moan, and, turning, he saw Miller lying about a rod north. He stopped, tied the lines, and went to Miller and asked who had done this. Miller said, "Indians." Bennett said, "When?" Miller answered, "Right now." Bennett asked if there was anybody at the mill and was answered, "Yes." He then lifted the old man off the cactus and drove up to the mill.

When we reached the place where Miller lay, I put my arm under his neck to raise him up for some of the others to pick the cactus briers out of his face, and in doing so I heard his back bone grate. I asked if it hurt him. He answered no, but that he was thirsty. One of the men stepped to the wagon to get some kind of a vessel in which to fetch some water, but the Indians had taken everything of that kind. He, however, picked up one of the bullets that had been fired by the Indians on the wagon.. I said "My hat will hold water," and ran to the creek, about

fifty yards distant, where I received a moment's
scare. On the opposite side of the creek some willows had been cut down and fire had been through
them. One willow about the size of a gun barrel had
been blackened by smoke so that it looked bright, and
lay in such a position that it pointed right at my
head. I thought that if I did not drop this instant, I
would be shot. As I squatted to the ground I saw
what it was. I obtained the water and let Miller
drink out of my hat, after which we held consultation and decided to make a litter of four small poles
and a pair of Higbee's blankets, using a pair of
overalls belonging to me for strings to lash it together. Gledhill was sent to the house after a bucket,
blankets and overalls. When he returned he
was sent upon an elevation to guard against a surprise by Indians.

The Spring City men made the litter while Higbee and I followed the trail of the Indians to learn
if possible, where they had gone. We were armed
with good "Henry" rifles, and followed the trail
to the mouth of Cedar Creek canyon, about two
miles, where the Indians had gone up a wide hollow with large oak brush on both sides. I told
Higbee that I was going there, as it gave the Indians
too good a chance to ambush us without our getting a chance at them. He then said that he would
go alone, and went on. I went onto a ridge where
I could look around and could see no Indians, but
saw one of Miller's mules feeding a short distance
north with the harness on. I feared it might have
been left there for a decoy to get us into a trap, but
as the mule was feeding contentedly, I concluded

that it had been left because it was too slow to make headway. I secured the mule and took it back to the wagon. When I reached the vehicle the men were ready to start with Miller. Some of the men had gone up to the mill and brought down my team.

The Spring City men carried Miller, one at each corner of the litter, and Gledhill took Miller's wagon with one yoke of my oxen. I drove my wagon with the other two yoke. Having travelled about half the distance to Spring City, Miller said he was tired and wanted them to lay him down in the road to rest. We all gathered around him. I asked him if he would like us to take any word to his family if he should not live to see them. His eyes were turning glassy. He said he had nothing on his mind, but would like to see his twins before he died. We learned later that a pair of twin baby boys had recently been born to him. We asked him if he wanted us to take vengeance on the Indians. He said, "No, they don't know any better." He said he knew some of the Indians, one was Taby-any, and there were five of them. Other things were said that I do not call to mind. We could see that he was too low to proceed, and in a short time the poor fellow expired. Colonel Allred came up with a wagon, and his body was carried down to Spring City. That night his family, who had been telegraphed at Nephi, came to Spring City and took charge of his remains.

Orson Hyde sent the following telegram to Salt Lake City, dated September 26th, 1872.

"The Indians are upon us. Several horses were stolen last night. This morning a man was shot off a load of lumber and his little boy wounded in the hip and wrist. The man is said to be Miller from Salt Creek.''

It was generally believed that the Indians mistook Mr. Miller for Bernard Snow, as they had the same kind of team, a gray and a bay mule, and Snow often had a boy with him. The Indians did not like Bernard Snow.

In one of the raids on Ephraim Bernard Snow, the veteran actor who was building a mill at the mouth of the canyon near the settlement sustained during several hours a lonely but heroic siege; the savages surrounded the mill, but the gallant defender kept up a fire so vigorous that they were forced to retire. (Copied from Whitney's History of Utah.)

GENERAL MORROWS RECOMENDATION TO INDIAN AGENT DODGE.

INDIANS GO TO WASHINGTON TO IN-TERVIEW PRESIDENT GRANT.

This was the last serious raid made by the hostiles, and matters soon quieted down to their normal condition. The settlers had suffered more severely than they otherwise would have done both in loss of life and property because of the proclamation of Governor Shafer, and Acting Governor Black, prohibiting the assembling of the militia. Governor Woods refused to rescind that order when applied to in July of the same year, even to enable the people to defend themselves. Of the action of the citizens in obeying the edict of the Executive, General Morrow said in his report to Indian agent,

Dodge: "I think I may say with truthfullness that there is not another American community in the nation which would have endured half the outrages these people have endured without rising up as one man to drive out the savage invaders at the point of the bayonet. On any principle of self defense they would have been justified in doing this. In the same letter the General made the following recommendation: "Now, sir, I have given you a plain statement of facts, and I desire to invite your attention, and through you the attention of the Indian Department, in the justice and propriety of making this people some recompense for their losses. This may be done, I believe, from the appropriation made by Congress for these tribes. It is only an act of simple justice to the poor people who have suffered so severely that it should be done. It is some time since I had occasion to examine the subject, but I believe there is a law of Congress, I think of 1834, which authorizes compensation to be made in cases like the present, and prescribes the manner in which it shall be done. If this course is pursued now, it will not only be proper in itself as an act of justice to the people, but it will also teach the Indians that they cannot commit depredations with impunity."

To General Morrow's letter, Colonel Dodge replied: "I fully concur with you in all the statements you have herein made," adding, "Your reference to the great losses on the part of the citizens of the disturbed district is eminently just, and I shall do everything in my power to bring such relief to the sufferers as the law will allow." He also supported

General Morrow's, application in behalf of the Indians, asking permission for a delegation of chiefs to visit President Grant. This application was favorably acted upon, and on October 17th, Chief Wandrodes, Antero, Tabiona, and Kanosh accompanied by Judge George W. Bean of Provo as interpreter, left Salt Lake City with Special Agent Dodge to confer with the "Great Father" at Washington. Since then depredatory acts by Indians in Utah have been rare.

UTE DIALECT, TRADITION AND LEGENDS.
By D. B. Huntington.

Numbers

One	Soos
Two	Wy-une
Three	Pi-une
Four	Wats-u-ene
Five	Man-i-gin
Six	Nav-i-une
Seven	Tat-su-ene
Eight	Ni-wat-su-ene
Nine	Sur-rom-su-ene
Ten	Tom-su-ene
Eleven	Tom-su-ene-soos spinko
Twelve	Tom-su-ene Wy-une spinko
Thirteen	Tom-su-ene pi-une spinko
Fourteen	Tom-su-ene wats-u-ene spinko
Fifteen	Tom-su-ene man-i-gin spinko
Sixteen	Tom-su-ene nav-i-une spinko
Seventeen	Tom-su-ene tat-su-ene spinko
Eighteen	Tom-su ene ni-wat-su-ene spinko
Nineteen	Tom-su-ene sur-rom-su-ene spinko

Robert Boardman   Oscar Wilkins   Henry Cluff   Joel Andrew Johnson   Thomas Vincent

PRESIDENT ANTHON H. LUND
First Telegraph Operator at Mt. Pleasant, Utah
Lieutenant, Capt. Frederick Neilsen's Infantry
Company.

Twenty	Wamp-su-ene
Twenty one	Wamp-su-ene soos spinko
Thirty	Pam-su-ene
Forty	Wats-u-ene tom-su-ene
Fifty	Man-i-gin tom-su-ene
Sixty	Nav-i-une tom-su-ene
Seventy	Tat-su-ene tom-su-ene
Eighty	Ni-wat-su-ene tom-su-ene
Ninety	Sur-rom-su-ene tom-su-ene
One hundred	Soos meh

THE TRADITIONS OF THE UTAH INDIANS IN RELATION TO THE CREATION OF THE WORLD.

When the gods made the world it was dark all over the face of the earth; and they said let us have light; and the chief said, I will make it; I have no arrow long enough to penetrate through the darkness. So he groped about and found some willows (Cannab), and broke the longest one he could find, put it upon his bow and shot upwards. In a short time a small star appeared. They watched it and it soon began to grow; light came in, the orifice expanded, the darkness disappeared, and they could see to divide the water from the land; and they made dry ground, and the rivers, lakes, springs, and small streams, and they all sang together.

THE FLOOD.

The people of the earth a long time ago became exceedingly wicked, and the Lord sent out a proclamation for all of the inhabitants of the whole earth to come together, for he wanted to talk to them. They met in a large valley and the Lord came down and stood, one foot on one mountain and the other foot upon another mountain; but the people would not listen to Him. He then called all of his friends to come to Him. They came two of every kind of beasts, and a few men, women and children, and they made a covenant to hearken unto Him. The others kept talking and would not hear Him. Then the Lord was angry; he stooped down and pulled up a large tree and whipped every living thing to death except his friends, and then He told them to go and throw or scatter their young upon all the face of the land and be His friends.

ELIJAH FED BY RAVENS.

A great many moons ago a woman strayed off and got lost from her lodge. She became very hungry, and cried to the Lord for food, and He sent ravens to carry her food for many days. After a while she found her lodge, and there was great rejoicing among here people when she told them what the ravens had done.

THE CRUCIFIXION OF CHRIST.

A great many years ago the Lord (Towats) lived in the Piede country. His house is standing at this time. He had a son who died and when he died the earth was broken up; there were earthquakes and terrible thunderings and lightnings. It was very dark for three days and nights. It was so dark the people could feel the darkness with their fingers; and all of this time they were howling and crying, for they could not make fire burn. They had to eat all their meat raw. The third day His son came to life and the darkness disappeared, and there was great rejoicing. The Lord had a brother, but they were not on friendly terms with each other. And he, the brother, had a son who died, and his father went to the Lord (his brother) to ask him why it was not dark. The Lord told him it was because he opposed him in all things. The Lord's brother's name was Shinnob. The Lord told him to go home, cut off his hair, burn up his lodge, kill his horses, howl, and lacerate his flesh, for the third day his son would stink; and it was so. Hence comes the tradition, which is; That when they die their spirits go to a large canon in the Sierra Nevada mountains where there is plenty of game, and they hate to have their relatives die and go poor to the hunting grounds. This is the reason why they kill the dead man's horses to go with him for him to ride. It is customary with them to kill a prisoner or some poor person to go with them to wait on them.

WAH-KER'S HISTORY.

Wah-ker was born about the year 1815, on the Spanish Fork River, Utah County, Utah Territory, and was one of the shrewdest of men. He was a natural man; read from natures books. He was very fond of liquor; but when in liquor you could not get him to make a trade.

Wah-ker means "yellow," or "brass." When about twenty five years of age he had a curious vision. He died and his spirit went to heaven. He

saw the Lord sitting upon a throne dressed in white.
The Lord told him he could not stay; he had to
return. He desired to stay, but the Lord told him
that he must return to earth; that there would
come to him a race of white people that would be
his friends, and he must treat them kindly. The
Lord gave him a new name. It was Pan-a-karry
Quin-ker (Iron twister) in 1846 or '47 he went to
California with a lot of Piede prisoners. He frightened the Piedes into giving him their children, which he
took to lower California to trade for horses to enrich
himself, taking many of his tribe with him. The Spaniards gave him numbers of beef cattle and charged
him for them, where upon he started for home. When
out two days he called a halt, held a council, and sent
the old men, women and children on towards home.
The third day ten men returned to visit the Spaniards. Each man visited different ranches, and took
a large number of horses. The Spaniards raised a
large force and pursued them, and recoverd many,
but lost six or seven hundred head of wild horses,
for which the Mexicans offered a large reward. The
Indians pushed the horses so hard that they lost
several on the desert.

He remained king of the mountains until about
1852, when he inaugurated what is called the Wah-
ker war, through which many whites lost their lives;
and which cost Utah Territory over a million dollars.

Soon after he was taken sick near Fillmore,
in Millard County, and was ill but a short time when
he was stricken with death, being blind for three
days. He would have the men raise him up, when

he would talk to them, telling them not to fight the whites as he had done. When he died there was a terrible howling. The men jumped upon their horses and killed seven head of horses, one Piede woman (a prisoner), and one boy, and carried Wah-ker up into the mountains, put his body into a cliff of rocks, walled it up and put a Piede boy in with him alive. Three days after, as some Indians were riding by, the boy called out to them and asked to be let out. He said Wah-ker began to stink and he was hungry. They laughed at him and rode on.

Wah-ker had three brothers: Ara-pene, Sam-pitch, and Tabby. Tabby is at present the head chief of the Utahs proper, and is on the Uintah reservation. (1872.)

Ara-pene was a great orator, but a hard-hearted man. At one time in Manti he got mad at his wife and burned her in a fearful manner with a frying-pan handle that was broken off the pan. She crawled to the settlement and the white women nursed her until she recovered.

At another time he came down out of the mountains with some deer-skins and a Piede prisoner, a small boy, to trade. The price was too high for the child, whereupon, in rage, he took the child by his heels and dashed his brains out by thrashing the ground with his head.

In 1849, when fifty of us were exploring the "Dixie" country, in the month of December, we met Ara-pene on his way from the mountains on the Sevier river, coming down to winter. An old squaw had a long roll of cedar bark, one end of which was on fire so as to light a fire quickly. We all camped

together. Ara-pene had one daughter, about nine
years old, and she was very sick with measles. She
died that night; and the Indians held a council whether to kill one of us or a Piede prisoner, a boy
about six years old, to send with the daughter. In
the morning two young men came out of Ara-pene's
lodge, loading their rifles and driving the Piede before them. I shall never forget how pitiful he looked,
for he knew what his fate was. He asked to take
off his moccasins and was refused. It was very cold.
They drove him about four rods from camp, when
both fired and the poor little fellow rolled down
from off the little knoll on which he stood. He was
buried along with the girl.

THE UTES.

Have no marriage ceremony. They buy and
sell their women and daughters. They have many
wives and the women do the hard work, dressing
all their skins. When the hunters return from a
hunt, if he brings in any game the women unload it
and unsaddle the horses. The hunter does nothing
more until the meat is gone, when the women bring
up the horse, saddle him, and he goes on the hunt.
The men are intensely fond of gambling, horse-rac-
ing and shooting at the target. The women love
to gamble with sticks for beads and paints, etc;
and are also fond of playing ball in summer time.
They are very affectionate to their children.

The Utes have no religious ceremonies, but are
great for doctoring. A "medicine-man" is looked
upon as one that can handle the thunder balls and
stand in the fire with his bare feet. Their medicine

RUDOLPHUS N. BENNETT
Vice-Commander
UTAH INDIAN WAR VETERANS

MORONI L. PRATT
Sergeant in A. G. Conover's Cavalry Company,
Late Adjutant-General.

HANS J. GOTTFREDSON
Who for seven years employed Indians to work for him. Boating
on the Colorado River, at Eldorado Canyon, 1872 to 1880. He camped with them and learned their language, traditions and legends.

is princpally singing and sucking.

I never saw an Indian with a bald head, and they have but very few decayed teeth. They pluck out their beards and eyebrows. They are very much afraid of witches and crazy people, and believe in making medicine on paper to kill people.

UTE AND PIUTE TRADITIONS.
By H. J. Gottfredson.

The Ute and Piute Indians have traditions very similar. Hans J. Gottfredson was in business at Eldorado Canyon on the Colorado River for about seven years, and employed Piute Indians to work for im. He camped out with them a considerable and from them learned some of their traditions with regard to the creation, and the Lord's dealings with his children. They believe when the earth was created that it was level and beautiful, that fruit and vegetation grew spontaneously. that game was plentiful everywhere and that all was peace, that God (Towats) lived in the south, and that the Lord had two sons. The elder son, who was independent and could always take care of himself, was the father of the Indians who inherit his nature: the younger was a cry baby always wanting everything he saw, and he is the father of the white people. The Lord granted him his desires, and the whites inherit his disposition, that is the reason why the white people are smarter in getting and in inventing and making things. But as orators they are not the equals of the Indians.

At one time the father became vexed at his children for some cause or other and tearing through

the country from south to north he tore up the land
as he went along, leaving it in the present condition, with mountains, hills and deserts and not fer-
tile as it was. But that he will sometime come back
and level the land and make it as it was before. Then
it will be the happy hunting ground. The Indians
are superstitious and believe there is some kind of
charm about writing and making pictures. They
also believe in Satan (Shin-nob) who is always bent
on doing harm, that he delights in seeing people do
wrong. They do not serve God, because he is good
and will not harm any-thing; but they serve Satan
through fear; they want to keep peace with him.
Many of them, when they eat, throw the first bite
over their left shoulders, and when asked what that
is for, they say that is to feed Satan to keep peace
with him. They believe that the white people can
write to him and he will cause sickness or trouble to
come onto others. And should you write the name
of an Indian on a slip of paper and tell him that you
was going to send it to Lucifer, the Indian would
risk his life, if necessary to get possession of it.
When trouble comes to them, they think, that if they
do something to please him, it will stop the trouble.

The writer had some acquaintance with the Indians in the early sixties, they were hospitable if
a person came to their camp hungry, and they expected the same from the whites. If they were
trusted with anything, they could as a rule be depended upon, and were generally truthful; they dispised a falsifier. There were many small bands of
Indians in the country at that time, and we could
run onto an Indian camp in many places. In the

summer of 1864 I was herding cattle and sheep in
Thistle Valley. Once I followed some cattle tracks
into the west mountains traveling over hills and
canyons for about fifteen miles to Mount. Nebo.
As it was late in the day, night soon overtook me.
I had with me my Kentucky rifle and a dog. The
night was dark and as I could not remember how
many canyons I had crossed I went down the
wrong canyon. Near midnight I was attacked by
a lot of dogs and I knew they were Indian dogs.
They were fierce and had it not been for my dog,
it is hard telling what the result would have been.
I yelled when some Indians got out of their blankets
and came up and called off the dogs. I went down
with them to their camp. They knew me and said
that I was the sheep captain. Some young squaws
came out and stirred up a fire and roasted deer
meat for me. They offered me some of their bread
which was made of berries and large wingless black
crickets the size of the end of my thumb, they call it
Queash. I showed them the cricket legs and said they
were "Kay-wi-no." not good. They laughed at me.
The Indians offered me blankets to sleep in but as
I told them that my folks would be worried about me
and would be out at daylight hunting for me. An In
dian went down the canyon with me about a mile
to where a trail led into Thistle Valley, and I got
to camp about daylight.

The Indians realized that they were being
crowded off their hunting grounds and would often
tell us so; they wanted cattle. horses or sheep in
payment for it They never stayed long on a camp-
ground. but moved to new hunting grounds and pas-

tures where feed could be found for their horses. In the morning before breaking camp. the Chief would call the Indians around him and talk to them for half an hour or so, instructing them as to their movements. Then each would go to their several tasks some would go hunting on the way to the new camp ground. The squaws did the packing and moving of camp while the men and boys gathered up the horses and did the easy work.

They loved hunting, and as scouts and trailers they were far superior to white men. If a twig had been newly broken, or a stone moved they always noticed it and learned the cause. They were so thoroughly acquainted with the mountain trails, canyons and watering places, and knew the hiding places in case of danger or pursuit so well, that they were hard to locate. They would often travel long distances without leaving any tracks or signs, by walking on rocks, or wading in streams, and thus conceal their movements. They generally made small fires and hovered closely over them, burning mostly sage brush, which made the best embers and coals and kept the fire better, when covered, than other wood. They thought white men foolish for making large fires and have to sit back. The Indians always smelled smoky because of sitting over their small fires so much. and being in their wickiups.

AN EXPLORING TRIP AND TREATIES WITH IN-DIANS IN GRASS VALLLEY AND VICINITY, BY A. K. THURBER, G. W. BEAN AND OTHERS.

On or about the 1st of June, 1873, President Brigham Young and Council called Bishop Albert

K. Thurber and Wm. Jex of Spanish Fork, George W. Bean, Bishop Abraham Halladay, General Wm. B. Pace and George Evans, of Provo and some others to take a party and explore the country southeast of Sevier Valley and make treaties of peace with the Indians in that vicinity. Consequently, on the 4th of June, 1873, a party of ten men left Provo, Pleasant Grove and American Fork. At Spanish Fork four other men joined and at Warm Creek (Fayette) one at Nephi, and at Salina one more man joined. From Richfield, Glenwood and Prattville came five more men. The noted Chief Tabiona accompanied them as guide. The party fitted out with saddle and pack horses, and started out on Indian trals southeast over the mountains. George W. Bean had previously acted as Indian interpreter for President Young, and also for the government. Bishop Thurber could also speak the Ute language and Chief Tabiona accompanied them both as guide and as mediator between the Indians and Whites. Interpreter Bean had obtained from the government two pack-horse loads of blankets, shawls, beads, butcher knives, calicos and numerous other articles, such as the Indians like, to give to them in order to obtain their good will, and keep peace with them.

We left Prattville June 11th, 1873 and camped at Brimhall Springs. Next morning we traveled up a nice narrow valley through grass which in places touching our stirrups, and at the head of the valley we found a large grizzly bear that had just been killed and skinned; it looked as large as a cow, so they named the place Bear Valley, and it still

retains the name. About half a mile farther on was
a bunch of quaking-asp, the largest about seven
or eight inches in diameter. We noticed that one
of the trees had the bark pealed off half way around
up about seven feet from the ground. We learned
later that the bear had an Indian up that tree for
about twenty-four hours, and he was in such a hurry
getting up that he dropped his gun, but later killed
the bear.

On the night of the 12th we camped on the
spot where Burrville is now located. Here we noticed the prettiest natural meadows that I ever saw,
and there was bunch-grass all over the hills. Hence
we named the place Grass Valley. Next day, the
13th, we reached Fish Lake about 3 o'clock p. m.
There we saw our first Indian; he was after fish;
but as soon as he saw us, he jumped onto his
pony and rode up the creek through the quaking-
asp timber as if he expected to be shot at every
minute. Tabiona called for him to stop, but he kept
going. Some of the members of our company became a little uneasy, knowing that the band was
camped not far away. I unsaddled right quick and
ran over to where the Indian had been fishing, and
there was about forty fish lying on the bank of
the creek and thousands more in the little creek
(Doctor Creek.) I ran down the little stream three
or four rods and started to throw out fish. By the
time the others had un-saddled and unpacked they
came and stopped me. I think I had about 300
fish and I was down on my knees throwing them
out with both hands. They threw back those that
were still alive but we took 210 to camp. It will

be well to state that the fish in this locality go up
the small streams to spawn in such numbers that
they can hardly move. We cleaned and salted what
we had taken, and got the Indians to dry and smoke
them and bring them to Cedar Grove in Grass Valley twelve days later—two seamless sacks full. We
prepared supper early, and after picketing and hob-
bling our horses (keeping them between our camp
and the lake) we made our beds scattered in the
brush. It was agreed that all were to keep quiet
and lie low. Tabiona, my father or A. K. Thurber
being the only ones allowed to talk. Not long after
dark, our horses began to snort and make an awful
fuss, trying to get loose. Tabiona called out and began talking; then also my father and Thurber. Tabiona spoke again, and finally two old squaws answered him and came into camp. We gave them
presents and sent them back to their camp; they
soon returned with about half the tribe. Old Poga-
neab (Fish captain) their chief, tried to keep them
from coming and was on the fight. A little later
most of his fighting men came in and said it was
safe to build fires, and about midnight the chief
and his two squaws, and eight or ten more, came
into camp.

We talked to them, and gave them presents till
about two o'clock in the night. We then sent them
to their camp, but told them to come back in the
morning.

We had a big talk all day. At the meeting
Tabiona spoke and said that when at Washington
visiting the Great White Chief (President U. S.
Grant) he saw three persons of fine appearance,

dressed in white robes and they had long white flowing beards; the friends to the Indians, the white men did not see them, but he did Some also thought that they might be the three Nephites spoken of in the Book of Mormon. Old Poga-neab became very friendly, and accompanied us on foot all the way round till we met the tribe at the council previously arranged at Cedar Grove. One of his sons went with us. We left Fish Lake June 15th and went to the place where Thurber is now located. A. K. Thurber liked the creek and location so well that we named the place Thurber in his honor. Next day we went to the lower end of Rabbit Valley, and during the day we caught a lone wild horse, and an antelope. Twenty seven of us circled round them and closed in on them. Where ever we went the deer were nearly as plentiful as the fish in the lake, and were quite gentle but we never killed more than we wanted to eat.

We camped in a nice grove of long-leaf pines which grew right down to the valley, and called the place Pine Creek; it is known as Pine Creek to this day. Here we picketed about half of our horses, hobbled the rest and built some nice big fires. All of a sudden several of our horses snorted and stampeded, running up the creek. Our ropes held fifteen animals I think. The night was dark, and as we had not been up the creek we let them go till morning. We knew there was another camp or tribe of Indians down there, somewhere, but not having seen any signs of them, we did not expect to see them till next day. Some of their scouts or guards, however, were out.

We put our fires out and all laid flat on the ground. It made old Poga-neab so mad, Tabiona said, that he swore at them He and his son went out on the trail and were gone about an hour, talking loud, telling the Indians to come in the morning.

We all rested next day and found our horses two or three miles up the creek. When the Indians came in, we gave them presents and made peace with them. Their squaws brought us forty nice trout that they had caught in their willow traps. The name of their chief was Angewetimpi. We noticed quite a difference in the Indians of the two tribes, though they lived only forty to sixty miles apart. Next day we started up Pine Creek through timber and grass and saw lots of deer which were quite tame. About sun-down we crossed a divide and came into a nice little flat where the water ran down into Grass Valley, as we learned later. We were just going to camp for the night, when we saw an old coyote with three young ones. We gave chase and caught the little ones, cut their ears and tails off short, tied a paper collar around one's neck and turned them loose. We named that stream Coyote It still retains that name and there is a settlement there now by that name. Next day we went south on to the Boulder Mountain, passing through big long leaf pine timber. We also saw springs and meadows and lots of deer, chickens, etc. In two days we reached the head of the east fork of Escalante creek, now called Potato Valley. Here we found a small band of Indians and after making peace with them. we came down the river and went up Grass Valley to the Cedar grove, just below the present site of Burrville, where we met the Fish Lake tribe of Indians.

We stopped there a day in council with the Indians; the next day we went back to Prattville, and then returned to our homes.

When the result of this trip was reported to President Brigham Young the result was that Bishhop Albert K. Thurber and George W. Bean were immediately called to settle in Grass Valley and assist the Indians who would gather there to cultivate the arts of peace and industry.

At the time of the meeting July 1st, 1873, a heavy snow storm came up which was a reminder that we were in the near vicinty of the top of the rim of the Basin, five or six miles distant. The Indian talk was highly satisfactory to all parties, and the promise made by the natives has been exceedingly well kept ever since.

In the spring of 1874, (about April 12th), these men with some of their sons and some others including the noted Porter Rockwell commenced operations in Grass Valley. Among the others who came into the valley were Tom and Billy McCarthy, James H. Clinger, Aaron and Dave Daniels from Provo, a man by name of Prator who had a family and a few others who took up ranches. We put up a lot of hay that summer.

THREE NAVAJO INDIANS KILLED IN GRASS VALLEY.

That fall four Navajoe Indians came into the valley to trade blankets for horses with the Grass Valley Indians. While in Grass Valley, it was reported, they had killed a calf belonging to the Mc-

Carthys and trouble arose. Just as they were leaving
they called at McCarty's cabin sullen and saucy. The
boys who were getting breakfast motioned for the
Indians to go. The boys guns were all in one corner of the cabin, and the Indians who got between
them and their guns, now motioned for the boys
to go. The boys went out to the corral and stable
to plan what was best to do and in the meantime
the Indians ate the boys breakfast. Mr. Clinger
had come to the cabin riding a fine horse, which
he tied to the fence just before the Indians came.
Though the Indians were in possession of the boys
guns there was no ammunition the boys carried that
in their belts and pockets. The boys finally tied up
a large bundle of hay in their lasso's and started to
roll it toward the house. The Indians got scared and
made a run, two of them getting on Clinger's horse,
and the other two taking their best horses.   The
boys got their guns and started to shoot, killing the
two on the Indian ponies not far off. The others
on Clinger's horse got away. The boys saddled up
fresh horses and followed the Indians down the valley. After getting quite close they killed one Indian and wounded the other as well as the horse.
The wounded Indian left the horse and went up a
rough canyon, as it was getting dark the boys returned to their cabin.

The wounded Indian was twenty-one days get-
tng home, eating anything he could catch, on the
way, as he had no matches to make a fire. As
word soon came that the Navajoes were coming to
kill the whites. All the whites left Grass Valley,
except Praitor and Family, Aaron Daniels, G. T.

Bean and E. P. Bean. We had to stay to feed the
stock. The Utes who were friendly said they would
take care of us. We wintered in the valley all
right till we run out of salt. We were snowed in
and it took three days on horse back to get to
Glenwood.

UTAH INDIAN WAR VETERANS ORGANIZE
AT SPRINGVILLE.

In the afternoon of July 4, 1893, a few of the
veterans of the Black Hawk War, met upon the
public square at Springville and talked over the
old troubulous war times and it was there agreed to
have a re-union of the Black Hawk warriors, their
families and friends, sometime during the ensuing
winter. The prime movers in the affair were George
Harrison, Edwin Lee, Joseph M. Westwood, Albert
Harmer, Francis Beardall and Walter Wheeler.
Another meeting was held January 1, 1894, at which
in addition to the above named, there were present
Thomas A. Brown, Eliel S. Curtis and Samuel Bulk-
ley, and it was there arranged to invite all the comrades of the Black Hawk war residing in the county
to meet at the Reynold's hall, January 24th, 1904,
for a grand ball and picnic. A local society was
organized about the same time called the ''Springville Comrades of the Black Hawk War.'' The
first captain was J. M. Westwood and Thomas A.
Brown was Adjutant and Quartermaster. From the
local Springville organization evolved the state organization, known as the ''Utah Indian War Veterans Association'' under whose auspices the great
encampment was held in (1900). Joseph M. West-

wood was made commander-in-chief, and Thomas A.
Brown, adjutant and quartermaster of this organization. During the previous year the "Home Guards'
and "Walker and Tintic War Veterans" held re-
ceptions, balls and feasts, which were patronized and
looked forward to as events to be prized for their
social and enlivening characters.

On the 25th day of January, 1894, the Black
Hawk War Veterans held their first re-union, at the
Reynolds Hall at Springville, commencing at two
o'clock, p. m. and continued, with an interval for supper until 4 o'clock a. m. next day.

There were one hundred and eleven veterans
present from various parts of the county.
On the arrival of the visiting delegations at Springville they were met with sleighs, under the direction
of George Harrison, and taken to the homes of the
Springville comrades, where old acquaintances were
revived and stories of the war times recounted. At
2 o'clock p. m. order was called by Captain F. P.
Whitmore and the Springville comrades opened with
a song, entitled "The Black Hawk War." F. C.
Boyer made an eloquent speech of welcome. At 6
o'clock, p. m., the supper hour arrived. A tent was
pitched outside and a fire kept burning, to remind
all of the early camping days. At intervals between dances, speeches were made by Orson Creer,
of Spanish Fork, an original poem was recited by
Milando Pratt, and Albert Jones sang an old-time
song, composed during the Sanpete campaign of
1866-67. Levi N. Kendall, a Utah Pioneer, made remarks and Colonel Page of Payson, recounted some
incidents of the war. Benjamin Driggs told about

campaigning in Sanpete; D. C. Johnson told of the
fight upon the Diamond and the gallant ride of
Noakes, Curtis and Stewart; John Tanner of Payson told how he got out of a certain scrape at Nephi;
B. W. Brown narrated his experiences at the fight at
Gravelly Ford, in Sevier County, etc. Thus with
music and song the first happy reunion of the Indian fighters of Utah passed into history. Since then
the reunions have been held annually, also a mid-
winter dance and festival.

All the counties which furnished assistance during the war have been organized into departments
of the organization, and most all the towns and cities
have had their local posts.

Local and State camp-fires and reunions have
been held, which have kept the fire of fraternal
friendship burning.

Through the efforts of Commander J. M. Westwood the organizations have been kept alive. I do
not know of another man, who would have continued
for twenty-five years or more to keep in touch with
the organization and lead it as long as he has done.
and I verily believe that if this organization had
not existed the Black Hawk Indian War Veterans
services would not have been recognized by the Fe-
deral Government, nor pensions granted. I feel
that we, as Indian War Veterans, owe him our sin-
cere gratitude as well as those who have stood by
him, of whom I will mention George Harrison and
Moroni L. Pratt.

We have held three State encampments, namely:
first at Ephraim, Sanpete County, the second at
Heber City, Wasatch County, August 12th to 15th,
1911, the 3rd at Springville, Utah County, August

20th to 23rd, 1912, and twenty-four annual camp-fires have been held in Utah County.

Camp-fires have also been held in other counties in the State where sufficient veterans reside. This year, A. D., 1918, the State Organization is composed of: Joseph M. Westwood of Springville, Utah County, Commander-in-Chief; Rudolphus N. Bennett of Mount Pleasant, Sanpete County, First Vice-Commander; Joel Andrew Johnson of Provo, Utah County, Second Vice-Commander and Peter C. Peterson of Ephraim, Sanpete County, Third Vice-Commander; Peter Gottfredson of Springville, Utah Co., as Adjutant-General, Israel E. Clegg, Sr., of Springville, Quartermaster General; George Harrison of Springville, Chorister, and Henry Moyle of Alpine, Chaplain; Dr. Seymour B. Young of Salt Lake City is commander of the Salt Lake Department; Judge John E. Booth of Provo, Commander of Utah County Department; Rudolphus N. Bennett of Mount Pleasant, Commander of Sanpete County Department, and Orson P. Lee of Monroe, Commander of Sevier County Department, James D. Shanks, Commander, Wasatch County Department. Some other counties have local posts.

REUNION AT MANTI, JOHN LOWRY STATES CAUSE OF BLACK HAWK WAR.

The occasion of the present re-union being opportune, in order to correct an erroneous impression that has become wide-spread as to what precipated the Black-Hawk War. I take this opportunity or means of placing the facts before the world.

But first let me state that I came here as a pioneer, and took part in the first battle fought with

the Indians under command of Col. John Scott. And
I have in one way or another been associated with
almost every Indian trouble in the early history of
this region. I served as Indian interpreter for years
in Manti, and have passed through many close places
in dealing with the red men. At times having been
surrounded by them when I knew that one word,
look, or action would have cost me my life in the
event that I showed fear. A man who betrayed cow-
ardice might be killed without any consideration,
but a brave man was always approached with consideration. Among them were some strange traditions and peculiar notions in relation to their spirit-
ual life, they served Satan, not God, the idea being
to placate the power bent on doing injury. The elder Brother (God) was good, and never harmed anyone, but Satan was served through fear. For instance, should a white man write the name of an
Indian on a slip of paper and give it out that it would
be sent to Satan, the Indian would sacrifice his life
if necessary to get possession of it. In 1864 a
small band of Indians were wintering at Gunnison,
many of them died, and they found reason for their
trouble in conclusion that the Mormons had written
their names and sent them to Satan. And he had
caused death to come upon them. So in their coun-
cils they were directed by their Chief to stop the
sickness among them by killing (Mormons) in retaliation. In February Black Hawk informed me
what the Indians were going to do when the snow
went off.'' They would kill the Mormons and eat
Mormon beef. I immediately went to my Bishop
with the information. He thought, as did many
others, that it was just Indian talk and amounted to

nothing; but the Indians told me several times what
they intended to do, and so I went the second time
to the Bishop. My story was received by his saying
"There are not enough of them." I then told him
that it did not matter how few the number as long
as they entertained the idea that it was the wish of
Satan, they would accomplish their purpose regardless of results to them. Shortly after I learned they
were killing cattle. I had some cattle on the range
myself, and in my search for them I found the skull
of an ox which I had owned. I operated a grist mill
at the time and the Indians would come there for
grinding, and I remember that it was about the sixth
of March that I informed them that I had found the
skull of my ox and asked them why they had killed
it, as I had always been a friend to them, as had the
Mormon people, generally. I talked to them in such
a way that they agreed to pay me for the animal
which had been killed by fetching me a horse, and
they did so next day. I agreed to meet with them at
Manti about the eighth of April and talk the matter
over of their killing our cattle. Accordngly the
council took place. It appeared the difficulty would
be settled amicably, but a certain young Indian present whose father had died during the winter continued to halloo and make demonstrations, saying that
he would (eat Mormon beef) and kill "Mormons"
when the snow went off. I told him a time or two
to stop and permit me to finish my talk. Just then
some one called out "lookout, he is getting his arrows!" I rode up to him and turned him off his
horse, and pulled him to the ground. The bystanders
interferred and we separated. I had fully exposed
what they intended to do. The next day as our

people were out hunting cattle a man named Peter
Ludvigsen was killed. I have always taken the position that that talk with the Indians "showed their
hand." I believe they started hostilities sooner than
they would have done had not the incident above
mentioned occurred. But the trouble would have
come just the same. I am confident many lives were
saved, because it put the people on their guard. The
chief, Black Hawk told Charles Whitlock of Ephraim, the same thing as had been told me concerning
the intention of the Indians. These are facts as to
the starting of the Black Hawk Indian depredations.
In those early days its was at times imperative that
harsh measures should be used. Hamilton killed an
Indian dog, and whipped some Indians too, but that
didn't start a war; I threw an Indian out of my
house and kicked him off the place, and no war
came of it. We had to do these things, or be run
over by them. It was a question of supremacy
between the white man and the Indian.

I have patiently borne the stigma placed upon
me, for I knew the facts, and to those who still
persist in looking upon me as guilty of precipitat-
ing the Black Hawk War I will say this, that I appeal from their decision to a higher court—Our
Creator, who will ultimately judge all men.

Signed, John Lowry.

Stamped with—Commissioners of Indian War
Records Seal.

Indians in Grass Valley, Piute County, Utah
did not want to go to the Uintah Reservation to live.

At the time the U. S. Government set apart the
Uintah reservation as a home for the Utah Indians

some Indians living in Thistle Valley, Sanpete County, and a few in Grass Valley, Piute County, were very much opposed to going to live permanently on the Uintah Reservation. Soldiers, Indian Agents and white traders were not esteemed by these Indians and they so stated.

President Brigham Young instructed President Albert K. Thurber and George W. Bean˜to visit these Indians and take them under their watchcare. Some of the Indians in Thistle Valley moved to Grass Valley; some also came up from Escalante and others came over from Wayne County to live at Greenwich in Grass Valley, Piute County, Utah. After the death of A. K. Thurber and George W. Bean about A. D. 1900, William H. Seegmiller, then president of the Sevier Stake of Zion, in reflecting over the situation of the Grass Valley Indians, concluded that in years to come the Indians there might feel that as their friends we had neglected them and did not inform them of the advantages that they might obtain in lands, money, blankets, clothing, farming implements, cattle, horses, education, etc., should they go to the Uintah Indian Reservation. Elder Francis M. Lyman, an Apostle, who had under his care these Indians was consulted about the matter, and of the welfare of these Indians, he consulted with Jos. L. Rawlins, then a Senator from Utah in Congress, 1893 to 1903 who presented the matter to the Committee of Indian affairs in Congress, who informed him that the Indians not on the reservation in Utah might still be enrolled with the Uintah Indians and receive the same advantages as those at Uintah had received, an instructed President Seegmiller to secure the services of the best

Indian interpreter he could get, and with him go over to Grass Valley and clearly inform the Indians there of the benefits that would come to them, if they would go to Uintah and enroll themselves with the Indians there. President Seegmiller had George Hatch informed the Indians that he and Archibald W Buchanan would be over on a certain date and wanted a meeting with them, as he had important matters to present to them for consideration.

The Indians assembled in the stack yard of John Hatch close to the Indian village near Greenwich. The Indians were sullen and said, they were members of the Mormon Church and why did we—, their old friends, want to drive them away to the Reservation? Did the Mormons want to get their land from them and make homes for themselves? They would rather starve here and eat dirt than go to the Reservation and have their squaws defiled and their generations cut off by decease, than to get money, land, blankets, etc., by going to the Reservation. They threw away (tarabbied) their Mormon friends, but would not go to the Reservation.

Interpreter Buchanan then told them we did not want to remove them to the Reservation; we wanted to be their friends as always, and for them to choose whether they would go or remain.

If they wanted to go to the Reservation and could see a benefit in it, well and good, but if not, to feel that we were their friends and would not force them to go.

President Seegmiller spoke to the Indians in a kind and fatherly way and said, they were to choose their course whether to go or stay, and in

time to come he did not want them to reproach their
"Mormon" friends for not informing them what
they could get by going to the Reservation. He desired that they should assimilate the conduct of their
"Mormon" friends, quit their begging and farm
industriously, fence their farms, build houses, raise
horses, cattle, hogs, sheep, etc., make gardens, go
to meetings on the Sabbath day, send their children to the District School and to the Sabbath school,
and thus become independent and sustain themselves.

After this was made clear to them by the visitors to their understandings, they seemed pleased,
took us back (cotch tarriby) to be their friends always, a great shaking hands was had and we and
the Indians were all (tic-a-boo) friends and have
been ever since.

GRASS VALLEY INDIANS IN 1914.

Peter Gottfredson, who has been collecting the
history of the Indians in Utah, writes interestingly
of a recent visit to the Grass Valley Indians at Koosharem, Mr. Gottfredson says in part:
"I visited their Sunday school class. It consists of about twenty members. The teacher is Louis
Hatch, who is sustained as missionary to the Indians
by the authorities of Sevier Stake. He is the son
of George A. Hatch, who occupied the position of
Indian Missionary for many years and who was
greatly beloved by the Indians. The elder Hatch
died four years ago. At his death the Indians
grieved very much, many of them crying at his

funeral. It was at their own request that a son of
George A. Hatch was appointed to have charge
of them.

Wappus, a venerable Indian of Koosharem,
says that he was twelve years old when Brigham
Young and his company came to Utah. Wappus is
now blind. Many Indians lose their eyesight due
to the fact, it is said, that they are in the smoke
of their wickiups so much of the time. When a
boy, Wappus went with his father to see the white
men. He was formerly of Thistle Valley, but sold
his farm there and placed his money in a Richfield
Bank.

"A much older Indian than Wappus, is "Chick-
ney shootem" or "Old Tom," as he is otherwise
known, he is the oldest Indian in the colony and is
said to be more than one hundred snows."

There are about forty Indians in the settlement.
Some of them own their land, holding patent, and
paying taxes, others have filed on land. but have not
yet proved up their claims. Some of the Indians
own horses, cattle. wagons, buggies and farm ma-
chinery. Last fall eight sewing machines were
purchased by the Indians there. A number of the
younger squaws are quite expert with the machines.

The Indians of Koosharem do not like to talk
of the Indian troubles of early days, and they don't
think that the re-unions of the Indian war veterans
are a good thing. They say their people have quit
fighting, are living as the whites do, and that the
old troubles should be forgotten. Nor do the Indians want to go to the Reservation. A few days
ago "Indian Pete" asked me why I was writing
about the Indians. I told him that perhaps I would

make a book, and he seemed to fear that my purpose was to complain against the Indians, so that they would have to leave their farms and go to the Reservation to live. I am hoping to gain their confidence, so that I shall be able to get more information about them. I have arranged to get some photographs of them.''

KANOSH KOOSHAREM INDIANS BEAR DANCE.

Peter Gottfredson. well know compiler of Indian war history, gives the following account of a unique celebration recently held by the Kanosh and Koosharem Indians:

The Kanosh Indians under Chief Andrew Hongkub, and the Koosharem Indians under Chief Walker Ammon, celebrated a ten days ''Bear Dance'' reunion between Richfield and Elsinore, Sevier County from March 7th to 17th. The legend on which the bear dance is based is an old one. It refers to two Indians who went hunting in the mountains. While they were out a heavy storm came up and they got lost. In roaming around they ran upon a bear's den. The bear was away and the two Indians sought shelter in the cave. Being hungry, they helped themselves to the nuts and other provisions which bruin had stored up for the winter.

''One Indian decided to remain in the den the rest of the winter, but the other found his way back to the village. The bear returned to her den and made friends with the Indian who was there.

''In the spring, when the snow was gone and the grass was getting green the Indians in the village went out in search of their brother who had been gone so long. They came to the cave, where they saw the Indian, the she bear and a cub, dancing joyously at the return of spring.''

"As observed now, the bear dance celebration is in part is a religious rite to show thankfulness that another winter has been survived, that summer is again at hand and all is well. It is a custom for friendly tribes to come together to renew friendship and cordiality.''

"In the bear dance the squaws form in lines opposite the musicians, two by two holding hands. With a chant, accompanied by the instrumental music, the lines step forward four steps, then the same distance backward, ending each advance and retreat with a kind of springing movement. One of of the squaws from each pair step out and touches a male Indian, who becomes her partner in the dance. Then she goes back and joins the other squaw, repeating the advance and retreat steps as before. The partner next steps forward and performs a chase in front of the women. Then he places a hand on the shoulder of either squaw, all the while keeping step with the music. The squaws separate and let the buck into line with them locking arms, the male with his back towards the music, the forward and backward steps are repeated and kept up until the music stops. It is considered a breach of manners for any of the dancers to stop before the music ceases.

"The orchestra consists of four Indians, a tin tub, bottom upward, and notched sticks. Each Indian places one end of a notched stick on the tub, to provide resonance, and see-saw up and down along the notches with another. The dancing is kept up

each afternoon and each night until towards midnight. There is not much moving around camp during the forenoon.

"Seventy-six Indians took part in the Kanosh-
Koosharem celebration, and hundreds of visitors
went to the camp and witnessed the dance.

"After a good deal of persuasion, the chiefs permitted photographer R. D. Adams to take a number
of pictures. Most Indans are shy of a camera.

BILL AWARDING MEDALS TO INDIAN
WAR VETERANS.

An act providing for a Medal of Honor for each
of the Indian War Veterans for actual service in
suppressing Indian hostilities in Utah during the
years 1850 to 1872 inclusive.

Sec. 1.—The Governor and Secretary are hereby authorized to procure a Medal for each of the
Veterans of the Indian Wars who actually served
in suppressing Indian hostilities in Utah during the
years 1850 to 1872 inclusive.

Sec. 2.—The design of said Medal shall be such
as may be determined upon by the Governor and
Secretary of State. And shall be made of Bronze,
and shall be attached to and suspended by a red,
white and blue ribbon. Upon the back of each medal
shall be inscribed the name of the Veteran entitled
to receive it, when completed and at such times as
may be expediant. And after the presentation of
proper evidence and proof of actual service in suppressing Indian hostilities between the years 1850
and 1872 inclusive, by each claimant to the Governor
and the Secretary of State, a medal shall be pre-

sented to each of said Indian War Veterans. Or in case of his death to his nearest relative.

Sec. 3—For the purpose of this act is hereby appropriated out of the moneys in the State Treasury not otherwise appropriated the sum of Five Hundred dollars, or as much thereof as may be necessary. To be disbursed upon the warrant of the State Auditor when duly authorized by the State Board of examiners.

Approved this 9th day of March, A. D. 1905.

LEGISLATURE APPROPRIATES $50,000.00 TO INDIAN WAR VETERANS.

An act providing for services rendered in the Indian Wars of the Territory of Utah.

And making an appropriation for such services.

And providing for the method of proving such services, and payment of said funds.

Be it enacted by the Legislature of the State of Utah.

Sec. 1st.—That the veterans who performed actual service in any of the Indian wars of the territory of Utah, in the regular Militia of the Territory, or if he be dead, then his widow shall receive from the State of Utah, compensation as follows:

1st. For expeditionary service while in the field away from home. (a) Cavalry, Infantry. Buglers, Teamsters and Musicians, at the rate of forty dollars ($40.00) per month. (b) For use and risk of horse at the rate of fifteen dollars ($15.00) per month.

2nd. Home guard service. Cavalrymen and Infantrymen at the rate of twenty dollars ($20.00) per month. The foregoing schedule for services shall govern without regard to the rank in which the person served. Provided that no person shall be paid for services for which he has heretofore received payment. And provided further that in no case shall payment be made to any one for a period exceeding one month. And provided that the provisions of this act shall not apply to any person who has been granted a pension from the United States. And provided further, that payments hereunder shall not be held to bar further payments in the future for services longer than one month as shown by the records herein after mentioned.

Sec. 2.—The affidavits of services in Indian Wars in the Territory of Utah on file in the office of the Adjutant General of the State of Utah shall be deemed conclusive proof of services therein respectfully mentioned. Such affidavits having been compiled by the Commissioners of Indian War Records as authorized heretofore by the Governor and Legislature of the State of Utah.

1st. Upon filing of proof of identity by any person rendering such service with the Adjutant General. He shall immediately list such person, showing the amount due hereunder.

At the end of ninety days the Adjutant General shall disburse said funds on a prorata basis, paying to each his proportionate amount of the sum hereby apportioned.

Sec. 3.—Identification may be made as follows:

1st. Of the rendering the service, By certificate of such person attested by two responsible witnesses.

2nd. Of a widow of the person rendering the service when the proof was filed by the widow, The certificate of said Widow attested by two responsible witnesses.

3rd. Of a Widow of the person rendering service when such person has died since the filing of proof of service: By certificate of such Widow attested by two responsible witnesses or by certified copy of marriage record of the Widow to the deceased.

Sec. 4.—There is hereby appropriated out of any money's in the State Treasury not otherwise appropriated. the sum of Fifty Thousand Dollars. For the purpose of carrying into affect the provisions of this act. The State Auditor shall draw his warrants on the State Treasurer in favor of the Adjutant-General for the sum hereby appropriated.

The Booth Bill asked for $321,837.00 to pay the Veterans for services. Affidavit of service made under the provisions of Chapter (55) Laws of Utah 1909.

1917. LEGISLATURE APPROPRIATES $25,000.00 to INDIAN WAR VETERANS.
APPROVED MARCH 2, 1917.

H. B. No. 33   By Mr. Ray

An act providing for an Indian War Veterans' Fund, making an appropriation therefor, and providing for the method of disbursement of said fund.

Be it enacted by the Legislature of the State of Utah:

Section 1. There is hereby created a fund to be known as the Indian War Veteran's fund; said fund to consist of any money appropriated by the

State for the purpose set out in this act, and any money appropriated or advanced by the Government of the United States for disbursement among Indian War Veterans, or persons herein mentioned, and any other funds donated or acquired for said purposes.

Sec. 2. There is hereby appropriated from the general funds of the State, not otherwise appropriated, the sum of twenty-five thousand dollars ($25,000.00), to be placed to the credit of the Indian War Veteran's Fund.

Sec. 3. The State Board of Examiners is hereby authorized and empowered to disburse the Indian War Veterans' fund to Veterans who have performed actual service in any of the Indian Wars of the Territory of Utah while such veterans were members of the regular militia of the Territory, or to the wives or widows of such veterans, as compensation for the services of such veterans.

Sec. 4. The State Board of Examiners shall examine into and investigate the merits of the claim of any person applying for a share of the Indian War Veteran's Fund. The findings of the said State Board of Examiners in regard to these matters shall be final.

If, in the opinion of the State Board of Examiners, any person applying for a portion of the Indian War Veterans' fund shall be entitled thereto, the State Board of Examiners shall determine the amount to be disbursed to such person, and upon such determination the State Auditor shall draw his warrant upon the State Treasurer for such amount in favor of the person so entitled; Provided, however, that no disbursement in excess of the

amount of money available in said fund shall be
made.

Sec. 5. This Act shall take effect on approval.
Approved March 2nd. 1917.

64TH CONGRESS.   H. R. 655
1ST SESSION

IN THE SENATE OF THE UNITED STATES

FEBRUARY 19, 1916.

Read twice and referred to the Committee on Pensions.

AN ACT.

The Act to pension the survivors of certain
Indian wars from January 1, 1859, to January, 1891,
approved March 4, 1917, grants a pension of $20 per
month to surviving officers and enlisted men, and
$12 per month to the surviving widows of said of-
ficers and enlisted men, who served in the campaign
in the Black Hawk Indian War in Utah from 1835
to 1867, inclusive

The Smoot amendment, which makes it possible for the Black Hawk War Veterans to prove
their service and grants them a pension without previous recognition or payment for said service by
Government, reads as follows:

"That when there is no record of service or payment for same in the War Department, the applicant may establish the service by satisfactory evidence from the muster rolls on file in the several
State or Territorial archives: And provided further,
That the want of a certificate of discharge shall

not deprive any applicant of the benefits of this
Act.''

That applicant for pension must establish his
service, or the service of her husband, in accordance with the terms of this amendment. The name
of the soldier, the name of the company and the
company and the date and length of service given in
the application must conform to the records found in
the State archives. Provided that the surviving widows of said officers and enlisted men shall have
married said survivor prior to the passage of this
Act; provided, that such widow has not remarried: *Provided further, That if any certain one
of said campaigns did not cover a period of thirty
days, the provisions of this Act shall apply to those
who served during the entire period of said campaigns; Provided further, that where there is no record of enlistment or muster into the service of the
United States in any of the wars mentioned in this
Act, the record of pay by the United States shall
be accepted as full and satisfactory proof of such enlistment and service*: And provided further, That all
contracts heretofore made between the beneficiaries
under this Act and pension attorneys and claim
agents are hereby declared null and void.

Sec. 2. *That the period of service performed by
beneficiaries under this Act shall be determined by
reports from the records of the War Department,
where there is such a record, and by the reports
from the records of the Treasury Department showing payment by the United States where there is
no record of regular enlistment or muster into the
United States military service.*

Sec. 3. That section forty-seven hundred and

sixteen of the Revised Statutes, relative to loyalty during the Civil War, is hereby repealed so far as the same relates to this Act or to pensioners under this Act.

Passed the House of Representatives February 16, 1916.

Attest: South Trimble, Clerk.

(Approved March 4th, 1917.)

(The Italics are Senator Reed Smooth's amendments.)

Printed in the United States
45753LVS00004B/46